D0977311

creativity

in education & learning

a guide for teachers and educators

arthur j cropley

First published in 2001

Kogan Page Limited
120 Pentonville Road
London N1 9JN
UK

Stylus Publishing
22883 Quicksilver Drive
Sterling, VA 20166
USA

British Library Cataloguing in Publication Data

A CIP record for this book is available from the British Library.

ISBN 0 7494 3447 3

Typeset by Kogan Page
Printed and bound in Great Britain by Clays Ltd, St Ives plc

Table of contents

Introduction

In 1949, in a seminal address to the American Psychological Association, the psychologist J P Guilford argued that conventional concepts of intellectual ability focused too strongly on speed, accuracy, correctness, logic and similar properties, aspects of what he called 'convergent' thinking. These are very important, it is true, but should not be allowed to dominate the conceptualization of mental functioning at the expense of branching out, generating alternative answers, seeing possibilities and the like – aspects of what Guilford called 'divergent' thinking. Publication of Guilford's address in the *American Psychologist* (Guilford, 1950) with the title 'Creativity' ushered in a new era of thinking about intellectual ability.

It would be incorrect to imagine that psychological and educational interest in creativity began with Guilford. There was a considerable literature in English, French and German in the 19th century as well as substantial interest prior to the First World War and between the two world wars. None the less, Guilford's address can be regarded as the beginning of the modern era. This was partly due to the fact that he was the right person in the right spot at the right time. A happy coincidence of events occurred that can be compared in some ways with an earlier situation when international hostilities led to the emergence of a defining moment in the history of the psychological study of abilities. At that time, in 1917, the concept of 'intelligence' was popularized almost overnight as a result of its usefulness in selecting officers upon the entry of the United States into the later stages of the First World War.

The key event in the case of creativity was the successful launching in 1957 by Soviet engineers of the first artificial space satellite, Sputnik I. The Soviets had won the first event in the space race. In the United States national survival seemed to be at stake and an explanation was urgently sought. Guilford's address provided a concept that was quickly seized upon to construct a plausible explanation: the problem was lack of *creativity*. US engineers were not creative enough. This view provided not only a concept (creativity) that led to an explanation (lack of creativity) but also a solution (train them to be more creative) and a ready-made and understandable approach to doing this (creativity

= divergent thinking), from which guidelines for the necessary training could be developed. The National Defense Education Act, which called for promotion of creativity in schools, came into effect and the wave of creativity research that followed set the stage for intense interest in the topic on a worldwide basis.

The year 50 GE (pronounced: '50 Guilford Era') has come and gone. Where do we stand? Guilford stressed the practical importance of creativity, the role of personality and ability in its emergence, and the possibility of fostering its growth. This book is concerned with precisely those issues. Creativity is understood here as *production of novelty*. Sometimes the novelty is acclaimed as sublime creativity but usually it is not. In the latter case we speak of 'ordinary' or 'everyday' creativity or even, where the novelty is banal and ineffective, of 'pseudocreativity'. In looking at creativity the book emphasizes *psychological states and processes* that lead to production of novelty, and *personal properties* that are related to those processes. The latter are found in all people although they are better developed in some than in others.

The third dimension of this book is fostering the actual production of novelty, whether it involves sublime or everyday products. Actual creative behaviour results from interactions among abilities and knowledge, personal properties, motivation and the *properties of the surrounding social environment*. Production of novelty involves both 'classical' creative factors such as divergent thinking, flexibility or risk taking and also 'uncreative' processes and properties such as convergent thinking, focusing on the single best correct answer, or seeking to complete tasks quickly. This combination defines the 'paradox' of creativity. The task of parents, teachers and other educators who wish to foster creativity is to provide conditions that foster the growth of both kinds of cognitive and non-cognitive factors that underlie production of novelty.

The book is intended for a broad readership. The first group I hope to reach consists of *teachers* at all levels: university teachers and graduate or senior students in education and psychology, to be sure, but also teachers in primary and secondary schools. A second group involves *creativity trainers* and *managers* in business and industrial settings. Just as important to me as readers are *parents* who wish to promote a rounded development of their children's potentials, as well as *individual people* who wish to develop their own ability to produce novelty. The intention is to provide readers with a clear, practical idea of creativity as well as vocabulary that will make it possible for them to articulate ideas about it and examine their own thinking and behaviour. The practical aim is to encourage parents, teachers and others to deal with children and adults in ways that will foster their ability to produce effective novelty.

This book does not conceptualize creativity as something that only applies to people with special gifts and talents and does not see fostering creativity as restricted to gifted education, although gifted education programmes should give great emphasis to it. Creativity as it is understood here is something for people at all levels and in many different settings: one brief case study in Chapter 1 involves housewives attending a one-day-a-week evening class on knitting, sewing and crocheting; another focuses on an under-12 football team.

The book has a practical orientation. However, it does not offer recipes for fast food creativity – something that is attractively packaged, quickly prepared, easy to serve and goes down well but offers little real nourishment. Rather the book seeks to provide parents and educators at all levels with guidelines for home-baked creativity. This may not be as appealingly packaged, well marketed, or easy to serve up as the fast food variety, but it reflects the special characteristics of the individual who prepares it, is wholesome and fosters healthy growth.

The book seeks to be academically rigorous and draws heavily on research findings. However, its predominant purpose is to tease out the main ideas in relevant publications and organize and present these in a readily understandable way. Thus, the book is not essentially a scientific treatise, although its conclusions rest on a framework of research findings. This scholarly material is supplemented by the observations and insights of 35 years' practical work. The book is also not a paint-by-numbers manual on how to foster creativity in the classroom. What it is, is an introduction to current conceptualizations of creativity in both adults and children and an attempt to work out general principles for fostering creativity in schools, where the main emphasis lies, in higher education and also in other settings where the production of novelty is prized.

Parts of this book were written in March–May 2000 while I was visiting professor at the University of Latvia. I am grateful for the hospitality provided in Riga by the Baltic office of the Association for the Advancement of Baltic Studies. Without their help I would not have been able to complete the manuscript on schedule.

1

Creativity: basic concepts

The purpose of this chapter is to look in a general way at the following questions:

- What is creativity?
- How can it be studied?
- How is it different from intelligence?
- What is its connection with education and childrearing?

The answers to these questions provide a framework for more detailed discussions in later chapters of creative thinking, personal properties connected with creativity and ways of identifying and fostering it.

What is creativity?

Emergence of the modern concept

There is well-documented interest in creativity going back to the ancient world. To take a single example, Plato's *Ion* emphasized society's need for creative people and urged the state to foster their development. Over the centuries painters, sculptors, poets, writers, musicians and other workers in the creative arts have frequently discussed creativity, usually seeing it as a medium for beautifying the environment, a form of self-expression and communication, or a way of understanding, opening up or coping with the previously unknown. More recently creativity has been seen by some as the only area where technology such as microelectronics cannot go. In this view creative thinking is a bastion of human dignity in an age where computers seem to be taking over.

Although creativity was initially looked at as an artistic/aesthetic phenomenon, in more recent times researchers have broadened the approach by looking more closely at creativity in mathematics and the natural sciences (eg Helson, 1983; Roe, 1952) as well as in the professions such as architecture or engineering (eg Facaoaru, 1985; MacKinnon, 1983). Creativity has continued to have the strong aesthetic and spiritual connotations it has in artistic discussions but recent work extends this by also giving emphasis to practical and professional considerations. The term has even been broadened sufficiently to be applied in areas such as sport, where discomfiting opponents via unexpected but effective tactics is equated with creativity (eg Herrmann, 1987).

In 1957 the successful launching of the first artificial earth satellite caused the 'Sputnik shock'. Despite the widespread impression that the space programme of the United States was vastly superior to that of its rival, the apparently inferior engineers and scientists of the Soviet Union (as it was then) had won the first event in the 'space race'. In the course of the soul searching that followed, creativity began to be seen as a way of achieving world supremacy. Adopting a human capital approach (see Walberg and Stariha, 1992) discussions of creativity have since become prominent in business and manufacturing, with creative people being seen as the vital resource needed to meet and conquer competition for markets and market shares, for instance through creative design and creative production or marketing. This has in turn led to considerable emphasis on creative leadership and the *management* of innovation (eg Rickards, 1994), not only in business and industry but also in government, the armed services and similar large organizations. This interest occurs despite the fact that there seems to be something inherently paradoxical about applying administrative procedures or management techniques to creativity. In technologically less developed countries where both physical survival and survival of the national identity are more important than world dominance, creativity is often seen as the key to rapid economic and social development, especially modernization and its hoped-for benefits of improved education, nutrition, health care, tolerance of minorities, democracy and political stability.

The three key aspects

It may thus seem that the term is so widely used that its meaning has become diffuse and uncertain. However, as will be shown in more detail in following sections there is a common core to all discussions, especially when educational or psychological considerations are emphasized. To anticipate, this core has three elements:

1. *novelty* (a creative product, course of action or idea necessarily departs from the familiar);
2. *effectiveness* (it works, in the sense that it achieves some end – this may be aesthetic, artistic or spiritual, but may also be material such as winning or making a profit);
3. *ethicality* (the term 'creative' is not usually used to describe selfish or destructive behaviour, crimes, warmongering and the like).

Creativity as cause, effect and interaction

Creativity as effect: creative products

As an effect creativity is a property of *products*. These are often tangible and material and frequently take the form of works of art, musical compositions, or written documents, on the one hand, or of machines, buildings or other physical structures such as bridges and the like. They can also be intangible although relatively specific, such as plans and strategies for solving problems in business, manufacturing, government and similar areas. Finally, they can consist of more general thoughts or ideas – systems for conceptualizing the world – as in philosophy, mathematics, or indeed all reflective disciplines. The special characteristics of products that make them creative were summarized in broad terms above (novelty, effectiveness, ethicality). A more detailed discussion is to be found in Chapter 5 (see especially Table 5.1 on p 113).

Creativity as cause: creative people

By contrast, as a cause creativity is a constellation or cluster of *psychological factors* within individual people that gives them the capacity or potential to produce products with properties such as those just outlined, but does not guarantee their emergence. It is thus a necessary but not sufficient cause for creative products. This psychological constellation involves abilities, knowledge, skills, motives, attitudes and values, as well as personal properties such as openness, flexibility, or courage (for more details see later chapters, especially Chapters 2 and 3). As Ericsson and Smith (1991) pointed out in a discussion of expertise, some aspects of this cluster involve attributes that apparently have a strong inherited component (eg special musical or artistic ability) but others involve attributes that are largely acquired through experience and/or training (eg domain-specific knowledge, special cognitive strategies). These latter are of particular interest to educators at all levels. The special characteristics of creative people are discussed in detail in Chapter 6 and are summarized in Table 6.1 (p 124).

Creativity as interaction: the congenial environment

Also important, however, is exposure to favourable or unfavourable life circumstances. Favourable circumstances involve factors like tolerance for novelty, encouragement and recognition, contact with models of creative behaviour and appropriate opportunities such as the presence of musical instruments, special tools, or specialized literature as well as people who foster creativity. Treffinger (1995) referred to the presence in the environment of 'resisters' (people or circumstances that inhibit creativity) and 'assisters' (people or circumstances that facilitate it). Potent assisters are people who provide models of appropriate behaviour or even merely encourage it, but they can also be such simple things as lucky timing or access to an important source. These define what Csikszentmihalyi (1996) called a 'congenial' environment. The role of the environment in creativity will be discussed more fully in Chapter 3.

This leads to the idea of *creativity as an interaction*. It involves psychological traits, to be sure. However, these do not express themselves in isolation but within the framework offered by the particular person's environment. The environment, broadly understood, includes the resources that it makes available (both human and material), the degree of divergence or risk taking that will be tolerated, or the kinds of rewards (or punishments) that it offers people who diverge from the usual. The quality, quantity and timing of these factors affect acquisition (or not) of knowledge and skills needed for creativity, as well as of favourable (or unfavourable) attitudes or motives.

The active role of the environment

The environment is not simply a passive recipient of whatever creative people offer, but itself determines what kind of novelty is produced. Only certain solutions will be tolerated by a particular environment. For example, a novel design for motor cars would be to arrange the seats so that all passengers except the driver faced the rear. This design would dramatically reduce deaths and injuries among occupants of motor vehicles involved in serious collisions and would thus not only be novel but also extremely effective. However, it has never even been tried by manufacturers because it is clear that car buyers would not accept it. The social setting thus determines what kinds of new ideas emerge by setting limits to the degree and/or kind of divergence that is seen, by guiding creative thinking into particular channels, or by affecting motivation: there is little incentive to produce novelty or surprise that no one else is willing to support. Despite this, exceptional individuals who swim against the current – such as Galileo, who was condemned for heresy – are still seen.

Simonton (see 1997 for a comprehensive summary) has shown that the effects of the environment are not only specific, affecting the creativity of a particular individual, but also general in that they influence the kind of novelty that is produced in the society as a whole. This occurs most obviously in the form of 'cycles' or styles in, let us say, art. However, different patterns of novelty production are also seen in times of economic prosperity or depression, during wars etc. For instance, 'melodic originality' of composers is higher during wartime (Simonton, 1998).

Focus on person and process

The problem of defining creativity via products

Defining creativity in terms of products raises a number of problems. It often proves difficult for different observers to agree on the creativity of a product, or when such agreement is obtained in one age future ages may come to a different conclusion. Shakespeare's plays, for instance, were judged to be indecent in Georgian England and had to be edited to make them respectable. In 1818 Dr Thomas Bowdler published the *Family Shakespeare* in which he removed expressions that could not with propriety be read aloud in the family (he *bowdlerized* Shakespeare's work, as we now express it). The problem of changing standards is possibly most obvious in the area of fine art where what is regarded as creative may vary from society to society and from epoch to epoch within a society, while the foremost experts may disagree on the creativity of a given work.

Similar problems also exist even in areas that are more objective and rely less on taste or judgement. In 1832, after his death in a duel at the age of 20, the French mathematician Galois was found to have left a body of mathematical writings that were examined and pronounced to be valueless despite the fact that he had frantically worked on them almost to his final moments. The mathematical propositions were novel, certainly, but were judged to have no basis in mathematical knowledge and to lead nowhere (ie to be lacking in effectiveness). It was only after the passage of several years during which mathematics advanced enough for the relevance and effectiveness of Galois's work to become apparent that their creativity was recognized. Other creative scientists such as Galileo have suffered extreme social disapproval even to the extent of being declared heretics because they introduced what was in effect a new paradigm whose relevance and effectiveness were beyond the ability of a particular age to appreciate. In Galileo's case this was the now commonplace idea that the earth revolves around the sun.

Jackson and Messick (1965) introduced a further element to the discussion by distinguishing between *external* criteria of the effectiveness of a novel product (eg its usefulness in solving a specific problem or issue) and *internal* criteria such as logic, harmony among its elements, and pleasingness. Miller (1992) emphasized 'elegance' as a property of creative solutions to mathematical problems, citing Einstein's view that the essence of creativity in science consists in spotting not just any solution that works but in recognizing the most elegant of all possible solutions. Whether a particular product really is the most elegant, however, sometimes becomes clear only after many years. Consequently, Albert (1990) recommended against using products as the core concept in studying the development of creativity and suggested concentrating instead on *processes* thought to be of particular importance.

Emphasizing the human element

Creative effects (products) without a corresponding cause (a creative product that simply appeared without any human inspiration) are difficult to imagine. If a cat crawled over the open keyboard of a piano and the pressure of its paws on the keys produced a new and pleasing melody, would that be an example of musical creativity? If a computer program used a random number generator to print a large number of different sets of 100,000 words from a stored copy of the *Concise Oxford Dictionary* and one of these turned out to be the manuscript of a brilliant novel, would that be literary creativity? Most people seem to answer 'No', believing that creativity requires a human element, especially one involving *purpose* or *intention*. In addition, the human element encompasses factors such as exercise of taste and judgement based on experience, knowledge and skill. Thus, a discussion that focuses on products seems to miss the central element of creativity, the person.

As a result, there is a tendency for discussions in education and psychology to focus on creativity as cause rather than as effect, ie to talk about creative people and creative processes rather than creative products. In the case of people, Torrance (1979) gave most weight to *skills* (eg critical thinking, divergent thinking, special problem-solving tactics) and *abilities* (eg concentration, imagination, problem finding), but also emphasized *motives* such as curiosity, willingness to take risks, or persistence. Albert (1990) emphasized among other things appropriate forms of decision making, goal setting and self-development. Parallel to approaches focusing on the abilities associated with creativity other authors such as Barron (1969) in the early years of the modern era or Helson (1999) in recent times emphasized the importance of the *creative personality*. Sternberg (1988) summarized the person-centred approach (as against the product-centred) by identifying six *facets* of creativity, of which five can be applied directly here: knowledge, insightful thinking, intrinsic motivation, self-confidence and facilitatory aspects of personality such as flexibility or willingness to take risks.

Creative potential

It is not difficult to conceptualize creativity as a set of personal properties within an individual that may lead that person to behave creatively – what might be called the *disposition to be creative*. In contrast with the difficulty of imagining a creative product without a creator, the unhappy idea of a creative disposition without corresponding products causes few conceptual difficulties: it is not hard to imagine, albeit as a sad case, a person who possessed the psychological properties needed for creativity but did not turn these into creative behaviour. Such a state of affairs would involve 'unrealized' creative potential and would be of particular interest for educators, the essence of whose job is turning potential into actual behaviour, or parents, who usually wish to see their children develop to the fullest whatever potentials they possess. Failure to realize potential could be caused by lack of exposure to a congenial environment (lack of opportunity) or, as will be shown in Chapter 3, by difficulties in other aspects of the personality. In later chapters the need for a differential diagnosis of the disposition for creativity will be discussed in greater detail and suggestions made for an appropriate system of assessment.

Levels of creativity

Sublime creativity

Even among those whose creativity has been recognized by the external world, ie 'validated' as Csikszentmihalyi (1988) put it, some products achieve widespread professional or artistic acclaim or commercial success and thus go beyond mere validation to be widely acknowledged. Of these, a few may go a step further and be regarded as outstanding by the world or at least relevant sections of it (such as art critics, literary reviewers, fellow scientists, or other professionals). Such products win or come close to winning awards like the Nobel Prize, the Booker Prize, the Archibald Prize or the Pulitzer Prize. They enlarge human experience and competence and can be referred to as involving 'sublime' creativity. Thus, even acclaimed creative products may have different degrees of creativity.

Everyday creativity

Nichols (1972) extended this view by introducing the important idea of creativity in people who will never produce anything novel, effective and ethical, ie the apparently paradoxical idea of creativity without acclaimed products. Essentially this approach treats creativity as a personal characteristic that exists in people whether they produce anything or not. It is regarded as a normally distributed trait that is found in everybody although to differing degrees in different people, highly in some, less in others and somewhere in between for yet others. It is impossible to have zero creativity just as it is impossible to have zero intelligence (short of being dead, of course). The creativity of those who never produce anything that is publicly acknowledged or acclaimed involves what Milgram (1990) and Richards *et al* (1988) called 'ordinary' or 'everyday' creativity.

Several studies in Hamburg offer concrete examples of what this can mean in everyday life. In one (Schwarzkopf, 1981) a group of women met one evening a week for a year and worked on sewing, knitting, crocheting and similar projects. A teacher encouraged them to produce work that differed from the usual, for instance by adapting well-known patterns in surprising ways. At the end of the year the participants were more confident in dealing with novelty, were more playful and more prepared to criticize their own work. They were also judged by close associates from their family and circle of friends – who had no knowledge of the purpose of the project – to be more independent, more goal-oriented, more determined and more willing to make decisions. (They also produced some interesting clothing.)

In another study (Herrmann, 1987) boys in an under-12 soccer team were constantly encouraged to make unexpected moves, even at the expense of technique and tactics. Such moves included withdrawing suddenly from one-on-one challenges for possession of the ball, deliberately passing to members of the opposition, or playing the ball in the wrong direction. These often caused consternation among opponents and frequently aroused anger in opposing coaches who saw them as somehow cheating. In comparison with a control group of similar boys playing in a team with conventional training methods, the boys coached to be surprising and unconventional obtained higher scores on a creativity test and showed greater self-confidence and less anxiety about their matches. In the first season with training oriented towards novel behaviours they lost every match but in the second they were champions of their league.

Scheliga (1988) studied amateur or semi-professional jazz musicians playing in clubs along the famous (or infamous) Hamburg Reeperbahn. They showed more spontaneity, higher ability to get ideas, greater breadth of associations and increased willingness to take risks than a control group of laboratory technicians. Apparently emphasis in jazz musicianship on individuality, lack of inhibitions, use of fantasy, expression of emotions and use of non-verbal communication frees latent creativity. A more recent discussion in greater detail of personality, creativity and musicianship is to be found in Woody (1999).

The idea of freeing the creative potential of 'ordinary' people (see also later chapters) was further pursued in the Hamburg project in a study of the motivation of hobby authors who wrote stories and poems for their own interest and pleasure without commmercial or literary ambitions (Petersen, 1989). Among other things it was found that amateur authors who received encouraging feedback in the form of praise and interest from the people around them developed strategies for avoiding writers' block and were therefore able to continue writing even when they felt discouraged. The study thus demonstrated the interaction between internal factors such as motivation and external factors such as relationships with other people.

Studying creativity

Quantitative vs qualitative approaches

In the *qualitative* sense creativity is something that a person either has or does not have. This approach restricts research on creativity to studying the chosen few who have been touched by the muse – they have it but the others do not. By contrast, the *quantitative* position adopted in this book is that there is a continuum of greater or lesser levels of creativity ranging from the unsung everyday form to the sublime. This approach rejects the view that some people are creative whereas others are not and assumes that everybody can display creativity, even if to differing degrees. Without denying the importance of validated, acknowledged or sublime creativity the study of everyday creativity is of greater importance for educators and parents, and of course, for children and college students, as well as for managers, administrators and leaders.

Methods in creativity research

Feist and Runco (1993) reviewed articles published in 50 issues of the *Journal of Creative Behavior* from its inception in 1967 until 1989. They found that three articles out of four were non-empirical, many of these focusing on theory and description, others on practical measures for fostering creativity. Empirical papers reported test-based studies, studies using questionnaires and interviews, archival and field studies (including studies in which several procedures were used) and to a much lesser degree longitudinal, meta-analytic and experimental studies. Mehlhorn *et al* (1988) distinguished two basic kinds of research on creativity: on the one hand biographical studies – essentially case studies – and on the other test-based studies. Case studies are more commonly used for investigating acclaimed creativity, test-based studies for research on everyday creativity. However, this is by no means exclusively the case as methodological cross-overs are also seen. Sternberg (1988) extended Mehlhorn's classification of research approaches by referring to: 1) case studies; 2) system-oriented studies; 3) phenomenological investigations. The latter involve looking at how creative people experience their own creativity – how it 'feels' to be creative. System-oriented studies are of considerable importance for the purposes of the present book because they emphasize the way in which creativity arises out of an interaction between the individual and the surrounding environment (including other people), which together form a system (Csikszentmihalyi, 1996).

Despite the focus in this book on everyday creativity it makes sense to seek insights into creativity by going beyond the study of children and adults in everyday situations and looking also at people and products that have been widely recognized (acknowledged and sublime creativity). Case studies have often involved retrospective investigations of people who in the past have become famous for their creativity: sculptors and painters, musical performers and composers, actors, authors and poets, mathematicians and scientists and inventors. Freud's retrospective study (1947) of Leonardo da Vinci is an example.

There have also been studies of living people and the fields covered have been expanded to include architects, engineers, even air force officers. Such people have frequently been identified by asking their colleagues and contemporaries to nominate creative workers in their field and have been investigated by means of interviews, psychological tests, self-descriptions, analyses of products and sometimes observation while they were actually at work. A number of studies of this kind have been summarized by Wallace and Gruber (1989) who emphasized the advantages of case studies, especially what they called 'cognitive case studies'. However, Simonton (1988b, 1994) showed that many creative people orient their answers in such studies to their own theories of creativity or to theories they are familiar with, while some researchers present studies in such a way that existing theories are always supported. Weisberg (1986) also criticized the case study approach by drawing attention to the problem of discrepancies between statements in autobiographies and objectively known facts.

Test-based studies, about which more will be said in Chapters 5 and 6, typically define creativity as a score on a so-called 'creativity' test and compare such values with scores on other tests (eg intelligence tests, achievement tests, personality tests, biographical questionnaires) or behavioural measures such as school grades or 'non-academic talented accomplishments'. A problem with such studies is that they may simply involve correlating scores on one test with those on another whose author has given it a different name from the first, ie the extent to which the studies actually involve creativity as the term is commonly understood can be questioned. Certainly, the activities needed for a high test score do not seem to bear much resemblance to the activities that lead to acclaim as creative. Indeed, acknowledged creative people sometimes refuse to participate in such studies. This issue of the validity of creativity tests will be discussed in more detail in Chapter 6.

Experimental studies are also possible although these are far less common than the other kinds just mentioned. In fact, Feist and Runco (1993) concluded in their review of published papers that experimental studies were 'practically non-existent'. Research of this kind involves approaches such as applying different reinforcement schedules to influence participants' behaviour on tasks, observing the production of products such as stories under differing conditions (eg with or without an audience), analysing protocols of thinking aloud during productive work, or manipulation of people's visual field during such work, to take several examples. These studies seem to offer a certain methodological rigour but their face validity is often low because the conditions under which data is gathered seldom seem to resemble the conditions under which real-life creativity occurs.

Key questions about creativity

Is everything that is different creative?

As was pointed out above the constant factor in virtually all discussions of creativity is *novelty*. This was already apparent long ago (Morgan, 1953) and has been reiterated in recent discussions (eg Amabile, 1996; Cropley, 1999; Engle, Mah and Sadri, 1997). Novelty was defined in a more psychological way by Bruner (1962) who regarded it as involving the process of achieving 'surprise' in the beholder. Surprise can be produced through mere unregulated self-expression (eg daubing paint on paper, writing text in any way that pleases the writer, or picking out notes at random on the piano) or by means of simple *production of variability* (doing things differently from the usual regardless of accuracy, meaning, sense, significance, or interestingness). However, it can also satisfy technical, professional, aesthetic, or scholarly criteria, as will be discussed below.

There is an obvious difference between the novelty involved in mere self-indulgence or simple uninhibited activity on the one hand, and novelty that meets external standards of goodness on the other. Heinelt (1974) summarized this by pointing out that variability alone may well cause surprise but is not a sufficient condition for genuine creativity. He added 'quasicreativity' to Cattell and Butcher's (1968) identification of 'pseudocreativity'. The latter is novel only in the sense of non-conformity, lack of discipline, blind rejection of what already exists and simply letting oneself go. Quasicreativity has many of the elements of genuine creativity – such as a high level of fantasy – but the connection with reality is tenuous. An example would be the 'creativity' of daydreams. Besemer and Treffinger (1981) also emphasized the importance of distinguishing between creativity and mere facileness, glibness or slickness. These may be observed in some genuinely creative people and thus confused with creativity but they are not actually part of it.

Genuine creativity requires a further element over and above mere novelty: a product or response must be relevant to the issue at stake and must offer some kind of genuine solution, ie it must be *effective*. Otherwise every far-fetched, outrageous, or preposterous idea or every astonishing act of non-conformity would by virtue of being surprising be creative. Thus, simply deviating from the customary is not enough. Of course, what is meant by 'effective' may differ between, let us say, fine art and business. In the former case criteria such as aesthetic pleasingness play an important role; in the latter more practical criteria do so, perhaps increased profit or avoidance of lay-offs or even simply survival of a company. These two aspects of effectiveness need not contradict each other although they are often seen as mutually exclusive. For instance, it is possible for a book to be commercially successful and at the same time written in elegant, even beautiful language. In the case of everyday creativity, effectiveness can simply mean that the novelty makes sense to open-minded observers.

The third crucial property of creativity arises from the fact that the term 'creativity' has highly positive connotations. It is difficult to think of the effective and relevant novelty of new weapons of mass destruction as creative, even though they might contain all the necessary elements discussed above. Indeed, revolutionary new ideas can have serious negative consequences regardless of the intent of the people producing the ideas. Nowadays this problem has become particularly acute in science (see, for instance, discussions of cloning human beings), in business, commerce and manufacturing, and in engineering, where the need for environmental responsibility is increasingly being stressed. Unfortunately, it seems that most creativity has the potential for misuse. The discoveries of people like Jenner and Pasteur, to take one example, laid the foundations for germ warfare! In a discussion of the 'dark side' of creativity McLaren (1993) referred to the 'general intoxication' with creativity that leads people to forget that much creativity serves negative ends. An obvious example would be the creativity displayed by a thief who developed a novel way to embezzle money from a bank. Thus, the *ethical* element takes on a particular importance (Grudin, 1990). In order to avoid a lengthy discussion of this issue, this book focuses on production of novelty with positive intentions.

Is creativity the same in all fields?

In recent writings (for a summary see Tardif and Sternberg, 1988) a number of authors (eg Csikszentmihalyi, Gardner, Johnson-Laird) argued that creativity can only be defined in particular areas such as fine arts or science. Shaughnessy (1988) concluded that Gardner's (1983) model of multiple intelligences (linguistic, musical, logical-mathematical, spatial, bodily-kinaesthetic, intuitive and personal) can also be applied to creativity. By contrast, Altshuller (1984) and Weisberg (1986) advanced general theories while Tardif and Sternberg also mentioned several other authors who adopted a more general position (eg Barron, Feldman, Gruber).

In the discussions just summarized the nature of the product is often emphasized. The importance of a domain-specific physical product is particularly obvious in fine art or performing arts (where specific works or performances are judged by specialized critics as well as interested members of the public), science (where peer judgement is of great importance), engineering, architecture and the like (where products are not infrequently sources of public and professional controversy), or in business. In some branches of natural, physical or social science such as mathematics or philosophy novel ideas or symbol systems rather than physical objects may well be the usual result of creativity. As has already been pointed out (see above), in this book novel 'products' will be understood in both senses: physical products on the one hand, new ways of symbolizing an area on the other. The two kinds of product are possible in all fields of creativity. Furthermore, more or less all creative achievements may have both tangible and intangible elements, the difference being more a matter of degree: concrete objects may be more prominent or dominant in some situations, symbol systems in others. Thus, there is specificity in creative products but a general approach is also possible.

A further area where there is both specificity and generality is that of *communication*. Various authors (eg Cropley, 1997b; Csikszentmihalyi, 1996) have emphasized that the results of creativity have to be communicated to the external world if they are to be validated; *Gone with the Wind* would never have been acclaimed if the manuscript had remained hidden in a cardboard box under Margaret Mitchell's bed in Atlanta. However, different areas of creativity (literature, fine art, science) have different forms of communication and different 'languages' (special terminology, systems of symbols, different kinds of physical object produced), which are mastered to differing degrees by different individuals. A particular creative person may not be able to express creativity with equal ease and effectiveness in all areas and as a result a certain field-related specificity can occur.

There may also be special knowledge and skills that are decisive in particular areas (for instance, discrimination of tones in music, special cognitive strategies in mathematics, mastery of musical notation in the former, of mathematical symbols in the latter) while certain *personal properties* (such as risk taking or goal directedness) may be of greater importance for one area than another, or under differing life circumstances. None the less, the position adopted here is that creativity in all areas involves specifiable internal properties interacting by means of describable processes with external circumstances. All three of these areas will be discussed more fully in later chapters. This way of looking at creativity permits a general approach that can be applied in principle to all fields.

Ludwig's (1998) comprehensive analysis of over 1000 eminent creators yielded a highly differentiated picture of the relationship among different fields of creativity, based on the demands of the field, on the personality of the individual. He defined four relevant dimensions for describing a field: impersonal vs emotive; objective vs subjective; precise vs imprecise (or structured vs unstructured, as it could also be stated); formal vs informal. He commenced by dividing the various fields of activity into two broad categories: 'investigative' and 'artistic'. Despite differences from field to field, investigative creativity involves ways of interacting with the fields' contents and modes of communication that are more impersonal, objective, precise (structured) and formal. Typical examples are mathematics, physics, biology, medicine, or social science (these are arranged in descending order of impersonality, objectivity, precision and formality, with allowance for a certain degree of stereotyping). By contrast, artistic fields as a group are more emotive, subjective, imprecise (unstructured) and informal. Examples are architecture, design, writing, composing, or visual arts (these are arranged in a hypothesized ascending order of emotiveness, subjectivity, imprecision (unstructuredness) and informality).

Of particular interest is that Ludwig showed that the four-dimensional framework just outlined (impersonal vs emotive, objective vs subjective, etc) applies not only to the broad division into investigative vs artistic fields, but that it also applies within fields, ie it is possible to divide both investigative and artistic fields into subfields that are more (or less) impersonal, more (or less) objective, more (or less) precise, or more (or less) formal. For instance, on the basis of the four dimensions the investigative field can be subdivided into 'natural' sciences such as mathematics, physics or biology vs 'social' sciences such as economics, sociology, or education. In a similar way the broad artistic field can be divided with the help of the same dimensions into relatively impersonal, objective, precise and formal subfields such as architecture or design, which can be contrasted with emotive, subjective, unstructured, informal subfields such as writing or visual arts.

Ludwig continued his analysis by showing that the same four dimensions can be used to divide fields at ever more specific levels. For instance, within the subfield of artistic creativity represented by writing it is possible to apply the four dimensions to make out even more specific subfields such as poetry and fiction writing (relatively but decreasingly emotive, subjective, imprecise and informal) vs biography, literary criticism and journalism (in theory at least increasingly impersonal, objective, precise and formal). He concluded that creativity is unified by possessing a structure defined by the mathematics of fractal geometry: this is the geometry of 'self-similar' objects that are characterized by possessing a structure that repeats itself again and again at progressively smaller scales. Applied to the question with which this section is concerned, this means that, psychologically speaking, the various fields of creativity are different, but that this difference occurs within the boundaries of a common or unified model.

Is simply letting ideas flow sufficient for creativity?

Although early studies of creativity (eg Ghiselin, 1955) supported the view that it frequently results from sudden bursts of inspiration, opinion on the role of inspiration is divided among contemporary researchers. In relevant case studies (eg Ghiselin, 1955; Simonton, 1988b; Wallace and Gruber, 1989) many acknowledged creators described the way their creativity seemed to appear without effort on their part: the mathematician Poincaré, for instance, reported that the Fuchsian functions (now known as 'automorphic functions') came suddenly and unexpectedly into his head in 1881 as he was about to enter a coach for a sightseeing drive and was not thinking about mathematics at all. Refinements of the equations appeared in a second burst while he was walking beside the sea. The poet A E Housman described how the lines of his poems simply appeared in his head. Mozart reported in a letter to his father that he never revised his work but wrote down complete music that came into his head in its final form. This has encouraged the idea that simply relaxing or letting ideas flow will lead to creativity or even that creativity and hard work are irreconcilable.

However, Poincaré had been working on his problem for many years and possessed a vast amount of relevant knowledge accumulated by hard work. Housman's descriptions of his effortless production of poetry go on to recount how after the first free flow of six or eight lines the next one or two took hours to emerge, and Mozart's account is inconsistent with the fact that corrected early versions of his music have been found. In describing their own creativity these men may have been influenced by the factors already mentioned as weaknesses of case studies, for instance an adjustment of their recollections and impressions to match their intuitive theories of creativity. As Miller (1992) put it, people being studied may be inclined to report mostly what is 'to their own advantage'. Although the main thrust of Miller's conclusions supports the idea of sudden illumination – what he called the 'nascent moment' – he accepted that this does not come from nowhere but requires preparation.

Contrary to the 'let it flow' approach a number of authors have emphasized the need for broad general knowledge, deep specialized knowledge of a field (see Chapter 2), ability to use special tools (eg sculpture), mastery of instruments (eg music) or skill in specific techniques (eg creative writing). In fact, relevant knowledge, special skills and techniques and similar factors play an important role in all fields of creativity. The relative importance of particular factors is greater in some domains than in others – knowledge is perhaps more important in science, technique in music, to take examples. The specific contents of these elements also vary according to the particular field or activity in question: the specific knowledge required in designing and building bridges may not be very relevant for creativity in, let us say, botany. However, both require knowledge and technique: for instance, both mathematical creativity and creative writing require mastery of a set of abstract symbols for representing ideas, although the two symbol systems may be quite different. It seems appropriate to adopt Edison's famous saying, replacing his word 'genius' with 'creativity': 'Creativity is 1 per cent inspiration, 99 per cent perspiration!'

A related question is whether creativity can result from chance or luck. There are many examples of apparently lucky combinations of events that led to acknowledged creative solutions (see Rosenman, 1988): for instance, Pasteur, Fleming, Roentgen, Becquerel, Edison, Galvani and Nobel all described chance events that led them to breakthroughs. Some famous thinkers have even concluded that chance and luck are dominant in creativity. For instance, Ernst Mach referred to 'die Rolle des Zufalls bei Erfindungen und Entdeckungen' (the role of chance in inventions and discoveries), Etienne Souriau concluded that 'le princip de l'invention est le hasard' (the basis of creativity is chance) and Alexander Bain acknowledged the importance of hard work in creativity but saw it as 'energy put forth… on the chance of making lucky hits'.

Austin (1978) identified four kinds of happy chance: *blind chance* (the individual creator plays no role except that of being there at the relevant moment); *serendipity* (a person stumbles upon something novel and effective when not looking for it); the *luck of the diligent* (a hard-working person finds in an unexpected setting something that is being sought – Diaz de Chumaceiro (1999) called this '*pseudo*serendipity' since in genuine serendipity the person would not be looking for what was found); *self-induced luck* (special qualifications of a person – such as knowledge, close attention to detail or willingness to work long hours – create the circumstances for a lucky breakthrough). Case studies suggest that genuinely creative people enjoy a combination of all four kinds of luck, which raises the question of whether it is a matter of luck at all! Pasteur put the matter succinctly: 'Chance favours the prepared mind!'

Perhaps the 'classic' example of this is an anecdote about Becquerel. In 1896, he is said to have left a photographic plate and a container with uranium salts in it in a drawer. On opening the drawer he noticed that the photographic plate had fogged. This unexpected event piqued his curiosity. He eventually concluded that the uranium had emitted some kind of radiation, which was responsible for the fogging. He then showed that this differed from X-rays in being deflected by electromagnetic fields, ie it was a previously unknown phenomenon. After initially being called 'Becquerel rays' the radiation subsequently became known as 'radioactivity' and ultimately led to Becquerel sharing the 1903 Nobel Prize for physics with Marie and Pierre Curie.

In the absence of factors such as the special knowledge that permitted Becquerel to realize that the event was unusual and important, a lively curiosity that led him to investigate the matter rather than simply throwing away the spoilt plate, and possession of scientific knowledge and skills that enabled him to pursue the matter further in an effective way, he would not have capitalized on the opportunity chance presented him with. Indeed, had he not already been engaged in relevant research the uranium and the photographic plate would not have found themselves in the drawer together at all. Thus Becquerel could be said to have created the lucky chance from which he profited. Additional factors that were shown to define the 'prepared mind' in a sample of prominent women (see Diaz de Chumaceiro, 1999) are curiosity, risk taking, self-confidence and competence.

Land, the inventor of the Polaroid camera, offers a more recent and even stronger example. He vigorously rejected the idea of sudden inspiration or chance in explaining his own creativity. He argued that he had had a purpose – the invention of a camera that developed its own pictures on the spot – and that all the necessary knowledge already existed. His achievement was to assemble this knowledge and work his way through it to the almost inevitable result, the Polaroid camera. Indeed, Land is recognized as an outstanding example of down-to-earth industriousness in creativity. Not only did he invent the self-developing film but he also played a substantial role in the conversion of his idea into a working camera (product development) and in the marketing of the camera.

Is creativity allied to psychopathology?

The ideas that there is a connection between creativity and madness is one of the oldest issues in modern psychology and was already a subject of empirical investigation more than 100 years ago (eg Lombroso, 1891). Over the years this theme continued to be the subject of investigations both before the beginning of the modern creativity era (eg Ellis, 1926; Juda, 1949) and after it (eg McNeill, 1971; Rothenberg, 1983). Research has shown that there are some similarities in schizophrenic and creative thinking, schizophrenics making for instance more remote associations and thinking more divergently (eg Heston, 1966; Karlsson, 1970; Walder, 1965). Similar findings were reported by Rothenberg (1983) who found that Nobel Prize winners, creative college students and schizophrenic patients all showed patterns of thinking that differed from those of less creative students. However, the creative people also differed from the schizophrenics, ie schizophrenic and creative thinking share some characteristics, but are not the same.

In a study comparing architects, writers and musicians with schizophrenic patients, Cropley and Sikand (1973) showed where these differences lie: both groups made more remote associations than members of a control group. However, the schizophrenic thinking did not favour production of effective novelty despite its divergent nature. The schizophrenics were frightened by their own unusual ideation whereas the creative people were positively motivated by it. This is consistent with Barron's (1969) finding that creative writers and architects scored in the upper 15 per cent on all psychopathology scales of the MMPI but that they were able to make use of the unusual associations and elevated mood because of their high ego strength. In his view, what would be pathological in conjunction with low ego strength was enriching in his creative people.

Contemporary research has adopted two approaches, either studying acknowledged creative people to see if they are more frequently mentally disturbed than chance would predict or working with people already regarded as mentally ill or at least 'eccentric' in order to see if they show more creativity than the general population. Studies in Britain (Weeks and Ward, 1988), where being eccentric is said to be accepted without great stigma, have shown that many eccentrics hold patents, some of them several. It has also been shown that mood disturbances are much more common among acknowledged creative people than in the general public (Andreasen, 1987). Jamison (1993) reported the results of a study carried out with famous British artists and authors in which she found that manic-depressive disturbances were six times more common in this group than in the general public. She concluded that mental states such as elation are vital for creativity. However, the connection between mood disturbance and creativity does not seem to involve a direct causal relationship. Instead, both mood disturbance and creativity seem to be related to emotional lability and greater sensitivity to external stimuli or internal mood fluctuations, thus producing an apparent causal relationship. Mood states such as manic disorders could also reduce fear of embarrassing oneself or promote self-confidence, once again creating an erroneous impression that the manic disorder causes the creativity.

Ludwig's (1998) data showed that there are 'exceptionally high rates' of mental illness among creative artists but not among creative scientists. This led him to conclude that there is no direct cause and effect relationship between creativity and mental illness. However, artistic creativity involves obtaining and communicating insights into human existence, and severe personal conflicts, drug-induced distortions of reality or even psychotic delusions may provide material for such insights, whereas they would be inimical to scientific creativity. Among other things, the latter usually involves systematic extension of and building on what already exists, something that would be inhibited by distortions of reality. (See, however, discussions of the problem of the inhibiting effects of expertise.) Artistic creativity also involves revealing a great deal of oneself: loosely applying an existing aphorism, an artistic product is the world seen through an ego. Applying the terms introduced earlier in the section on similarities and differences between fields of creativity, Ludwig concluded that the more informal, imprecise, subjective and emotive a particular field, the greater the chance that mental illness will facilitate creativity because it provides unusual ways of experiencing and feeling about the world, and frees communication of insights obtained via these experiences and feelings.

Generally, the position of clinically oriented researchers on creativity is that it requires a *high* level of mental health (Maslow, 1973; May, 1976; Rogers, 1961). Helson (1999) demonstrated empirically that sound mental health was necessary for the realization of creative potential. Women with problems in this area did not fulfil in their lives the creative potential they had shown as students 30 years earlier. It can even be argued (eg Cropley, 1990) that creativity *promotes* mental health. Studies of highly creative people indicate that creativity is connected with psychological properties such as flexibility, openness, autonomy, humour, willingness to try things, or realistic self-assessment. These are usually thought of as prerequisites for the emergence of creativity. However, research on normal personality development also emphasizes similar properties as core elements of the healthy personality. Adopting a psychoanalytic position, Anthony (1987) argued that creativity is related to ego autonomy and ego autonomy to mental health, with the consequence that creativity and mental health are related. In humanistic psychology (eg Maslow, 1973; Rogers, 1961), healthy personality development requires openness, flexibility and tolerance, characteristics of the creative personality. Krystal (1988) showed that uncreative people had difficulty in 'self-caring' and lacked 'self-coherence'. Fostering creativity in such people would promote self-realization.

Emphasizing cognitive processes, Hudson (1963) made the point that non-creative people tend to be narrow and rigid in dealing with information from the external environment whereas creative individuals show openness and flexibility in dealing with such information. Narrowness and rigidity help achieve a sense of certainty and security but this occurs at the expense of healthy personality development. According to Burkhardt (1985) modern life is marked by a 'mass psychosis' that has at its core an obsession with sameness and uniformity. Creativity is, of course, concerned with novelty and difference and would counteract the mass psychosis. Thus, it can be argued that creativity, far from arising from or causing madness, is important in maintaining mental health. Although it is not clear whether there is a cause and effect relationship between the two, creativity and mental health seem to be connected at least at the level of everyday creativity. Thus, in urging teachers to foster creativity in the classroom this book is not proposing that psychopathology should be given free rein but is arguing for more emphasis on psychological dimensions that are valuable in achieving or maintaining a healthy personality.

Creativity and intelligence

The two-track approach

Conventional intelligence is heavily dependent on recognizing, recalling and reapplying, and requires among other things substantial knowledge of facts, effective acquisition of new information, rapid access to the contents of memory, accuracy in finding the best answer to factual questions, and logical application of the already known. Creativity, on the other hand, involves departing from the facts, finding new ways, making unusual associations, or seeing unexpected solutions. The initial position adopted in the 1950s and 1960s by psychologists was that creativity and intelligence are therefore separate, more or less competing or even mutually exclusive dimensions of intellect. However, later theory has emphasized that the two work together. Some writers have referred to this as involving 'true' intellectual giftedness (eg Cropley, 1994), with neither intelligence nor creativity alone leading to effective gifted behaviour. Both early and later studies of achievement at school or university level have shown that by and large the highest achievers display both creativity and intelligence (Hudson, 1968; Sierwald, 1989). In her research on practical creativity Facaoaru (1985) showed that engineers rated as creative displayed a combination of characteristics: plentiful knowledge, swift recall, accurate application (intelligence) on the one hand, generating possibilities, seeing unexpected connections, introducing novelty (creativity) on the other.

Overlapping skills

Ward, Saunders and Dodds (1999) identified two major approaches to conceptualizing the relationship between intelligence and creativity. According to the *overlapping skills* model certain cognitive skills such as problem definition, selective encoding, shifting context, or transcending limitations are common to both (Finke, Ward and Smith, 1992; Sternberg and Lubart, 1995), while others are specific to one or the other (swift and accurate memorization, for instance, is vital for intelligence but not for creativity). The result is that the two aspects of intellectual functioning correlate but are not identical. Sternberg's (1988) 'facets' of creativity (see above: knowledge, insight, intrinsic motivation, the courage of one's convictions, special personal factors such as flexibility and willingness to take risks, relevance) overlap partially with facets of intelligence. Knowledge is closely linked with intelligence and is indispensable for a high IQ as well as being important in creativity. Insight seems to play a role in creativity while it may also be favourable for high intelligence although it is probably not absolutely necessary for obtaining a high IQ. Intrinsic motivation is favourable for the acquisition of knowledge but it is possible to operate rapidly, accurately and logically without it. Flexibility and risk taking may even detract from performance on an intelligence test but are central to creativity.

Subcomponents

The second approach is typified by Renzulli's 'three-ring' model (eg Renzulli, 1986) according to which creativity and intelligence – together with motivation – are *separate subcomponents* of a more general concept of intellectual power that Renzulli called 'giftedness'. Hassenstein (1988) adopted a similar position and argued that what he referred to as *Klugheit* (literally 'cleverness' but used by Hassenstein as a label for a more encompassing concept of intellectual ability) incorporates both factual knowledge, accurate observation, good memory, logical thinking and speed of information processing (eg intelligence) and inventiveness, unusual associations, fantasy and flexibility (eg creativity).

Intelligence threshold

Summing up, creativity and intelligence are neither identical nor completely different but are interacting aspects of intellectual power. As early as 1966 it was shown (Cropley, 1966) that the correlation is about 50. A combination of the two is needed for high levels of creative achievement. An early conceptualization of the way they combine was the *threshold model* (for a discussion, see Runco and Albert, 1986) according to which a minimum level of intelligence (corresponding to an IQ of perhaps 130) is necessary before creativity is possible. A slight extension is the idea that as intelligence approaches this threshold from below the possibility of creativity rises (ie creativity and IQ are positively correlated below the threshold). When intelligence lies above the threshold, increases in intelligence have no consequences for creativity (ie IQ and creativity are uncorrelated once intelligence is high enough).

This view has been expanded somewhat by the idea of a 'one-way' relationship between creativity and intelligence (Guilford and Christensen, 1973). Intelligence determines the upper limits of a person's ability to obtain and store information without actually being itself part of creativity. The degree of creativity depends upon the amount of novelty created in the processing of the information made available by intelligence. If as a result of either low intelligence or environmental deprivation a person does not have access to information, there is nothing to be retrieved and creatively processed. An approach even more clearly oriented towards information processing is the idea that intelligence involves channel capacity (the amount of information flowing in, in a given time). Creativity results from flexible and versatile handling of this information. Lack of creativity results from merely conventional use of the information. Channel capacity in the sense of an upper limit on the number of 'bits' of information that can be assimilated is intuitively compatible with the concept of intelligence while the versatility and extent to which an individual can manipulate, reorganize and recombine those bits is compatible with the notion of creativity.

Creative 'style'

Another approach is to regard creativity not as a level at all but as a style for applying intellectual ability. Gardner (1983) referred to it as *a way of applying intelligence* and Runco and Albert (1986) defined it as *intelligence in action*. Application of intellectual ability to produce *novelty* was contrasted with using it to produce *singularity* or *orthodoxy* (Cropley, 1999). The two styles are possible at all levels of ability so that the crucial difference between production of novelty and production of orthodoxy (ie between 'creativity' and 'intelligence') is qualitative rather than quantitative. As has already been emphasized production of novelty only occasionally leads to sublime products, although it sometimes does. Sublime products require high levels of specific and general knowledge, a strongly developed connection to reality, well-grounded self-evaluation, a high level of command of a medium of expression and communication, and a superior grasp of what the surrounding environment can tolerate. All of these are aspects of what is usually regarded as intelligence.

Thus, creativity involves both intelligence and creativity. Acclaimed creativity both resembles everyday creativity and is also different from it. The resemblance is qualitative: both involve a *kind* of intellectual functioning that is different from 'mere' intelligence. The difference is quantitative: acclaimed creativity differs from everyday creativity because it requires a high *level* of performance. For this reason, confining the study of creativity to acclaimed products would confound kind and level of performance and would ignore the people Nichols (1972) drew attention to (producers of ordinary creativity, a group that includes most children) since they may well display the kind but seldom the level.

Summary

As an aid to clearer understanding of what is meant by the term 'creativity' as a psychological constellation it is contrasted with 'intelligence' in Table 1.1. The entries in the table concentrate on thinking (ie on cognitive aspects of intelligence and creativity) and thus do not offer a comprehensive summary of all its characteristics. However, it is the cognitive aspects of intelligence that are most commonly emphasized and most widely understood so that the difference between it and creativity can most easily be grasped by contrasting the two in the way it is done here. The entries in Table 1.1 are merely examples. Thus the entries 'recalling' and 'problem solving' are examples only of abilities related to intelligence, not an exhaustive definition.

Table 1.1 Examples of differences between creativity and intelligence

Psychological Domain	Intelligence	Creativity
Function	acquiring factual knowledge perfecting the already known (producing orthodoxy)	developing new ways changing the known (producing novelty)
Abilities	recalling problem solving	imagining problem finding
Skills	convergent thinking memorizing	divergent thinking critical thinking
Thinking Processes	recalling the known recognizing the familiar reapplying set techniques	inventing linking disparate domains branching out
Desirable Properties of Thinking	logic accuracy speed	novelty surprisingness variability

The approach of this book

In this book the people/process approach will dominate. Emphasis will not be on the production of acclaimed works but on:

- the psychological factors within the individual – such as those mentioned above – that give the person in question the *potential to behave creatively*. This involves what Runco (1995) called 'individual' creativity. These factors will be divided into two groups: on the one hand processes, on the other personal properties;
- the aspects of the environment that promote turning potential into creative behaviour.

This focus not only avoids difficulties associated with defining creativity of products but it is also more productive for a discussion of creativity in the family, in educational institutions (both schools and colleges), as well as in business, commerce, law, politics and similar fields. Because few young people produce acclaimed products during their school years, emphasis on products would exclude almost all children from the discussion. It is also true that despite exceptions high achievement in childhood in many creative areas such as music (Howe and Sloboda, 1991) is only occasionally followed by prodigious achievement in the adult years so that products in childhood are, in any case, only a rough guide to later acclaim for creativity. This approach views creativity as a psychological potential of *all* people regardless of level. In other words production of novelty can be fostered in everybody not just the chosen few.

Focusing on person and process does not mean that products will be ignored in the book. For instance, eminent creative people can most easily be identified by means of their products. The concept of 'effectiveness', seen here as central to creativity, is a property of products. The interaction between internal characteristics (thinking, personality and motivation) and external factors (the congenial environment, exposure to models, opportunity) can most easily be studied by looking at the emergence of products, for instance via a stage or phase model (see pp 71–74). Products are left out of consideration here only in the sense that – with one or two exceptions (eg the discussion of creativity tests) – the book is not concerned with laying down rules or guidelines on how to assess the creativity of products, with determining the creativity of specific products, or with comparing certain products with others, nor does it restrict its discussions to people with acclaimed products.

In this book the family, schools and institutions of higher education, as well as businesses, firms and other practical settings are seen as environments that need to be made more congenial. In other words they can do more to promote the growth of the psychological properties defining creative potential and can encourage their realization in the form of creative behaviour. Furthermore, since all people are capable of developing their abilities, knowledge, skills, attitudes and personal properties in a creative direction the measures outlined in later chapters are intended for everybody, not just a small group of the highly creative. (This does not mean that the measures may not foster the emergence of highly acclaimed creativity, however, since it is perfectly possible that some people may go on to achieve widespread acclaim.)

Educational discussions of creativity have tended to concentrate on schoolchildren and this is scarcely surprising. Creativity seems to be part of the essence of being a child. After all, children are more or less free of preconceptions about the world (the *tabula rasa* model) and are in a sense engaged in the creative process of building their own internal map of the external world. *Creativity seems to be an inherent part of childhood.* Furthermore, it seems important that children should be creative. It is the ability to look at things differently, for instance to find new approaches to old problems, that society needs and the young through their inexperience and consequent freshness seem to be our best chance of developing such new approaches. *Creativity in children is necessary for society.* Finally, creativity offers classroom approaches that are interesting and thus seems to be a more efficient way of fostering learning and personal growth of the young. *Creativity helps children learn and develop.*

While accepting the validity of the points just made the present book will also extend the school-focused approach by paying some attention to creativity in adults. Chapters 2–4 discuss various aspects of the developmental psychology of creativity. Chapters 2 and 3 define in more detail the psychological components of creativity: the skills, abilities, motives, attitudes, personal properties and similar factors that need to be fostered in an appropriate environment. The social nature of creativity will also be emphasized in Chapter 3 along with its implications for facilitating creative thinking and doing. Chapter 4 emphasizes differences between children and adults and presents a concept of children's creativity. This focuses on psychological processes and characteristics and is also consistent with the quantitative approach outlined above. The purpose of the review of theoretical material contained in these chapters is to crystallize out guidelines on what it is that needs to be promoted in order to foster creativity. The closing chapters will focus on these guidelines and on teaching and learning methods that can be applied in order to foster creativity both at school and also in higher education.

2

The role of thinking in creativity

Thinking involves:

- *structures* (internal representations of the external world such as patterns, categories, or networks) that are built up on the basis of information coming in from the outside;
- *processes* such as exploring, recognizing, organizing, interpreting, associating and applying, through which this information is processed;
- *control mechanisms* such as perceptual styles, combinatorial tactics, decision-making rules, or evaluation strategies that guide the processes and affect the kinds of structures they lead to.

The present chapter will review the special forms these must take in order to lead to creativity.

Creative cognitive structures

The nature of internal structures

Cognitive structures are internal representations of the external world that are built up on the basis of experience – they reflect and summarize the accumulated experiences of the individual and are stored in memory. Thanks to the phenomenon of language they also contain much of the accumulated experience of the whole society, passed on mainly by means of language by parents, teachers, books, media and similar sources of information. The structures make it possible to interact with the external world without direct physical action via what is usually called 'thinking'. As a result, when they receive information about a situation people can work out what will probably happen next, try out one or more courses of action in their head, rehearse what to do if certain further events occur and so on. Of course, the conclusions reached are not always accurate and they are sometimes even catastrophically wrong. None the less, in general cognitive structures make it possible to perceive the world as systematic and largely understandable, not as an unpredictable chaos, although there are substantial differences from person to person and within an individual person from situation to situation in the accuracy, efficiency, flexibility, or similar properties of cognitive structures. Some of these differences are of great importance in creativity (see below).

The usefulness of conventional structures

Despite the emphasis in this book on novelty, it should not be overlooked that the building of conventional structures is helpful, even necessary, for dealing with everyday life. Parents and teachers usually want children to develop accurate internal representations, for instance of how to read or count, but also of how to use public transport, borrow a book from a library, or surf the Net. Passengers have a keen interest in pilots acquiring a formally correct internal picture of how to fly a jet and how to navigate it, while patients would undoubtedly prefer brain surgeons to possess a conventional, unsurprising mental map of the anatomy of the brain. In fact, accurate, novelty-free internal representations of the external world are vital for the fundamental act of physical survival. They are also important for social survival – getting along with other people. If an individual's understanding of events departs too extensively from that of others the person in question will have difficulty not only in communication but also in fitting in to social structures, and may even be adjudged 'strange', 'weird' or 'crazy'. Thus, creativity does not involve abandoning conventional understandings of the world. What it does require is going beyond them and building structures that contain novelty while at the same time retaining the capacity to function in the social environment.

Creative cognitive structures

Guilford (1976) focused on the *organization* of the information that internal structures contain. They consist of *units* (single, discrete 'ideas'), *classes* (sets of linked units), *relations* (linked classes with defined principles or rules specifying the nature of their connection with each other), *systems* (complex sets of relations with a high level of abstractness and complexity), *transformations* (systems, relations or classes that see lower-order structures in a new way) and *implications* (structures that draw attention to further possibilities arising out of existing knowledge). To lead to creativity the structures must contain novelty (eg classes must link units not usually combined with each other, relations must go beyond the usual rules for linking classes, and systems must be based on unusual or unexpected relations). Helson (1996) linked these directly to creativity by defining it as the 'renewal and revising of symbol systems'.

Adopting a Piagetian position, Case (1978) identified three levels of what he called 'schemata' in building cognitive structures. According to him 'figural' schemata yield a concrete internal representation of information, 'operational' schemata identify the general aspects of the information and 'executive' schemata lead to transformations of data. He saw creativity as occurring when figural schemata are applied to yield accurate structures, operational schemata identify their abstract properties and executive schemata are flexible, complex and differentiated and lead to novel transformations. Under these circumstances, cognitive structures can be closely related to reality (ie relevant and effective) but at the same time yield novelty.

This can, however, be a struggle as will be emphasized more strongly in Chapter 3 in a discussion of social influences on creativity. Increasing maturity is accompanied by pressure to 'grow up', which means among other things, taking over the conventional structures: as has just been pointed out this is to a considerable extent necessary for physical and social survival. None the less, it is not necessary to think conventionally all the time and in every situation as the result of this would be no variation from the usual and no production of novelty. What is necessary is that people retain or develop the capacity to build structures displaying novelty, while continuing to be able to function in the surrounding world. Following sections will discuss the processes through which this occurs and the thinking strategies and styles that facilitate it.

Creative cognitive processes

Producing effective novelty

Finke, Ward and Smith (1992) distinguished two phases in producing effective novelty: on the one hand *generating variability* by building novel structures (unusual units, classes, relations and systems) and on the other *exploring* these new structures to discern the effective ones. In the case of generation of structures it has been argued (Cropley, 1999) that particular processes such as synthesizing different elements of information, transforming it, shifting perspective, or constructing analogies (ie changing, seeing differently, branching out) lead to novelty, whereas others such as recognizing the familiar, retaining what already exists, or reapplying the tried and trusted generate not novelty but orthodoxy or conventionality. As Finke, Ward and Smith pointed out, processes of the first kind generate variability, to be sure, but are not sufficient for creativity on their own. The second step (exploration), which occurs via processes like attribute finding, reinterpreting, inferring, shifting context, or testing limits, makes it possible to find the effectively novel elements in the variability that has been generated. Thus, a discussion of the processes leading to construction of effectively novel structures (ie of creativity) needs to examine both generation and exploration.

Bearing in mind what has just been said, it is possible to crystallize out some of the special characteristics of cognition that are involved in the production of effective novelty. Several of these are discussed in the following sections.

Special forms of thinking

Divergent vs convergent thinking

The crucial distinction made by Guilford in his seminal 1950 paper was between *convergent* thinking – quickly equated with conventional intelligence – and *divergent* thinking, which was seen as the cognitive basis of creativity. Convergent thinking is oriented towards deriving the single best (or correct) answer to a given question. It is effective in situations where a ready-made answer exists and needs simply to be recalled from stored information, or where the answer can be worked out from what is already known by conventional and logical search, recognition and decision-making strategies. Convergent thinking with its emphasis on accuracy, correctness and the like seems to be necessary for effectiveness (see earlier and following discussions) but it focuses on recognizing the familiar, reapplying set techniques and preserving the already known, and thus does not produce novelty. Divergent thinking, by contrast, involves processes like shifting perspective, transforming, or producing multiple answers from the available information and thus favours production of novelty. These answers may never have existed before, at least in the experience of the person producing the novelty in question. In a given situation it may be possible to produce large numbers of novel structures and many of them could, at least in theory, be equally useful. Although both convergent and divergent thinking lead to production of cognitive structures there is a qualitative difference: convergent thinking involves *production of orthodoxy*, divergent thinking *production of variability*.

Other concepts of creative thinking

Other authors have also emphasized the idea of a special kind of 'creative' thinking, often in the form of two contrasting strategies. Bartlett (1932), for instance, distinguished between 'open' and 'closed' thinking, while Rothenberg (1988) introduced the idea of 'janusian' thinking, naming it after the Roman god Janus who had two faces and could look in two directions at the same time so that he had the ability to deal simultaneously with pieces of information that would not normally be processed together. Rothenberg also introduced the term 'homospatial' thinking. This kind of thinking is able to unite apparently conflicting or mutually exclusive ideas, thus producing novelty.

Psychoanalytic theory distinguishes between 'primary process' and 'secondary process' thinking. Primary process thinking takes place in the unconscious. It is concrete and irrational (not bound by strict adherence to 'reality'). It is not restricted by the rules of the conscious mind and is thus capable of forming unlimited associations without regard to the restrictions imposed by experience and knowledge. In other words primary process thinking produces novelty. By contrast, secondary process thinking is conscious, rational, logical and oriented to reality. The ego functions strictly in terms of secondary process thinking and thus does not allow the fantasies of primary process thinking to enter consciousness, ie it acts to preserve what is rational, well known and socially acceptable. In doing so it inhibits the production of novelty. To gain access to novel material a person must be willing to 'regress in the service of the ego' (Kris, 1950; Kubie, 1958) by admitting the novelty into consciousness. For this reason creativity involves 'biphasic' thinking, which consists of an initial phase in which unfettered associations are made in the unconscious via primary process thinking (ie variability or surprisingness are generated) followed by a phase in which these associations are admitted into consciousness in the 'realistic' form of secondary process thinking (ie they are explored and made acceptable). Thus creativity involves 'tertiary process' thinking (Arieti, 1976) in which primary and secondary process thinking are combined to yield effective novelty.

According to Gestalt psychology the essence of thinking lies in the building of 'gestalts', well-rounded, closed 'wholes' that are formed by combining ideas. This may involve ignoring some aspects of a new stimulus or exaggerating others in order to absorb the new into what already exists. This process involves 'reproductive' thinking. Novelty is produced when instead of retaining an existing gestalt new experience is used to form a novel one that is surprising or unexpected. This is referred to as 'productive' thinking. The driving force behind productive thinking (see also later discussions of motivation) is the perception of 'dynamic gaps' in an existing gestalt; it simply does not stand up to the full facts of the situation (see sections on problem finding). Dynamic gaps arise out of the perception of contradictions, unexpected implications, inexplicable properties, inadequacies, or similar weaknesses of existing gestalts. As Birch (1975) showed, knowledge of the field is necessary for the detection of such gaps.

Although his work is essentially of a popular nature, deBono (eg 1991) made an interesting contribution to the discussion of creative thinking. Initially he emphasized 'lateral' thinking. Unlike conventional thinking, which is strictly sequential in nature and follows a set of logical steps, lateral thinking involves detours or sidesteps. Marginal characteristics of a concept or object that are not central to its usual definition are emphasized and brought into juxtaposition with similar characteristics of other concepts and objects to yield unexpected associations. To take an example, the fact that a paper clip consists of metal is emphasized in order to 'see' it as a device for conducting an electric current. By contrast, a matchbox can be regarded as a non-conductor that also has movable parts. Seeing these two objects in this way makes it possible to utilize them in an emergency situation as the basic materials for the construction of an electric switch.

Recently deBono has extended his model to distinguish between 'rock logic' and 'water logic'. Application of the first leads to thinking step by step in a straight line according to conventional logic. Decisions on what the next step should be are based on correctness and this is decided in terms of absolute norms such as 'truth', 'justice', or 'beauty', which change only slowly. Water logic, by contrast, allows ideas to flow together from many directions according to the 'natural' pathways in the material in question, just as water flows along cracks and depressions in the ground where there is no resistance and forms pools and eventually rivers (creative ideas). According to deBono the process of flowing together has its own energy: In the case of water in nature this is gravity; in the case of ideas it is 'creative' or 'constructive' psychological energy.

Special cognitive processes

Cognitive processes use existing information to produce further information and when this further information contains effective novelty it is customary to speak of 'creativity'. These processes include, among others:

- *selecting* from among the masses of information available at any moment (perception is not simply a passive acceptance of everything that impinges on the senses or is already stored in the mind);

- *relating* new information to what is already known;
- *combining* elements of new and old information;
- *evaluating* newly emerging combinations;
- *selectively retaining* successful combinations (which may then function as new information, returning the process to the phase of relating elements of information);
- *communicating* the results to others.

In his three-facet model of creativity Sternberg (1988) differentiated between three components: the 'intellectual', the 'personal' and the 'style'. The creative style will be emphasized here. It arises from special cognitive processes such as adapting successfully to special circumstances, recognizing opportunities, finding order in chaos and building broad categories. Creative people can cope with new information, recognize possibilities, cross boundaries, or find order in apparent chaos. They also generate larger numbers of ideas more quickly and express them in a more understandable way. Mehlhorn and Mehlhorn (1985) showed that the variance of such traits was at its lowest in a group of highly creative people (ie they resembled each other on these traits) but increased steadily in groups with successively lower creativity.

Torrance and Hall (1980) supported this approach by concluding that creative thinking involves special aspects of the processes just outlined. In particular, they emphasized:

1. uniting disparate ideas by putting them into a common context;
2. being able to imagine, at least as a theoretical possibility, almost anything;
3. enriching one's own thinking through the application of fantasy;
4. adding spice to one's thinking through the use of humour.

Although Necka's (1986) 'triad model' of creativity goes beyond thinking to encompass motives and skills, thinking is still of great importance in his approach. The aspects he emphasized include: forming associations; recognizing similarities; constructing metaphors; carrying out transformations; selectively directing the focus of attention; seeing the abstract aspects of the concrete.

Creativity-enhancing cognitive tactics

Particular forms or 'styles' (see Chapter 1) of some of these processes seem to be especially favourable for the production of effective novelty and thus of creativity. A number of these will be discussed in following sections.

Constructing 'remote' associates

The idea that cognition largely involves seeing connections between bits of information has already been mentioned (eg recognizing patterns, synthesizing). This involves making associations. Mednick (1962) argued that what is necessary for creativity is that associations go beyond the traditional, conventional or orthodox, and are 'remote'. He described the formation of remote associates and their connection to novelty production in the following way. In the course of experience people learn a number of possible responses to any given stimulus. Those responses most frequently linked with a particular stimulus whenever it was encountered in the past have a high probability of being selected as appropriate when the stimulus is encountered once again (ie they are common). Responses seldom paired with the stimulus in the past have a low probability of being chosen (ie they are uncommon). When the stimulus recurs in a new situation most people select a common response (they have often made it to this stimulus in the past). This means that people's reactions to familiar stimuli have the advantage of being consistent, but are repetitious: they interpret stimuli in the same way over and over again. In other words, they do not create novelty. 'Mouse' is a common associate to the stimulus word 'cheese', since these two ideas often occur together. Similarly, common associates to cheese are 'sandwich' or 'milk'. An uncommon associate (except to readers of Dr Seuss) would be 'green', as in green cheese. A similarly remote associate to 'cheese' would be 'moon' (according to children's tales the moon is made of cheese). A person with a high preference for close associates might associate 'green' with 'grass', whereas another who preferred remote associates might create novelty by associating 'green' with 'moon' via their common (remote) links to cheese.

Building unusual categories

Bruner's (eg 1964) approach goes further. On the basis of experience, events that repeatedly occur together are recognized as belonging to the same 'category'. The properties that are common to a number of individual exemplars of a category are seen as typical for members of that category: all members of the category of 'weapon' are useful for fighting, those of 'food' for eating. (It is interesting to note that, initially, belonging to the same category is understood on the basis of simple temporal or spatial proximity, or concrete resemblances such as similar colour or shape. In the course of cognitive development, however, people come to understand that events have generalized abstract properties, and that these are the basis of belonging together. This point will be discussed more fully in Chapter 4.)

The process of assigning events to categories is referred to as 'coding'. A new event is seen to have distinctive and characteristic properties. When these are judged to match the definitive properties of a particular category (ie *pattern recognition* occurs), the new event is encoded into that category. The new event is then treated as though it has all characteristics of the category, even characteristics that have not been directly observed. Thus, coding is a special form of 'going beyond the information given' (Bruner, 1964). Furthermore, once an object has been coded into a category it is difficult to see it as anything other than a member of this category. A simple example is the difficulty people have in seeing a hammer as anything other than a device for driving in nails. It could also be a weight, a hook, or a can opener, but encoding it as 'tool' shuts out most other interpretations. A further example is the difficulty experienced in eating kangaroo by many Australians despite the fact that kangaroo is a plentiful, tasty, healthy and cheap source of protein. This animal is coded as 'lovable and cuddly' or 'symbol of our country', categories that are incompatible with the behaviour of eating them. Eating kangaroo is something like eating one's national pride or dignity, an obvious impossibility. Sheep on the other hand have the misfortune to be coded into the category 'food' and therefore readily eaten, despite the fact that they are woolly and much more cuddly, while they also contribute far more to Australia's economic well-being than kangaroos.

Coding is very useful in everyday life. Without it every situation would have to be dealt with anew as though the person concerned had had no prior experience with the external world. It makes it possible to deal with the familiar swiftly and efficiently by activating the category to which a well-known stimulus belongs and thus knowing what it is and what to do about it. It also makes it possible to deal with the unfamiliar: once something new has been assigned to a familiar category on the basis of whatever information is available it has a meaning and the person knows how to deal with it. This gives life consistency and predictability and engenders a high level of confidence in one's own behaviour. Consistency and predictability are, however, the very opposite of creativity. When new stimuli are coded into existing categories and the categories remain intact in their existing form no novelty is created: under these circumstances going beyond the information given simply protects the status quo or produces orthodoxy, to use the term introduced earlier in this chapter.

In order to produce novelty, coding needs to go beyond the obvious and dominant properties of a stimulus so that its membership of categories other than the most obvious can be recognized. Coding also needs to be flexible so that a stimulus can be seen to be capable of belonging to more than one category or of being recoded as the situation demands. How a stimulus is coded depends not only on the properties of the stimulus itself but is strongly affected by contextual factors. For instance, in a library rectangular paper objects are likely to be coded as books, while a *hungry* person is likely to code a spherical object about the size of a tennis ball, yellowish-red in colour and with indentations like those on a golf ball on its surface as an orange. Contextual factors act like a key that increases a category's accessibility by unlocking and leaving the door to it ajar. Codings usually reflect past experience in a particular context and are thus usually commonplace and lacking in novelty. They may, of course, be sensible and socially acceptable as well as being readily available, so that coding into these categories trades off production of novelty for ease of processing and avoidance of 'cognitive strain' (Bruner, 1964).

As just described, the context predisposes people to code new events into certain categories. This induces a *set*, ie a tendency to see the world in fixed ways. The conventional coding of a wristwatch would be to class it as a device for telling the time. However, it is possible to break sets and code stimuli into unexpected categories such as coding the watch as an object with weight instead of as a timepiece. This recoding of the watch draws attention to previously ignored properties that it possesses and the person is then in a position to use the watch to solve problems where a weight is required but time of day is irrelevant, for instance by using it as a sinker on a fishing rod. Andreasen and Powers (1974) demonstrated empirically that creative writers displayed 'over-inclusive' thinking, ie they constructed wide categories in which ideas coded as separate by most people were treated as belonging together.

An amusing anecdote about the famous physicist Nils Bohr shows how a common object can be coded not only in the commonplace way but also in a number of divergent ways that are all none the less capable of solving a problem. In about 1905 in a physics exam at the University of Copenhagen, Bohr was required to answer a question on how to use a barometer to measure the height of a building. Since the customary coding of barometer is 'instrument for measuring air pressure' the expected answer was to use the barometer to measure the air pressure at ground level and at the top of the building, calculating the height of the building from the difference between the two. Bohr suggested tying a piece of string to the barometer and lowering it until it just touched the ground, adding the lengths of the string and the barometer together to obtain the height of the building, thus coding 'barometer' as 'rigid object with fixed length'.

He was failed but appealed on the ground that his method would work – in the terminology of this book it was effective, while it was also surprising. A referee ruled that Bohr was correct but that his answer showed no knowledge of physics. He was then given a few minutes to answer the question in a way demonstrating such knowledge. He responded by suggesting:

1. Throw the barometer off the roof and count the seconds until it hits the ground. Calculate the height of the building with the formula $s = \frac{1}{2}at^2$ (barometer coded as 'object with mass').

2. Measure the length of the barometer and of its shadow and calculate the ratio of the two. Measure the length of the shadow of the building and multiply it by the same ratio (barometer coded as 'object with fixed length').
3. Tie a piece of string to the barometer and set it swinging as a pendulum. Time the period of the pendulum at ground level and at the top of the building. Use Huygens's formula $T = 2\pi L/g$ to calculate the difference in g at ground level and at the top of the building and then calculate the height of the building from this (barometer coded as 'object with weight').
4. Use the barometer to calculate the difference in air pressure at ground level and at the top of the building, calculating the height of the building from this difference.

Finally he had coded barometer as expected, and given the conventional answer!

However, the irrepressible Bohr apparently could not stop himself and he went on to suggest climbing up the fire escape and marking off the height of the building in barometer lengths with a piece of chalk and then adding up the number of barometer lengths, thus placing 'barometer' in the same category as 'yardstick' or 'metre rule'. Finally, he suggested using some creativity and offering the janitor the barometer as a bribe to reveal the height of the building (barometer coded as 'object with monetary value'). What mark Bohr received for this answer is not known, but he received the Nobel Prize in 1922!

Building broad networks

In an analysis of the creative thinking of Poincaré and Einstein, Miller (1992) concluded that the essence of creative thinking is 'network thinking'. Building broad networks involves combining apparently disparate concepts. Miller defined the mechanism of combination as 'proper choice of mental image or metaphor'. In terms of concepts outlined above, the building of networks is an extension of the process of coding. Different categories may share properties. For instance, weight, balance, a convenient length, rigidity and portability are all properties of weapons but also of bats and rackets used in sports such as baseball, cricket, hockey, or tennis, as well as of walking aids such as a walking stick or a crutch. The three categories overlap and can thus be combined to form a system or *network* (for a relevant discussion of networks in thinking, see Anderson, 1976). Broad networks linking categories that are usually kept apart would make it possible to break the boundaries of a particular category, in the present example by combining the categories of 'sporting equipment' and 'walking aid' and using a baseball bat as a walking stick, thus producing novelty.

The concept of networks of interlocking categories was stated somewhat differently by Koestler (1964) who saw knowledge as existing in *matrices*. Information processing usually involves linking elements from within the same matrix and thus produces no novelty. By contrast, when two matrices are linked via 'bisociation', or three are 'trisociated', variability is produced. In the extreme form it would be possible to speak of 'omnisociation' where in principle all matrices could be linked to one another. The potential for production of novelty would then be very high.

Producing novel 'configurations'

Simonton (1988b) advanced what he called the 'chance configuration' model of genius; his approach can, however, be applied to creativity. He concluded – somewhat adapted for present purposes – that creativity requires possession of a large number of mental elements (pieces of information, memories, ideas, concepts). Production of novelty involves making a large number of associations more or less randomly or blindly until the chance occurrence of a 'configuration' – a happy combination that is just what is needed to solve the problem in question. The creative person is especially good not only at producing associations but also at recognizing that a configuration has occurred and grasping that it offers a solution.

According to this approach creative behaviour requires a combination of processes. These interact in the following way. As a result of convergent thinking (knowledge acquisition, development of skills), human beings possess a range of what Simonton (1988b) called 'mental elements'. When confronted with a situation requiring production of effective novelty the individual works through the available mental elements, selecting or discarding, bringing them into juxtaposition, etc, until a 'configuration' occurs: this could involve an idea, a model, an action, a way of arranging words, musical notes, shapes or forms and so on. The divergent thinker produces configurations that are unexpected and surprising. Construction of divergent configurations requires not merely divergent and convergent thinking but also motivation (for instance a drive to produce better solutions), appropriate personal characteristics (eg openness for the new), social elements (societal tolerance of non-conformity) and communication skills. It is also accompanied by feelings and emotions but these non-cognitive aspects will not be discussed here since they are the subject of Chapter 3.

Intuiting

Sometimes creative ideas seem to pop into the head of a particular person out of the blue. Ghiselin (1955) gave examples of famous creators who described their own production of effective novelty in this way. In his classical stage model of creativity Wallas (1926) identified a stage of *incubation* during which ideas seem to churn and work in the creative person's head until – apparently coming from nowhere – the required answer pops up. This phenomenon is frequently interpreted as indicating the existence of unconscious processes, in the psychoanalytic sense (eg Kubie, 1958). Indeed, psychoanalytic creativity theory regards unconscious thinking (primary process thinking) as an important element in creativity. However, the psychoanalytic approach will not be discussed in detail here although the idea of thought without conscious awareness will be developed further in a cognitive context.

Some cognitive writers such as Simonton (1988b) and Weisberg (1986) reject the notion of unconscious processes but others acknowledge the role of intuition (for a relevant discussion see Policastro, 1995). The basic idea of intuition in a cognitive sense is that people sometimes already have in their head a rough outline of the solution they are seeking. Their task is that of defining and refining this rough idea into effective novelty. The outline may be acquired via *implicit learning* (ie learning that occurs without the learner being aware of it), for instance in the course of everyday life. To take a simple example, during the course of riding to work every day in a public transport bus and sitting just behind the driver a person might learn a great deal about the work of a bus driver without realizing it and without ever having thought of the ride to work as a learning experience.

Implicit learning leads to *tacit knowledge* that people do not know they possess. Such knowledge can prestructure thinking about an issue. For instance, an engineer who had often ridden to work in a bus as in the example above might possess a great deal of tacit knowledge about the design of buses. As a result, upon being hired to design a new bus this person would already possess a preliminary framework that could suggest where the required answer might be found or approximately what the eventual solution might look like. When this tacit knowledge leads to production of effective novelty it is experienced as intuition. When it narrowly focuses information processing and leads to production of singularity it is experienced as a set or corset that blocks ideas.

A striking description of intuition is to be found in the writings of Poincaré, as summarized in Miller (1992). Poincaré experienced his own creativity as involving unconscious processes. He regarded creativity as a process of selection in which knowledge elements from widely separated domains are combined (ie remote associates are formed without conscious awareness). However, according to Miller nearly all of the possible combinations that arise from vast knowledge of many fields – as was the case with Poincaré himself – are 'filtered out', leaving only the ones that are 'harmonious' and 'beautiful'. In his view 'sensible intuition' acts as a guiding mechanism that makes it possible to filter out the mass of unproductive combinations. The nature of such guiding mechanisms will be discussed more fully in the following section.

Mechanisms guiding thinking

Some contemporary authors have gone so far as to argue that creativity results from random processes. An example is Simonton's (1988b) 'chance configuration' model that has already been mentioned. However, many authors argue that information processing leading to effective novelty cannot proceed by 'brute force' (Simon, 1989) in a process of perceiving, blindly associating and occasionally recognizing that a new combination is the required solution. This would lead to a 'combinatorial explosion' (Simon, 1989) involving huge numbers of 'empty' trials (Altshuller, 1984) and leading to cognitive strain (Bruner, 1964). Thus, combinatorial processes must be guided in some systematic way if they are to produce effective novelty. Several approaches to understanding these guiding mechanisms are now summarized.

Preference for accommodating

Martinson (1995) identified two 'strategic dispositions' in thinking: some people consistently seek to deal with the new by reapplying existing knowledge and tried and trusted solution strategies, whereas others try to construct new approaches when dealing with new situations. Horn (1988) made a similar point. He differentiated two contrasting ways of reacting to novelty, uncertainty, or ambiguity: the one seeks to absorb the novel into what is already known (ie to make it familiar and preserve what already exists), the other to alter the already known (ie to produce novelty). This disposition can be characterized by borrowing from Piaget and emphasizing *assimilating* and *accommodating*. In the present context, assimilating involves fitting new information in with existing mental structures and thus preserving the status quo, whereas accommodating is based on recognizing that current structures are not adequate and revising them. Intuitively, assimilating (making the new fit the known) is related to intelligence, accommodating (changing the known as a result of contact with the new) to creativity.

However, Ayman-Nolley (1999) cited Piaget himself and pointed out that it is the interaction between assimilating and accommodating that produces a creative product. The external world must first be assimilated and then the assimilatory schema 'adjusted' to take account of the form it takes in a number of diverse situations. The second step is accommodation. Piaget seems here to be emphasizing the importance of what has earlier been called knowledge of the field (ie assimilated experience) or of a preliminary step of convergent thinking, which is then followed by divergent thinking.

Creativity-facilitating cognitive styles

Cognitive styles are consistent and stable differences between people in the way they obtain information from the world around them, utilize their experience (sort, organize and recall information) and cope with demanding situations. (For a detailed discussion see, for instance, Messick, 1994.) Cognitive styles are often stated in the form of bipolar dimensions such as 'levelling versus sharpening', 'focusing versus scanning', 'field dependence versus field independence', 'preference for wide versus narrow categories', or 'seeking cognitive complexity versus seeking simplicity'. Some of these styles (eg field dependence, wide categories, or preference for complexity) are favourable to creativity.

Although their work does not belong to the mainstream of cognitive psychology, Myers and McCaulley (1985) discerned four bipolar types that in some ways resemble cognitive styles: extraversion (E) vs introversion (I); sensing (S) vs intuiting (N); thinking (T) vs feeling (F); and judging (J) vs perceiving (P). In theory the combination I–N–F–P is the creative profile. Myers and McCaulley reported that creativity is particularly related to the sensing–intuiting dimension with creatively gifted people very frequently being intuiters (N). Meisgaier and Meisgaier (1997) summarized nine studies with gifted students and concluded that the combination I–N–P is typical. They also showed that creative graduate students showed a strong tendency towards the N–P combination (intuitive perceivers as against sensor–judgers).

Early in the modern era, researchers attempted to identify *the* cognitive style or strategy that leads to creativity (eg Bloomberg, 1967). In my own early research on creativity and personality (eg Cropley, 1967), I linked it to field dependence. Other studies emphasized preference for complexity (as against simplicity), openness to novel information, tolerance for ambiguous information, tolerance for discrepancies and tolerance for incomplete information (eg Barron, 1963, 1969). More recently, however, as Puccio, Treffinger and Talbot (1995) concluded, there is no single cognitive processing strategy that is uniquely favourable for creativity. The relationship has come to be seen not as a matter of which strategies lead to it and which do not but rather of how various styles and strategies are connected with creativity. For instance, it could be speculated that production of variability would increase arousal by increasing uncertainty. In view of the known tendency for high arousal to narrow and rigidify thinking, production of novelty might well be easier under conditions of low initial arousal, especially in individuals with low tolerance for arousal. Issues like this suggest that there is a need for further research.

Heuristics in production of effective novelty

Favourable associational hierarchies, permeable category boundaries and loosely structured networks promote production of novelty. However, the number of individual ideas that could be produced in any given situation is very large: for instance, the total number of situations that could in theory emerge during the course of a chess game is larger than the total number of atoms in the universe. Despite this, champion players produce effective novel moves. Since it has been known formally for nearly 50 years that human information processing capacity is limited (Miller, 1956) such players must make use of tactics for dealing with very large quantities of information very quickly (for a more detailed discussion directly related to chess see Chi, Glaser and Farr, 1988). This is presumably done by editing out the high proportion of alternatives that lead nowhere. Thus, the first step in generating effectively novel moves is to produce variability, to be sure, but to confine this to the promising alternatives. The number of possibilities this yields is admittedly large in comparison with the small number suggested by orthodoxy, but is small in comparison with the number theoretically possible through blind associating. The second step is to identify the effective novelty in this mass of material. This division of the process into two steps is reminiscent of Finke, Ward and Smith's (1992) discernment of two phases – generating and exploring – in the production of effective novelty. These two steps would be greatly facilitated by *heuristics*. These have two aspects: on the one hand they involve rules or techniques for recognizing blind alleys from the start and ruling them out, or the opposite, homing in on particularly promising lines of attack; on the other hand they involve evaluation skills that make it possible to see that a line of attack is proving inadequate or the converse, to recognize that a solution is at hand (for example, blueprints or patterns of what an effectively novel solution might look like and techniques for matching the present state with this blueprint).

Metacomponents of novelty production

The properties of heuristics just outlined can be seen as elements of *metacognition*. This involves the 'executive processes' (Resnick, 1987) in thinking that allow people to organize and keep track of their own cognitions. According to Resnick these processes include review of knowledge, direction of attention and marshalling of resources. Sternberg (1988) emphasized further metacognitive processes such as defining the problem, selecting an appropriate set of processes for solving it and combining these into a workable strategy. To these can be added evaluation of one's own progress, effective changing of course should the evaluation make this necessary and sensing of one or more promising alternatives. The ability of people to articulate their own metacognitions is also of considerable importance. Articulation permits conscious self-reflection, identification of precise differences between approaches, discussion of progress with other people and the like. Rosenblatt (1986) concluded that there are two kinds of metacognitive process: those based on internal criteria and those based on external. In the case of creative writers it was found that both kinds of self-direction of the writers' own work could be observed.

Expertise, problem solving and creativity

Expertise

Langley *et al* (1987), Brown (1989) and Walberg and Stariha (1992) among others emphasized the importance in creativity of deep knowledge of a field, what Feldhusen (1995) called the 'knowledge base' of creativity. Weisberg (1986) examined self-reports and case studies of famous creators and combined this information with data obtained in experimental studies. This led him to conclude that creativity arises from 'chains' of ideas connected associatively in a long series of strictly logical small steps for which deep knowledge of the field is vital. Such knowledge is often referred to as involving 'expertise'. A striking example of its importance is Einstein's recognition – as a result of his deep understanding of them – that existing theories of the electrodynamics of moving bodies were inadequate (Fromm, 1998). This led to his development of the special theory of relativity. In general (eg Elshout, 1990; Walberg and Stariha, 1992), an 'apprenticeship' of 10–15 years seems to be necessary for acquiring the fund of knowledge and skills necessary for creativity, even in the case of famous youthful prodigies such as Mozart who produced creative music in his teens, it is true, but who started his musical education by playing at the age of four!

Expertise and creativity

However, despite its importance, research has shown that high expertise does not always facilitate novelty production. A very high level of familiarity with a field and with existing solution strategies can preorganize thinking so effectively that it leads only to production of orthodoxy (tried and trusted, correct approaches). A concrete example is to be found in the fate of a German chemist between the two world wars. He was interested in finding what would nowadays be called an antibiotic. Each evening before leaving his lab he set out bacteria colonies on Petri dishes so that they could grow during the night and he could attempt to kill them next day. After a while he noticed that his work was being impeded by because the bacteria were often dead when he arrived in the morning. He observed that the colonies of dead bacteria all had mould spores on them, whereas those that survived did not. He concluded (correctly) that the spores came from mould growing in dark corners of his lab and that this mould was killing the bacteria. He arranged for the entire room to be cleaned and decontaminated. This action was successful and he reported in a chemistry journal that the mould had been eliminated without trace and he was now able to carry on with his research on killing bacteria. Unfortunately he had not yet had any success in finding a chemical substance that was effective! Had he had expertise as a biochemist or botanist or biologist or been able to break the set imposed by his training as a chemist he might have won the Nobel Prize that later went to Sir Alexander Fleming.

By contrast, a very low level of expertise and consequent absence of preorganizing or constraining factors might seem at first glance to favour novelty production (ie ignorance is bliss). However, although absence of an adequate knowledge base makes taking the first step in Ward and Finke's two-stage model (production of novelty) easy by permitting a flood of simple variability (a large number of admittedly unexpected but ineffective suggestions), it leads to great difficulty with the second (identification of the effective elements of that novelty). Thus, both ignorance and expertise would be associated with low creativity, producing the U-shaped relationship identified by Martinson (1995).

Without questioning the importance of familiarity with a field, recent research (eg Ericsson and Smith, 1991; Root-Bernstein, Bernstein and Garnier, 1993) has looked at this interesting problem: although working successfully in an area over a long period (ie becoming an expert) can provide a knowledge base that can be manipulated to yield effective novelty it can also produce a kind of tunnel vision that narrows thinking and restricts it to the conventional. In order to achieve effective surprise, experts need appropriate personal properties such as openness to the spark of inspiration (Cropley, 1992a). They must be capable of seeing the contents of their field in a fresh light. In an empirical study of almost 1000 employees and managers van der Heijden (2000) showed that expertise has five dimensions, including special knowledge and specific skills as would be expected, as well as two further important dimensions: 'meta-cognitive knowledge' and 'growth and flexibility'. The former involves self-insights, the latter the combining of fields. The fields may be adjacent so that combining them produces only orthodoxy or, more interesting for present purposes, radically different or remote, in which case combining them leads to production of novelty. In other words, deep knowledge is only favourable for creativity when it is accompanied by insight, flexibility and similar properties.

Indeed, despite their high expertise highly creative experts often show a freshness and openness that is more typical of beginners. This has been referred to by Root-Bernstein, Bernstein and Garnier (1993) as the 'novice effect'. I once attended a lecture by the then 70-year-old Hans Selye, discoverer among other things of the stress syndrome, who apologized for being in plaster from his toes to his hip – a few days before he had fallen out of a tree after he saw something that seemed odd and interesting in its branches and climbed it in order to have a better look! A less creative senior researcher would have been too busy with current research problems to bother with something in a tree or would have sent a junior staff member to investigate.

Problem solving

Creativity as problem solving

Early in modern discussions Guilford (eg 1959) linked creativity directly with problem solving. He concluded that the creative process has four stages:

1. recognition that a problem exists;
2. production of a variety of relevant ideas (ie divergent thinking – see above);
3. evaluation of the various possibilities produced;
4. drawing of appropriate conclusions that lead to the solution of the problem.

Newell, Shaw and Simon (1962) also defined creativity as a special form of problem solving.

Creativity researchers speak of 'problem awareness', 'problem recognition' and the process of 'problem finding' or 'problem definition', which they see as major elements of creativity. Tardif and Sternberg (1988), for instance, stressed the importance in creativity of *sensitivity to problems*, especially finding 'good' problems. Getzels and Csikszentmihalyi (1976) concluded that this is as much the case in artistic as in scientific creativity. As Dillon (1982) pointed out it is possible to distinguish between *recognizing* problems that are already evident in the present organization of available information and are obvious to any qualified observer, *discovering hidden problems* as a result of an intensive analysis of a situation and *inventing problems* that are only apparent after the available information has been reorganized according to novel principles. The latter is more closely related to creativity (see above) than 'merely' solving problems (Jay and Perkins, 1997). A striking example already mentioned (Fromm, 1998) is Einstein's recognition that existing theories of electrodynamics were inadequate in dealing with moving bodies (ie his 'invention' of the problem where others saw none).

The question also arises whether creativity always involves solving problems. If 'problem' is understood broadly enough, effective novelty could indeed be argued always to lead to the solution to a problem. This could be, for instance, the problem of communicating a poet's sense of awe or the problem of capturing on canvas the beauty of a sunset. Using such broad definitions it could be argued that creativity always involves a product that solves a problem. An important aspect of problem solving is the distinction between solving by eliminating a difficulty or removing an impediment, and solving in the sense of envisaging, posing or formulating questions that need to be raised in order to deal more effectively or elegantly with an existing situation. The latter was referred to above as 'problem finding' and is proactive and constructive rather than reactive and destructive, since it involves bringing into existence a new way of looking at the issue in question.

Expertise and problem solving

Expertise plays an important role in problem solving. This is particularly noticeable in the case of problem recognition and reformulation. Experts seem to spend a higher proportion of solution time than beginners on (re)formulating problems (Rostan, 1994), and less on searching for solution strategies. Experts code (reformulate) problems on the basis of recognition of their definitive patterns. Once they have encoded the problem into a category the process of going beyond the information given means that the solution is at hand, since this is part of the category. Thus, in a sense, experts already know the solution, and the task is to encode the problem. This is done by means of identifying its deep structure (its systematic and metasystematic properties). Beginners, on the other hand, believe that they already know the problem, which they define on the basis of its surface structure (its immediate, concrete, highly specific properties). They thus code it into simple, superficial categories that contain little deep information about instances belonging in the category and therefore offer limited prospects of going beyond the information given. The consequence of this is that beginners believe that they 'understand' the problem since they have encoded it, but cannot find the answer, whereas experts have more difficulty encoding the problem but know the answer as soon as they have done so.

The interaction of creativity and problem solving

The role of the problem

One way of showing the relationship of creativity to problem solving is to focus on the problems themselves, dividing them according to:

- their degree of definition;
- the degree of specification of the way they are to be solved;
- the clarity of the criteria for recognizing a solution.

Clearly defined problems that are solvable by means of standard techniques and for which there are obvious and well-known criteria identifying the solution constitute 'routine' problems. They can often be solved without the help of creativity, although when existing knowledge is applied in settings where it has previously been treated as irrelevant a certain technical or inventive creativity in the sense of Taylor (1975, see Chapter 4) occurs. None the less, creativity is not absolutely necessary and is probably not usual. By contrast some ill-defined problems require in the first instance becoming aware that there is a problem at all and finding a way of defining it, secondly working out techniques for solving the problem and thirdly developing criteria for recognizing a solution. Such 'complex' or 'intractable' problems demand a high level of creativity. This raises the possibility that certain kinds of problem (routine problems) may actually inhibit creativity (see also earlier discussions of high expertise and creativity). It is also conceivable that the reverse could occur: creativity could inhibit the solving of routine problems, for instance, by making the solver overlook perfectly effective and obvious solutions and look for obscure ones, or by encouraging the solver to go beyond the actual problem at hand and define it in an excessively complex fashion. In the case of intractable problems, on the other hand, creativity may be indispensable.

Cognitive processes in problem solving

Brophy (1998) turned attention to the processes within individual people, and concluded that 1) finding, 2) identifying and 3) clarifying problems are the aspects of problem solving that lead to creativity. Kirton (1989) distinguished between people who, when confronted with a problem, seek to solve it by making use of what they already know and can do (adaptors) and people who try to reorganize and restructure the problem (innovators). He constructed an appropriate test, which is discussed in more detail in Chapter 6. Mumford and co-workers (for a recent summary, see Mumford *et al*, 1997) have made a more differentiated analysis of the cognitive processing skills that are decisive in creative problem solving. They identified dimensions such as *problem construction*, *information encoding*, *category selection* and *category combination*.

A further aspect of creative problem solving involves the ability to recognize a solution (eg Ghiselin, 1955) even if it falls outside traditional boundaries. The example of the chemist who failed to recognize that the killing of bacteria by a living organism (mould) rather than by a chemical means was the solution he was seeking provides a good illustration of how a failure to recognize a solution that is at hand can block problem solving. It also seems, however, that a too narrow definition of the required solution may hinder problem solving. An example is to be seen in the now almost infamous Australian 'submarine project'. The Department of Defence has spent several billion dollars on designing and building a revolutionary new submarine. Unfortunately, despite the protests of the apologists, the submarine is said to be as loud as a rock orchestra at full blast, to have a weapons system that cannot hit anything and a propulsion system that cannot guarantee to move the submarine. Although they were asked to build something effectively novel the designers and engineers were given excessively narrow specifications of the nature of the end product including, even, stipulation of the material of which the screw was to be constructed, ie the solution was overdefined. A truly open task statement would have been something like: 'Design and build an effective device for defending Australia's coastal waters at a cost of no more than six billion dollars.'

Limitations of the cognitive approach

The cognitive approach to creativity ('production of effective novelty') just outlined sounds admirably straightforward. However, it raises the danger of reducing creativity in a rather mechanistic way to a defined set of processes and guiding mechanisms regardless of the characteristics of the person in whom they are occurring or of the setting in which they occur. It would thus ignore the goals and motives underlying the production of novelty and the social, occupational, or educational context in which it occurs. Treffinger, Sortore and Cross (1993) stressed the importance of what they called the 'full "ecological system" of creativity'. This involves recognition of creativity's interaction with other psychological properties of the individual, aspects of the creative process, effects of the situation, characteristics of the task itself and the nature of the desired product. They concluded that these must be specified in discussions of how to foster creativity.

It is also unclear whether novelty means novel in a specific time and place, in which case it is partly determined by the external context and not solely by the cognitive processes or the structures generated. Similarly unclear is whether a product must be novel for a specific person, in which case an ignorant person could most easily produce novelty, or novel for all societies in all history. For instance, transferring procedures from one work setting where they are familiar to another where they are unknown may produce effective novelty but this is obviously different from inventing ideas previously unknown in any context. Case studies (eg Ghiselin, 1955; Weisberg, 1986) also indicate that some highly creative individuals regard the novelty they produce as obvious or even the only logical conclusion to be drawn from available data, ie it is conceivable that some effective novelty may not involve special forms of cognition at all. This is one of the 'paradoxes' of creativity (Cropley, 1997a). The following chapter turns to non-cognitive factors within the individual (personality, motivation) and to influences within the social environment, and shows how they interact with processes in the production of effective novelty.

3

Creativity: the role of personal properties

In addition to thinking, creativity requires willingness to produce novelty and personal properties that permit this. It is also accompanied by feelings. Creativity as a psychological potential is as much determined by these as by thinking processes. The present chapter looks at:

- *personality traits* associated with creativity such as openness, self-confidence, or flexibility;
- the aspects of *motivation* that favour creativity, including courage and risk taking;
- the interaction of personality with the *social environment*.

The search for the creative person

Helson (1996) referred to the search for the creative personality as 'one of the exciting adventures' in creativity research. The first step is usually that of identifying 'creative' people either on the basis of demonstrated creative behaviour or of scores on instruments thought to measure creative potential (see Chapters 5 and 6 for discussions of such instruments). The test approach is particularly common in research with children although it is not confined to this group.

Identifying creative people

Sublime creativity

The search often focuses on people who have already produced highly acclaimed products especially in the arts and science (ie it concentrates on *sublime* creativity). For instance, Freud (1947) carried out a retrospective analysis of Leonardo da Vinci. As Runco and Charles (1997) pointed out, focusing on sublime creativity is 'safer' since it is certain the people involved really are creative (after all their products have been acclaimed). In the present book everyday creativity and potential creativity are of greater interest because the purpose here is not to explain after the fact what made the famous great but to work out how to encourage unacclaimed people to realize their potentials, even if only in humble forms. None the less, it makes intuitive sense to draw upon knowledge about acknowledged creators in looking for the vital characteristics that underlie creativity, and this will be done here.

Occupational creativity

It is also possible to focus on creative behaviour without setting the bar so high by studying people who pursue occupations regarded as inherently creative such as writer, musician, or actor, treating the people as creative simply by virtue of the area in which they work (*occupational* creativity). Examples are the work of Barron (1972), Cattell and Drevdahl (1955), Drevdahl and Cattell (1958), Eiduson (1958), Götz and Götz (1979), or MacKinnon (1983). One finding is that such people possess special personality characteristics that set them off from less creative colleagues in their own disciplines or from people in less creative occupations (ie creative people vs less creative).

A variant of this approach is to study people in occupations not regarded as necessarily inherently creative but offering opportunities for creativity (eg architect, research scientist), or even occupations thought (rightly or wrongly) to offer few opportunities for creativity, such as engineer, business manager or officer in the armed forces. Creative members of these professions are then compared with less creative colleagues. Participants are often identified as creative by virtue of patents, awards, publications, or similar more or less objective criteria. Identification by means of ratings of their creativity in their job by colleagues or other qualified persons is also commonly employed. MacKinnon (1983) showed differences between creative and less creative architects while Helson (1983) also reported similar differences for creative mathematicians. Barron (1969) reported that creative members of several groups, including air force officers, had greater ego strength than the less creative.

Some researchers (eg Cattell and Butcher, 1968; Roe, 1953) looked at possible differences in personality between people who had achieved creative eminence in different areas (eg chemists vs psychologists, social scientists vs physical scientists, scientists vs artists). This involves comparing creative people with other equally creative individuals, the difference being the field of creative eminence. A more eclectic approach is to compare producers of sublime creativity with 'ordinary' people or even with psychiatric patients. An outstanding example is Rothenberg's (1983) comparison of Nobel Prize winning scientists with schizophrenic patients and college students rated as either highly creative or less creative on the basis of creativity test scores. The results showed among other things that creative scientists (sublime creativity) and creative students (potential creativity) showed similar patterns of thinking (divergent thinking, remote associates) and differed in similar ways from less creative students.

Unacclaimed behaviour

Without losing sight of the importance of actual creative behaviour, however defined, the criterion of creativity can be set lower by concentrating on 'humble' activities that none the less produce novelty (ie *everyday* creativity). This is often identified by biographical inventories (see Chapter 6) in which people report their degree of participation in their daily life in activities regarded as creative: acting in an amateur theatre group, writing a family history, collecting something surprising and unexpected such as spider webs, sewing unusual clothing, developing new recipes and similar activities. Finally, it is possible to study people – especially children – who have not yet displayed creative behaviour but seem likely, for instance on the basis of test scores (especially tests of creative thinking – see Chapter 5), to become creative if they receive appropriate encouragement (ie *potential* creativity).

Dynamics of personality and creativity

It is usually assumed by researchers that personality influences creativity, although it is theoretically conceivable that the reverse is true, ie that creativity influences personality. For instance, the experience of producing novelty and having this accepted or rejected by other people seems very likely to increase self-confidence, willingness to deviate from the commonplace, openness for new ideas and similar traits. It is also possible that people gravitate to a particular field that suits their personality (eg music, painting, poetry, literature, biography, journalism, architecture, social sciences, mathematics, natural sciences, engineering). These fields differ according to the degree of formality and precision they require, as well as according to the degree of self-revelation involved, approximately in the order in which they are listed above. People who preferred informality and imprecision associated with a high degree of expression of feelings and emotions would cluster together in fields that permit these, while those who preferred formality, precision and low levels of self-revelation would be found in different fields. A particular field would thus be associated with a certain personality type, not however because this personality type makes the people in question creative but because the particular kind of creative activity 'draws' certain people, the creative field also probably encouraging, rewarding and amplifying appropriate personality characteristics.

However, in the first comprehensive review of research on personality and creativity in the modern era Dellas and Gaier (1970) concluded that personality traits are determinants of creative behaviour, rather than the reverse. In any case, the question of the effects of personality on the expression of creativity is of central interest in this chapter, since this book is concerned with fostering creativity. Does personality make people creative, allow them to become creative, or increase the likelihood that they will be creative? Five possibilities will be looked at in this section:

- *causal* relationship (certain personality traits actively trigger creativity almost perforce);
- *threshold* relationship (certain traits are necessary for creativity);
- *facilitatory* relationship (certain traits make being creative easier);
- *common source* relationship (personality and creativity both derive from the same fundamental roots);
- *interaction* relationship (personality and creativity affect each other).

Personality as a compelling cause

It is conceivable at least as a theoretical possibility that certain personality characteristics may directly trigger creative behaviour. In fact there are writers, especially psychoanalytically oriented authors including Freud himself, who emphasize a link of this kind. The most obvious examples of such characteristics would be negative properties like lack of impulse control or rejection of social norms. These would lead more or less inevitably to *surprising* behaviour as antisocial impulses were expressed, ie they would 'cause' production of novelty. Such behaviour would not usually be regarded as creative but rather as unwelcome, annoying, delinquent, criminal, or even psychotic and would often have negative consequences for the person concerned, ie it would involve at best pseudocreativity. However, someone who was active in a setting where unbridled expression of impulses and ignoring the conventions were regarded as admirable – in, perhaps, avant-garde theatre or dance – might be fortunate enough to have this behaviour accepted as not only surprising but also effective, and thus creative.

Not only negative traits as in the example above but also *positive* characteristics could also more or less force people to be creative. For instance, a strong sense of justice could impel a person to turn to literature, the theatre, or medical research in the hope that these would provide a pathway to righting what the person regarded as social wrongs. To take one example, Emile Zola was moved to write *Germinal* by the outrage he felt at the injustice experienced by French coal-miners. Other admirable traits, too, such as determination and strength of character could energize a person who had experienced misfortune and hardship to turn to literature or art to communicate to others the sorrow and disappointment these experiences had caused, or they could cause a person who had been refused a research grant to work hard to achieve a major scientific breakthrough against all the odds.

Creativity need not always be a reaction to negative factors either in the individual's personality or in the environment as might seem to be the case from the examples just given. It is also apparent that positive personality characteristics such as the drive for self-realization in the sense of Maslow (1973) or generative motives in the sense of Necka (1986) may lead to the production of effectively novel products even without deprivation, injustice, or the like. Indeed, some acknowledged creators are born into environments of wealth and privilege or at least of acclaim and success and seem to become creative either because the production of effective novelty is simply a natural part of the ethos of their environment or because their social privileges give them the time and facilities to pursue their interests.

The three generations of Becquerels – Antoine César, Alexandre Edmond and Antoine Henri (Nobel Prize in 1903) – are an example of the former. They successively held the chair in physics at the Museum of Natural History in Paris from 1837 to 1895, each becoming one of the creators of modern knowledge in his particular field: electrochemistry, the nature of light and radioactivity respectively. An example of creativity in an atmosphere of wealth and privilege is to be seen in the achievements of the cousins Charles Darwin and Sir Francis Galton. After studying medicine in London and then graduating from Cambridge, Galton travelled widely before accompanying his cousin on the voyage of the *Beagle*, apparently motivated by curiosity. He published books in geography and meteorology and went on to lay part of the foundations of modern statistics, which he invented because he needed it to pursue his interest in quantitative analysis of the inheritance of ability (which he called 'genius' although he later retracted the term).

It is important to notice, however, that *effective* novelty can only occur if the cognitive elements such as knowledge, skills and divergent thinking are also present: these would determine what *level* of creativity the novelty achieved. Zola displayed extraordinary imagination and poetic fantasy in his work, it is true, but without his mastery of the French language, painstaking research and detailed drafting of plot his manuscripts would still have been surprising, even shocking, but would have lacked effectiveness and may well have produced no more than quasicreativity – surprisingness unaccompanied by effectiveness. A striking further example is to be seen in the case of Vincent Van Gogh. His early work was driven by impulses (personal disappointment in love and a desire to bring other people beauty and consolation) that he initially tried to express by becoming a missionary, before turning to painting. However, he lacked technical knowledge and returned at the age of 32 to the Academy of Art in Antwerp where his flair for colour and light came to fruition in the course of training. Technical skills had to be learnt before his work produced effective novelty.

Personality as a facilitator/blocker

Personality may function not so much as a sufficient cause – a press or goad that almost drives a person to production of novelty in the way just outlined – but rather as an assister. This would mean that certain personality characteristics may be necessary or at least helpful for creativity without actually causing it. In the case of some negative traits it may be their *absence* that is necessary or helpful. This approach involves the idea of personality as a *necessary but not sufficient cause*. Relevant personality characteristics may include courage, interest in the novel, self-confidence, a generative or growth orientation and similar factors. These will be looked at more closely in later sections of this chapter.

This way of conceptualizing the relationship between personality and creativity can be grasped easily by examining *negative* personality characteristics that seem to inhibit production of effective novelty. For instance, a person could conceivably be cognitively equipped to produce effective novelty and even highly motivated to do this but be inhibited by personality characteristics such as fear of looking foolish, excessive need for certainty, or exaggerated social conformity. In this case the personality characteristics in question can be thought of as *blocks* to creativity (eg Cropley, 1992b). Not encouragement but weakening of such characteristics would facilitate realization of creative potential.

Although it is fictional, an episode in the American soap opera *Providence* illustrates this point in a striking way. One of the main characters is a woman who has a child but lives at home with her father (a widower) in the house where she has spent her entire life. She even works for her father whose practice (he is a veterinary surgeon) is located in the family home, ie she does not even need to leave the house to go to work. (Her sister had broken away temporarily and been a medical specialist in Boston but returned home to live with her father, sister and brother in Providence, also in the family home.) She has very little money, knows hardly anyone and leads a dull and uneventful life. Not surprisingly she is bored and frustrated. Unexpectedly, she develops her own formula for clam chowder (how is amusing but irrelevant for present purposes) and is offered a contract worth billions of yen by a Japanese firm. However, this would mean living in Japan for several years. Without even thinking it over she rejects the offer, horrified and repelled by the prospect of leaving the house and town in which she has spent her entire life in order to live for some time in Tokyo. This reaction is completely predictable from incidents in the rest of the series, is accepted without question by the other characters and is presented by the writers of the series as being obviously correct. Although the whole thing is fictional the episode dramatically presents the inhibiting effects of exaggerated clinging to the familiar even at the cost of abandoning financial security, recognition and acclaim.

The common cause explanation

Although she was studying the possible relationship between creativity and psychosis (see Chapter 1), Jamison's (1993) conclusion that mental states such as elation are vital for creativity but do not *cause* it is of considerable interest here. Traits such as excitability, non-conformity, or risk taking may well be an expression of more fundamental characteristics such as emotional lability, greater attentiveness to internal mood fluctuations, or greater sensitivity to small changes in external stimuli. These also underlie production of novelty. The result is an apparent direct relationship between excitability, non-conformity and risk taking, and creativity. To give a more concrete example, elevated mood could lead to flamboyant (non-conforming) behaviour in people by reducing fear of embarrassing themselves (ie it could remove a blocker). Simultaneously it could promote making remote associations and thus lead to production of novelty. It could then seem logical to conclude that the non-conformity had led to the production of novelty whereas in reality both might be the result of euphoric mood resulting from emotional lability.

Eysenck (1997), one of the strongest proponents of the idea that creativity is a matter of personality, has emphasized that many apparently causally related personality characteristics may in fact be indirectly related because they both stem from a single more fundamental cause. He identified a very small number of biologically determined fundamental dimensions of individual difference that are anchored in the central nervous system (ie extraversion, psychoticism, stability) but express themselves in a larger number of more superficial observable characteristics. These observable characteristics reflect the interaction of the fundamental dimensions with each individual person's particular environment and are correlated with each other because they are derived from a common cause (the fundamental characteristics).

This model makes the problem of pseudocreativity easier to conceptualize. A fundamental state – let us say impulsivity – might lead some people to behave in ways that the majority regards as rude, wild or antisocial. At the same time it might promote production of novelty. If the antisocial behaviour were repeatedly seen paired with production of novelty it might come to be regarded as essential for creativity, or even be regarded as a cause of it. Ultimately it might even be mistaken for creativity itself, thus reducing creativity to non-conformity (pseudocreativity). Pseudocreativity is attractive to some people because it eliminates the need for *effective* novelty and the hard work this often entails.

Qualitative vs quantitative approaches

The relationship between personality and creativity can be looked at in two ways. The first posits a threshold effect, the second a linear relationship. According to the threshold model possession of certain decisive personality traits beyond some minimum level (the threshold) is necessary for creativity to occur (a qualitative approach: if you have the personality you are creative; if you do not, you are not). According to the second model certain special characteristics would increase the likelihood of creativity the more strongly a person possessed them (a quantitative approach). As the strength of the 'necessary' traits increased the probability of creativity would also rise. The quantitative approach is more optimistic for educators and parents since strengthening existing traits (or weakening negative ones) seems intuitively easier than inculcating what is not there. The idea of personality as a stable set of behavioural dispositions whose fundamental form is laid down in early life supports this view.

Creativity and personality

Several comprehensive reviews of research on creativity and personality have appeared over the years including Dellas and Gaier (1970), Farisha (1978), Barron and Harrington (1981), Motamedi (1982), Treffinger, Isaksen and Firestien (1983), Dacey (1989), Albert and Runco (1989) and Eysenck (1997). These summaries confirm that a fairly stable set of findings have emerged, although different authors name traits somewhat differently or give differing weight to particular traits according to their own areas of interest.

Dellas and Gaier (1970) concluded that creative people are characterized by a special pattern of traits that distinguish them from the less creative. By and large this pattern cuts across content areas. They identified 11 typical traits of which 9 would generally be regarded as positive:

- independence (both in attitudes and in social behaviour);
- dominance;
- introversion;
- openness;
- breadth of interests;
- self-acceptance;
- intuitiveness;
- flexibility;
- social poise.

The remaining two (lack of concern for social norms and antisocial attitudes) are less positive. Dellas and Gaier also identified two further traits that differentiate between people who are creative in aesthetic fields such as art or literature and those who are creative in science: radicalism and rejection of external constraints.

According to Dacey (1989) there are nine traits that characterize creative people:

- tolerance of ambiguity;
- stimulus freedom;
- functional freedom;
- flexibility;
- risk taking;
- preference for complexity;
- androgyny (possession of both male and female characteristics);
- acceptance of being different (ie self-acceptance);
- positive attitude to work.

Eysenck (1997) concluded that researchers typically emphasize:

- autonomy;
- non-conformity;
- openness to stimulation;
- flexibility;
- tolerance of ambiguity;
- inner directedness;
- ego strength.

More specific studies have given particular weight to a smaller number of traits that are thought to be of central importance. Barron and Harrington (1981) listed preference for complexity, autonomy, self-confidence, the ability to tolerate contradictory aspects of one's own self and high evaluation of aesthetic qualities. Parloff *et al* (1968) emphasized autonomy and complexity, while Albert and Runco (1989) focused on independence. Barron (1969) showed the importance of ego strength, including acceptance of conflicting aspects of one's own self. Basadur and Hausdorf (1996) drew attention to the importance of placing a high value on new ideas.

Dellas and Gaier (1970) concluded that the personalities of young creative people are similar to those of creative adults and this is supported by studies focusing on children. Heinelt (1974) studied schoolchildren identified on the basis of test scores as highly creative and came to the conclusion that they were significantly more introverted, self-willed, intellectually active, flexible and possessed of wit and a sense of humour than less creative youngsters. According to Neff (1975) they are flexible, tolerant and responsible as well as being sociable and success-oriented. They are also characterized by being less satisfied and less controlled than children who display lower levels of creativity. In social situations they are less willing to conform and less interested in making a good impression.

Since early studies (eg Getzels and Jackson, 1962) humour and playfulness have been emphasized as personality characteristics associated with creativity in children. More recently, Graham, Sawyers and DeBord (1989) demonstrated the relationship between playfulness and creativity in schoolchildren. Isen, Daubman and Nowicki (1987) showed that children did better on creativity tests after they had seen a comedy film. A playful approach fosters creativity because play is not chained to the strict rules of reality and is freed from social pressures (Bruner, 1975). Play is also less risky than real life because situations imagined in play can be cancelled out if they prove too problematic and everything returned to what it was before. This means that in play novel situations can be tried out without risk. Picasso's well-known observation that he played with ideas is often cited as support for the importance of play even for acknowledged creators. Torrance and Safter (1999) saw play as a central element in what they called 'making the creative leap'.

Motivation and creativity

Studies of famous creative people from the past have confirmed that *motivation* plays an important role. For instance Cox (1926) showed that geniuses such as Newton, Copernicus, Galileo, Keppler and Darwin were marked by tenacity and perseverance in addition to high intelligence. Goertzel, Goertzel and Goertzel (1978) also showed the importance of motivation in their case studies of historical figures while Hassenstein (1988), too, commented on the obsessive nature of the work of gifted individuals. Biermann (1985) concluded that fascination with the subject matter and consequent extreme motivation was one of the most important characteristics of creative mathematicians of the 17th to 19th centuries. Facaoaru (1985) showed that creative engineers were characterized not only by special intellectual characteristics but also by motivational factors, and Csikszentmihalyi (1988) emphasized the importance of motivation in creative musicians. Baldwin (1985) gave the discussion a new perspective by arguing that intense motivation for activity in a particular area may be the best indicator of creativity in members of disadvantaged groups.

According to Perkins (1981) creativity is the result of six elements, of which four are closely related to motivation: the drive to create order out of chaos, willingness to take risks, willingness to ask unexpected questions and the feeling of being challenged by an area. Henle (1974) gave a Gestalt psychology perspective to the drive to create order out of chaos by emphasizing that perception of 'dynamic gaps' (inadequacies, inconsistencies) in gestalts (eg existing knowledge) leads in creative people to a drive to build a good gestalt by reorganizing knowledge. Einstein's (Miller, 1992) description of how his recognition that existing theories of thermodynamics were inadequate motivated him to develop the special theory of relativity is an example of this phenomenon. Lehwald (1985) also identified *Erkenntnisstreben* (thirst for knowledge) as a central characteristic of successful creators.

Intrinsic motivation

A widely accepted position is that creativity is based on intrinsic motivation (Amabile, 1996), the wish to carry out an activity for the sake of the activity itself. This can be contrasted with working for external rewards such as praise, prizes, even avoidance of punishment (extrinsic motivation). This approach strongly supports the view that children are only creative when they are intrinsically motivated. Otherwise, it is argued, they become active only in order to gain the extrinsic reward and shape their behaviour in order to conform to whatever is necessary to receive that reward. Conformity is, of course, the opposite of creativity.

More recently, however, the possibility of fostering creativity in the classroom by the application of external rewards has been demonstrated by Eisenberger and Armeli (1997). They showed that extrinsic reward led to enduring improvements even in a creative area such as music when children were rewarded for specific 'creative' behaviours such as incorporating unexpected elements or producing alternative possibilities. These findings have been severely criticized by, among others, Joussemet and Koestner (1999). None the less, they indicate that children and teachers need a clearly defined concept of creativity that specifies what behaviours are necessary in order to be creative, where and how each individual's behaviour needs to be changed and what aspects of personality, attitudes and motivation are facilitating as well as blocking of such behaviours. Cropley and Cropley (2000) demonstrated this by showing that engineering students who received a concrete definition of what was meant by 'creativity' in a particular class and were counselled individually on the basis of a personal profile of their own specific strengths and weaknesses were more original than the members of a control group on creativity tests and built more creative models in a laboratory exercise, despite the fact that they were working for grades. This study will be discussed in greater detail in Chapter 8 (pp 164–65).

Openness

Perkins (1981) regarded openness as one of the basic characteristics associated with creativity. McCrae (1987) defined this as interest in novelty for its own sake: the open person likes to go beyond the conventional and enjoys the unexpected. The difference of an open person as just defined, from the woman in the *Providence* case study above, is very striking. She was open to almost no variation in her life. McCrae demonstrated the relationship between creativity and openness empirically, and Treffinger, Feldhusen and Isaksen (1990) also emphasized openness as well as tolerance for ambiguity and self-confidence. In my own work I have particularly emphasized 'openness to the spark of inspiration' (Cropley, 1992a).

Openness vs closedness seems to be a fundamental dimension of personality on which differences from person to person are already visible in early childhood. Many people reject out of hand anything that departs from the familiar by more than a small amount, preferring novelty to arise, if at all, out of small, barely perceptible changes to the status quo. The size of the maximum tolerable change in the status quo may correlate with creativity. In view of the well-known importance of 'collative variables' (incongruity, unexpectedness, unpredictability) in the environment for maintenance of optimal cognitive and emotional functioning (Berlyne, 1962) and the negative effects of monotony as seen in, for instance, the hospitalization syndrome in small children (Bowlby, 1979), the drive in many people for maximum sameness and stability seems to be unhealthy. In studying the effects of stimulus deprivation on mental and emotional functioning Heron (1957) described the 'pathology of boredom'. Sternberg and Lubart (1995) highlighted the problem of creativity in a 'culture of conformity' while Burkhardt (1985) went further and identified society's '*Gleichheitswahn*' (psychosis of sameness).

Preference for complexity

Early research in aesthetics (eg Eysenck, 1940) showed that two fundamental dimensions of visual preference are involved in judging the pleasingness of works of art: on the one hand good taste, on the other preference for simplicity vs preference for complexity. The latter is of particular interest here. Research (eg Götz, 1985) has shown that this dimension is stable and can be measured reliably. Gestalt psychologists also emphasized preference for complexity, and developed instruments for measuring it (eg Welsh, 1975). Shaughnessy and Manz (1991) reported a substantial number of studies that showed that preference for high complexity and asymmetry is an indicator of creativity. In creative people complexity and asymmetry energize behaviour aimed at creating 'good' gestalts that none the less contain original and unexpected combinations. Barron and Harrington (1981) also identified preference for complexity as a dimension of personality that is associated with creativity while Nardi and Martindale (1981) showed that the preference for asymmetry goes beyond visual perception. They found that creative people preferred dissonant tones when passages of music were played to them.

The material just reviewed demonstrates the existence of two fundamental dimensions of individual difference that are central to the present discussion: openness vs closedness on the one hand, preference for complexity vs preference for simplicity on the other. Taken together, these seem to define two basic approaches to life. The one involves welcoming the new and different and being positively motivated by incompleteness, disharmony and uncertainty, the other rejection of novelty and preference for neatness, harmony and closure. The first combination is favourable for production of novelty; the second favours retention of the status quo. It is not being suggested here that this distinction provides an exhaustive definition of the motivational aspects of creativity, but it appears to be well founded both in terms of research and also of practical observation of youngsters and adults confronted with novelty.

Society and creativity

The courage to create

As Moustakis (1977) put it, being creative means living your life your own way. Barron (1969) concluded that there is a connection between creativity and 'resistance to socialization'. In discussing the problems of the culture of conformity Sternberg and Lubart (1995) introduced the term 'contrarianism' to refer to creative people's resistance. Such people defy the rules, even when they do not call attention to themselves through antisocial behaviour.

Otherwise they would simply echo whatever was accepted in their society. As was pointed out above, however, the production of novelty requires readiness to diverge, defy conventional opinion, or expose oneself to the possibility of being wrong. Motamedi (1982) saw this as requiring a special form of courage – the 'courage to create'.

The social rules

In principle all people are capable of a wide range of responses to life situations but in the process of growing up they learn that most of these are forbidden and usually restrict their responses to a narrow range of socially tolerated behaviours. Anderson and Cropley (1966) studied the reactions of schoolchildren in social situations where a number of alternative courses of action were possible, of which one was highly socially desirable (eg 'You have promised to visit your grandmother but are tempted to go to the cinema instead'). They concluded that the children were guided by 'stop rules' that forbade most of the wide range of possible reactions in a particular situation in favour of the socially approved 'correct' one.

A high level of conformity with social norms has the advantage that life becomes predictable since it is more or less known what can be expected in everyday situations. However, the disadvantage is that unusual, unexpected behaviour is discouraged and becomes rare. There are rules not only about behaviour but also about which opinions are correct, indeed about the right way of thinking and the contents of correct thought. Societies have 'filters' (Fromm, 1980) through which behaviours and ideas must pass, and carry out constant 'surveillance' (Amabile, Goldfarb and Brackfield, 1990) in order to detect and deter deviance. They are prepared to tolerate the breaking of the rules to a certain degree, the rules that can be broken and the degree of deviation is accepted varying from society to society and from time to time, as well as according to the age, social position, occupation and other characteristics of the individual doing the rule breaking. For instance, the British or North American societies would tolerate deviations from the norms for behaviour at a wedding by a 21-year-old art student that would not be tolerated from the local bank manager.

Degree of openness of the society

Thus, openness or lack of it is a characteristic not only of individual people but also of environments. People who produce novelty in settings that are not open for it are likely to suffer various kinds of negative sanctions. The situation of such people is exacerbated because some traits associated with creativity may lead to disorganized even chaotic behaviour or to behaviour that is regarded as antisocial or arrogant (eg impulsiveness, lack of concern about social norms, lack of interest in making a good impression, tendency to lose themselves in their work). Cognitive characteristics such as making remote associations that are too remote for most observers worsen the situation. The result may be that the effectiveness of the novelty creative people produce is difficult for others to recognize.

A good example is the PhD dissertation of the mathematician Henri Poincaré, who possessed vast knowledge of his field associated with very high creativity. His dissertation was highly original but after the first 30 or so pages the novelty became increasingly difficult for the examiners to understand (their report is still in the relevant files in Paris). They criticized it on the grounds that after a good beginning it became progressively more disorganized. Fortunately for Poincaré the examiners showed a degree of openness. They eventually concluded that the level of mathematical knowledge and original thinking displayed at the beginning was so high that the dissertation could be accepted anyway. Not all highly original thinkers have been so fortunate – to take one famous example, Einstein's dissertation was rejected by the Technische Hochschule in Zurich.

In general, there are rules about breaking the rules. People publicly acclaimed as creative break the rules but succeed in staying within acceptable limits. If they do not they are likely to be regarded as eccentric, immoral, mentally disturbed or criminal rather than creative, with the possibility of being criticized, shunned or even locked away. A conversation a number of years ago with the coach of a team in the Canadian Football League demonstrated this point very clearly. He was asked why his team had not made use of the legal but never-used drop goal (worth three points) in a game in which they were in possession of the ball for the last play of the game, were only 30 yards out and trailed by only two points. Instead of trying for the match-winning three points with a kick that would have been quite easy, the team preferred instead a conventional, completely predictable long pass into the end zone. The opposition – since it knew what was coming – had its defence perfectly organized for this play and it was more or less inevitably unsuccessful. The coach explained that had he called for an attempted drop goal he would have been written off as an idiot who had 'lost it' when the pressure went on. Even if the kick had succeeded, far from being celebrated as the creative genius who had engineered an unexpected victory when all had seemed lost, he would have been regarded as some kind of cheat or 'hot dog', who had somehow succeeded by trickery. An unsuccessful long pass, by contrast, caused great excitement among the spectators and sent them home feeling that their team had fought bravely to the end and only lost through bad luck. Creativity is allowed in sport as in other areas but only within the limits of what the environment can tolerate.

Creativity assisters

Despite what has just been said many people produce novelty. This is regarded here as in a sense a successful fight against the influence of society. Such success is facilitated by 'assisters' in the environment. In a study of 20th-century British novelists Crozier (1999) argued that differences in productivity were largely attributable to the influence of 'social support factors'. Csikszentmihalyi (1988) postulated that 'social support networks' are vital determinants of creativity in the lives of individual creators: these include parents and teachers, spouses, mentors and colleagues. Such groups or networks seem to be important not only for acquisition of a high level of technical skill but also for development and maintenance of the intense *motivation* that has already been discussed. Petersen's (1989) study of hobby authors showed that support from such people was vital in their ability to avoid 'writer's block' and maintain their motivation to write, thus demonstrating the importance of the social support system not only in acclaimed but also in everyday creativity. Subsequently Csikszentmihalyi (1996) encapsulated the necessary environment by referring to what he called a 'congenial' environment. Among the properties of such an environment are openness, positive attitude to novelty, acceptance of personal differentness and willingness to reward divergence. These factors define a society that 'assists' novelty production.

It is not only the groups to which a person belongs – intimate groups such as the family, more public groups such as playmates or friends, or more or less formally defined groups such as experts/critics, colleagues, or workmates – that foster creativity by offering a social environment marked by recognition and encouragement of novelty production (or, of course, hinder or block it by withholding such positive feedback). Research indicates that individual people too can function as assisters of creativity. One way they do this is by energizing, activating or releasing it in others without necessarily producing effective novelty themselves. As Bloom (1985) showed, such creativity assisters can be humble and unsung people such as a grade school teacher. In adults, working in a team may provide contact with assisters. An important function of such people is to offer creative individuals a safe space where they can break the rules without sanctions. Another is to offer them a positive perspective on themselves, for instance the view that their ideas are not crazy but creative. This recognition can help to foster the courage to deviate from what everyone else is doing, among other things by offering an opportunity to test the limits of the acceptable without risk or feelings of guilt.

The interaction approach

The creativity-facilitating pattern of motivation and personality characteristics stressed in earlier sections of this chapter is very plausible. Traits such as non-conformity, flexibility, intuitiveness, possession of broad interests and self-acceptance, or motivational states such as risk taking or tolerance for ambiguity, fit well with what common sense suggests would be expected of creative people. However, precisely this plausibility raises problems. Who could possibly expect creative people to be narrow-minded, rigid, conforming and lacking self-confidence? The list of properties of creative people has the taste of mother's apple pie about it!

This is not to suggest that discussion of the relationships among creativity, personality, motivation and society is valueless. However, the traits identified contain little surprise value – they do not produce much novelty. Thus, the question of *how the necessary personality and motivation develop* is of greater interest than the simple listing of traits that could easily have been guessed without any research. If the necessary characteristics are biologically pre-programmed there seems to be little point in attempting to foster the 'creative' personality. Although it is now well known that personality really is partly inherited, patterns of personality are – to a considerable degree at least – acquired as a result of interactions with the social environment. The section that follows will look at this interaction.

A dynamic system

In his 'typology' of creative giftedness Necka (1986) emphasized that it requires a combination of ability, personality and motivation. He saw these as defining an individual 'profile' for each person. More important for the present purposes he argued that this profile is dynamic in nature – it changes as the person acquires new knowledge or as different motives become more important. Gruber and Davis (1988) went into greater detail about this dynamic. They regarded the achievement of an effectively novel product not as an isolated event that stands alone but as the result of a long developmental process that can last for years before coming to fruition. In the course of this process knowledge, opinions and attitudes are not only acquired but are constantly subject to *reorganization*. They called this the 'evolving systems' model. Three systems are involved: knowledge and abilities, motives and feelings, and goals. All three change continuously as a result of interactions between them and the external environment (for instance, new knowledge is acquired, emotions and attitudes change and new goals emerge) as well as among themselves.

Shaw (1989) extended this approach by considering not only the interaction of cognitive and non-cognitive factors but also incorporating consideration of the product. He called the interactions 'loops'. To give some examples, acquisition of information interacts with stewing over a problem in what he called the 'Arieti loop', thinking about a problem interacts with the 'Aha' experience of unexpectedly seeing a solution (the 'Vinacke loop'), seeing a solution with verifying its apparent effectiveness (the 'Lalas loop'), verification with communication of the product to other people (the 'communication loop') and communication with validating the product in public (the 'Rossman loop'). (With the exception of the communication loop these are named after creativity researchers. Rossman, for instance, carried out research with people holding successful patents so that the appropriateness of his name for the phase of communicating and validating a product is obvious.) Shaw concluded that there must also be more complex loops involving three or more aspects. The complexity of the interactions among the elements of creativity is emphasized by the fact that, for instance, the information obtained when a product is tried out in public could affect the stewing-over process of incubation, thus providing the possibility of a new 'Aha' experience (Vinacke loop) and so on.

Feelings and emotions in creativity

Shaw extended his analysis by expressing concern that creativity research has not paid sufficient attention to further non-cognitive aspects of novelty production such as the feelings and emotions experienced by creative people when they are producing novelty. Basadur and Hausdorf (1996) emphasized a related aspect of the personal correlates of creativity: *attitudes* favourable to creativity (eg placing a high value on new ideas, believing that creative thinking is 'normal', admiring creative people in one's immediate environment and not just in the abstract). In a study of acknowledged creative engineers and physicists Shaw showed that they experienced at various points of the production process feelings such as fascination, self-confidence or self-doubt, frustration, relief, excitement and satisfaction. These various feelings can be regarded as part of the *joy of creating*. Shaw's respondents seldom mentioned negative feelings and emotions such as aggressiveness or triumph at having beaten someone else, perhaps because they knew that these are socially undesirable but perhaps because it really is more a matter of *joy* in creating. When Shaw looked at emotion and loops he found that particular loops were accompanied by specific feelings: the Arieti loop, for instance, was accompanied by fascination and excitement, the communication loop by hope and anxiety. A dynamic approach to the development of the personality and motivational aspects of production of novelty and the role of society in the developmental process needs to take account of the interactions involved.

The expanded phase model of creativity

Problems of the personality approach

Helson (1996) drew attention to the tendency, especially in the 1950s and 1960s, to idealize 'the creative type' by assuming that people acknowledged as creative represent all that is good and desirable in human beings. One result was to regard less creative individuals as less worthy or even as failures. The problem is even more fundamental. The very idea of a unique personality type that can be labelled 'creative' has been questioned strongly by some writers (eg Helson, 1996). Indeed, she concluded that there is no unitary, differentiated personality profile that is typical of all highly creative people and also distinguishes them as a group from the less creative. Pursuing a similar point Treffinger, Sortore and Cross (1993) concluded that there is no evidence that specific measures for fostering creativity are effective with particular kinds of people and not with others, or that specific kinds of people can be identified that react in different ways to creativity training. Thus, there may be no 'typical' creative personality at all. However, this does not negate the idea that certain traits (see above) are related to creativity.

Another problem with the study of creativity and personal properties was the tendency to ignore evidence that there is a 'dark' side to creative people. One example of this is the link between creativity and psychopathology already discussed in Chapter 1. Another is the fact that creativity could be used for evil ends (see the discussion in Chapter 1 of the ethical aspect of creativity). The negative side of the creative personality is also visible in social relations. More than 30 years ago Cropley (1967) mentioned evidence that not all was sweetness and light in the families of highly creative children. Some families displayed coldness, indifference and exaggerated parental expectations of independence, negative aspects of family life that seem, however, to foster independence, non-conformism and intense motivation for a particular area of interest. These latter properties are generally regarded with approval as necessary for creativity but they apparently come at a cost for family life. The creative architects in MacKinnon's (1983) study were *lower* than the less creative on sense of well-being, communality and sociability as well as being less well socialized. Feist (1993) reported that creative scientists were arrogant and competitive. This simultaneous linkage of personality with positive and negative personality traits is part of the 'paradox' of creativity described by Cropley (1997a) and discussed in greater detail below.

The paradoxical personality

Quite early in the modern era McMullan (1978) concluded that despite the high level of interest in the issue there is no simply definable creative personality. On the contrary the evidence shows that creative people are characterized by seven 'polarities':

- openness combined with drive to close incomplete gestalts;
- acceptance of fantasy combined with maintenance of a strong sense of reality;
- critical and destructive attitudes together with constructive problem solving;
- cool neutrality combined with passionate engagement;
- self-centredness coexisting with altruism;
- self-criticism and self-doubt together with self-confidence;
- tension and concentration side by side with relaxedness.

These polarities appear to be mutually incompatible and when they occur together they define according to MacMullan a *paradoxical personality*. More recently Csikszentmihalyi (1996) made a similar point when he emphasized the importance in creativity of a 'complex' personality, combining among others sensitivity with toughness, or high intelligence with naïveté.

One aspect of the apparently contradictory characteristics combined in creative people is they often simultaneously display stereotypically 'masculine' traits (autonomy, self-confidence, toughness) and yet stereotypically 'feminine' ones too (sensitivity, intuitiveness, responsibility), a combination that is nowadays referred to as involving 'androgyny'. (The terms 'masculine' and 'feminine' are not used here to describe real men and women but are simply stereotypes.) This finding implies that both rigid maintenance of strict gender roles as well as insistence on a well-balanced or harmonious personality would inhibit creativity. What is needed seems to be an 'integration of opposites' (Urban, 1995a, 1997). A dynamic, developmental approach offers prospects of solving some of the problems of the paradox just described.

A 'phase' approach to creativity

The 'classical' analysis of the emergence of creative products is the phase model, first introduced into creativity research about 75 years ago (Wallas, 1926). Wallas distinguished four phases or stages. In the first, referred to as the phase of *information*, a person becomes thoroughly familiar with a content area. In the *incubation* phase the person 'churns through' or 'stews over' the information obtained in the previous phase. The phase of *illumination* is marked by the emergence of a solution, not infrequently seeming to the person involved to come like a bolt from the blue. Finally comes the phase of *verification* in which the person tests the solution thrown up in the phases of incubation and illumination. The solution may emerge into consciousness all at once, thus seeming to have appeared from nowhere and creating the subjective feeling of creativity without perspiration. This would explain why some creative people overlook the phases of information and incubation in describing their own creativity.

Empirical studies of the process of creation in people actually engaged in producing something new, as well as retrospective studies in which acknowledged creators described how they obtained new ideas, have cast doubt on the validity of the phase model (see Glover, Ronning and Reynolds, 1989). None the less it offers a helpful way of disentangling a number of issues in the discussion of creativity. In particular, as will be seen below it helps to resolve the problem of the paradoxes of creativity. It also helps clarify the interactions among psychological elements. For this reason it will be retained here as an aid to the present theoretical discussion.

The discussion of the role of society in creativity, for instance Csikszentmihalyi's (1996) emphasis on the importance of socio-cultural validation, indicates the need to take account both of the communication of novelty to other people and also of their assessment of its effectiveness. For this reason, Wallas's four stages need to be extended by adding after verification further stages, of *communication* and *validation*. Furthermore, discussion in Chapter 1 of the necessity for creativity of a human agent acting with intention suggests that an initial stage of *preparation* should be taken into account. In this stage the necessary problem awareness and intention develop. These considerations yield an extended model involving seven phases (see Table 3.1).

When the processes of production of novelty outlined in Chapter 2 and the personal characteristics and motives associated with the processes are related to the expanded phase model just outlined, specific processes, motives, personal traits and feelings can be associated with specific phases. Table 3.1 presents an outline of the results of such an analysis. The processes, motives, personality caracteristics and feelings shown in the table do not provide an exhaustive list, but are merely examples.

Table 3.1 Creative processes, traits and motives in the phases of production of novelty

Phase	Process	Result	Motivation	Personality	Feelings
Preparation	– identifying problem – setting goals – convergent thinking	– initial activity – general knowledge – special knowledge	– problem-solving drive (intrinsic) – hope of gain (extrinsic)	– critical attitude – optimism	– dissatisfaction
Information	– perceiving – learning – remembering – convergent thinking	– focused special knowledge – rich supply of cognitive elements	– curiosity – preference for complexity – willingness to work hard – hope of gain	– knowledgeability – willingness to judge and select	– interest – curiosity
Incubation	– divergent thinking – making associations – bisociating – building networks	– configurations	– freedom from constraints – tolerance for ambiguity	– relaxedness – acceptance of fantasy – non-conformity – adventurousness	– determination – fascination
Illumination	– recognizing a promising new configuration	– novel configuration	– intuition – reduction of tension	– sensitivity – openness – flexibility	– excitement
Verification	– checking relevance and effectiveness of novel configuration	– appropriate solution displaying relevance and effectiveness	– desire for closure – desire to achieve quality	– hard-nosed sense of reality – self-criticism	– satisfaction – pride in oneself
Communication	– achieving closure – gaining feedback	– workable product capable of being made known to others	– desire for recognition (intrinsic) – desire for acclaim or reward (extrinsic)	– self-confidence – autonomy – courage of one's convictions	– anticipation – hope – fear
Validation	– judging relevance and effectiveness	– product acclaimed by relevant judge (eg teacher)	– desire for acclaim – mastery drive	– toughness – flexibility	– elation

In each phase (see left-hand column), psychological processes (second column) produce a result (usually a psychological state) shown in the third column, which forms the material for the next phase. The psychological processes are made possible or at least facilitated by motivational states (fourth column) and personality characteristics (fifth column) and are accompanied by the feelings shown in the right-hand column. Table 3.1 depicts a process culminating in a socio-culturally validated product. Naturally the product can also fail to achieve validation, ie be judged by observers not to be effectively novel. The process can also be broken off before being communicated, for instance when executive or metacognitive processes indicate that the current configuration is doomed to failure. The creative process can also start part-way through such as when a person who has in the meantime learnt more returns to a configuration previously abandoned, thus restarting the incubation phase without first passing through preparation and information.

Dividing the emergence of effective novelty into phases as in Table 3.1 shows how apparently contradictory aspects of creativity can work together to produce an effectively novel product. For instance, in the stage of *information* convergent thinking, naïveté and intrinsic motivation might be of paramount importance whereas in the stage of *illumination* divergent thinking, general knowledge and openness might predominate. In the stage of *verification* by contrast toughness, courage, extrinsic motivation, specific knowledge and convergent thinking might be vital. The table also offers insights into fostering creativity, a topic that is discussed in greater detail in Chapter 7. For instance, it is necessary to specify which phase of the production of novelty is to be fostered by a particular activity. To take one example, promoting *preparation* might well require different activities from those needed to foster successful behaviour in the stage of *verification*.

4

Creativity in adults and children

Three main issues lie at the heart of this chapter:

1. Is creativity something for children only?
2. Is the creativity of children and adults the same?
3. How can adults remain creatively productive?

The answers can be summarized in a few words:

- Adults are capable of producing novelty into old age although there are age-related changes.
- There are differences between typically 'juvenile' and typically 'adult' novelty production.
- Adults can take steps to preserve their creativity.

Age and intellectual performance

The traditional view: the adolescence peak

Early psychological research on the relationship between age and intellectual performance in general (ie not focusing on creativity) supported the still-widely prevalent stereotype encapsulated in the *adolescence peak* hypothesis. This can be summarized in a simple manner. A rapid increase in early life is thought to lead to a peak in performance in adolescence or early adulthood. This is followed by a plateau lasting until the age of perhaps 60 or 70 (unless disease or injury intervenes). At this point a rapid deterioration is thought to set in and accelerate rapidly once old age makes itself felt, ending ultimately with death. In other words it is all downhill after adolescence, with late adulthood a time of catastrophic deterioration. This point of view is represented in Figure 4.1.

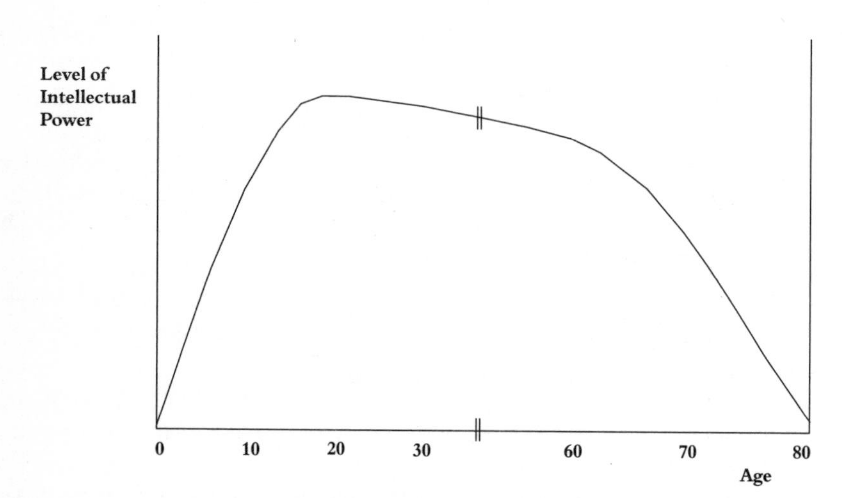

Figure 4.1 Stereotype of intellectual growth and decline with age

Weaknesses of this approach

The hypothesis concerning age and level of intellectual functioning depicted in Figure 4.1 is not without foundation. However, it is only a rough representation of the situation and is marred by a number of weaknesses that will be reviewed in following sections.

Narrow range of abilities

The graph is based primarily on findings derived from studies that used IQ scores as the measure of intellectual performance. These are an average score obtained by combining different cognitive skills such as word knowledge, numerical fluency, or resistance to distractions. As a result the graph does not take account of differences in the shape of the curve for different aspects of ability. It also focuses on knowledge and skills that are closely related to conventional school activities such as speed of problem solving, rapid and accurate access to the contents of the memory, or familiarity with the most up-to-date technology, and thus favours children and young adults. In effect, the adolescent peak hypothesis reflects the one-sidedness in conceptualizing ability referred to earlier.

Differences from person to person

Figure 4.1 involves a *nomothetic* approach. In other words it adds together information from a large number of people in order to make generalizations that apply to people as a group. In doing so, however, it blurs differences between individual people. For instance, some individuals show consistently low levels of intellectual activity from an early age, some are active early but slow down early, some are active from young adulthood and continue into advanced age or even until death and so on. The focus on development within an individual person involves the *ideographic* approach. Differences in the pattern of development from individual to individual within an age group (ie ideographic differences) are so large that it may well be more profitable to examine the factors that give rise to these differences than to look at average differences between age groups.

Post-mortem studies show that except for situations involving the sudden onset of debilitating illness or injury many people maintain a high level of intellectual activity until the point where a final decline culminating in death occurs, regardless of chronological age. In other words it is not age itself that is correlated with reduction in intellectual activity but rather entry into the final phase of life. This may at first glance seem to be saying the same thing. However, there are large individual differences in the chronological age at which the final decline begins as well as in its length. One determinant (once again leaving aside injury or illness) is the extent to which people remain intellectually active. According to the principle, 'Use it or lose it', those who start resting on their laurels earliest are often (although not always) the ones who slip into the downhill part of the curve earliest, not the people who are oldest according to the calendar. A social factor influencing level of activity is career choice or career pathway. Those who follow occupations with little intellectual challenge from the start or who gravitate with increasing age into passive positions show the strongest tendency to 'lose it'. Occupational patterns are themselves correlated with education as well as with socio-economic status and related variables such as degree of intellectual stimulation in the family via books, demanding hobbies, challenging conversations with parents and the like.

Methodological weaknesses

The hypothesis represented by Figure 4.1 is not only nomethetic in nature but is also based on *cross-sectional* studies, a method in which different groups of people of different ages are tested at the same time and compared with each other, eg a group of, let us, say 20-year-olds and a different group of 50-year-olds are tested at the same time and then the conclusion drawn that the performance of the 50-year-olds shows what the 20-year-olds will be like in 30 years' time. This method ignores *differences between generations* such as greater familiarity of young people with test procedures, greater knowledge about technology, or broader experience of adolescents as a result of increased prosperity of the parents and consequent greater opportunities for travel, membership of clubs, or exposure to books or special tuition. Even if there really were a constant increase throughout life *within* a single generation, cross-sectional studies could yield a curve similar to that in Figure 4.1 purely as a result of differences *between* generations in the average level of scores on the various tests. Thus, cross-sectional studies tend to *over*estimate the degree of deterioration with age.

Methodological analyses (eg Baltes, Reese and Lipsitt, 1980) have shown that *longitudinal* studies in which the *same* people are tested several times at intervals during their lives are likely to produce different results, generally demonstrating less deterioration. However, this method may *under*estimate the decline because, for instance, of selective drop-out of participants (eg those who have had particularly unfavourable life experiences cannot be found for follow-up studies, refuse to participate, or die early). By the early 1980s there was conflicting evidence from the two sorts of studies as well as better understanding of the methodological issues, which led to pronouncements on the 'myth' of decline in intellectual functioning during adulthood, accompanied however by counterarguments that the myth was itself a myth (see for instance Horn, 1982): in other words, there really is a decline. This conclusion will be supported although with a considerable degree of differentiation in a later section.

The more recent position

The generalization depicted in Figure 4.1 is not completely inaccurate but is a highly simplified summary that both reveals and conceals the truth of the matter. Apart from methodological and technical issues this is because the relationship between age and intellectual performance is complex. The level of intellectual performance at any age results from a compromise between two age-related aspects of cognition: the 'mechanics' on the one hand, the 'pragmatics' on the other (Lindenberger, 2000).

Mechanics vs pragmatics

The *mechanics* are the biologically based dimensions such as sensory and motor capacity, perceptual skills, memory, the ability to direct attention selectively, the capacity for associative learning, or the ability to build categories – they resemble what is commonly called 'fluid intelligence' (eg Cattell, 1971). They are part of the biological inheritance of each individual so that differences from person to person in mechanics are to some degree inherited, although the precise way in which they are transmitted by genes is not yet clear. There is a tendency for the mechanics to deteriorate with increasing age after reaching a peak in adolescence or early adulthood (ie to confirm the adolescence peak hypothesis). However, the age at which deterioration commences and the speed with which it proceeds vary from person to person and according to each individual's life circumstances (see the discussion above), thus partly *dis*confirming the adolescence peak hypothesis.

The *pragmatics* are the knowledge and skills acquired as a result of experience with a particular environment (in Cattell's sense 'crystallized' intelligence). They are learnt via interactions with adults (eg parents and family members, teachers, media, sports and entertainment figures) as well as with other children such as siblings, playmates, or classmates. Differences from person to person in pragmatics are highly dependent upon the particular environment in which each person grows up. Pragmatics arise out of mechanics. To take a simple example, someone who lacked the mechanics needed to distinguish between tones could not acquire pragmatics based on the experience of hearing music. To take a further simple example, a child who possessed the mechanics of hearing but heard only French in the surrounding environment and no other language would acquire the pragmatics of speaking French, no matter what language its biological parents spoke.

Interaction of mechanics and pragmatics

Mechanics and pragmatics interact with each other. For instance, the ability to perceive clearly, remember accurately and recall information rapidly (mechanics) obviously affects the quality and quantity of material acquired via experience. To return to the example just given, a child with defects in the mechanics of hearing would be handicapped in acquiring the pragmatics of speech. Thus, mechanics affect the development of pragmatics. At the same time, however, acquired skills developed through training (pragmatics) affect mechanics. For instance, musical training leading to pragmatics in this area enhances the ability to perceive fine differences in auditory stimuli (mechanics). Since the improved mechanical ability to perceive sounds would in turn foster the further development of the pragmatics of musical skill a circularity or interaction is established. Factors affecting acquisition of pragmatics are not exclusively cognitive.

Acquired interests and values and development of a self-image, for instance as a musician, would also lead to closer attention to certain kinds of stimuli (music) and thus foster the further acquisition of knowledge about music.

It is true that mechanics deteriorate in adulthood as capacities like memory, speed, or ability to resist distractions fade, thus conforming to the adolescence peak hypothesis. On the other hand pragmatics may continue to grow, for instance as vocabulary gets larger or as motivation becomes more intense. The level of performance at any age is a trade-off between the two aspects of mental functioning. In younger people factors such as speed, sharpness of perception, accuracy and speed of memory (ie mechanics) are more important determinants of performance than acquired knowledge, ability and skills (ie pragmatics) – indeed, in the theoretical situation where no pragmatics had yet been acquired mechanics would be entirely responsible for differences in performance from person to person. As people get older, however, acquired pragmatics tend to play a more and more important role, knowledge and skill, as well as attitudes, motives and self-image becoming more important than raw mechanics.

Peak performance

Peak performance occurs at that age where the sum of falling mechanics and rising pragmatics is at the optimum level. However, this would vary according to the particular task in question and the conditions under which it is to be dealt with. Sometimes the relationship can be compensatory, improved pragmatics making up for worsened mechanics. For instance, in some situations the increasing 'cunning' associated with age and experience may permit peak performance despite loss of physical prowess. This might occur, for instance in some areas of commerce, in the form of routinized business acumen or in management where acquired skill in dealing with people might compensate for failing intuitive quick-wittedness.

A concrete example from real life of how pragmatics can compensate for mechanics is to be found in observation of the on-field performance of the ageing Franz Beckenbauer in his last season as a player in the German national soccer league. While the younger, fitter, faster, stronger players fought for the ball in scrimmages and then raced after it with flying legs and arms and no doubt wildly beating hearts, Beckenbauer would glance at the situation, identify it (whether consciously or not) as something he had already experienced a hundred times and jog at his leisure to the spot where his experience told him the ball would arrive in a few seconds. He would reach this spot just before the ball and ahead of the racing youngsters and deliver a pinpoint pass to a team-mate standing alone. In this way he was able through the application of the pragmatics he had learnt in a long football career to make a major contribution to his team's success despite the greatly reduced mechanics associated with an ageing body.

Pragmatics may become so important for performance that they more or less completely replace mechanics. The danger is then that the person in question will focus all effort on perfecting and maintaining the pragmatics (learnt ways of dealing with the world) even in new situations, thus maintaining the status quo and rejecting novelty. (See earlier discussions of *expertise*.) For instance, it would be logical and understandable for a senior player like Beckenbauer to reject any changes in the rules of soccer or in the basic tactics for playing the game (ie introduction of novelty) because such changes would render null and void his acquired advantage in the form of wisdom about the game.

The precise combination of pragmatics and mechanics that leads to peak performance is partly dependent upon the task or the conditions under which the task is undertaken. A good example is to be seen in the fact (Bosman and Charness, 1996) that the average age at which champions such as Bobby Fischer or Viktor Korchnoi win the world chess championship in *tournament* play is 30, whereas the average age at which world *correspondence* champions win their titles is 46. The factor that favours older players in correspondence chess seems to be that in this form they have three days to consider their next move whereas in tournament play they have on average only three minutes! (The latest rules require 40 moves in 100 minutes plus 30 seconds per move.) It seems that where there is sufficient time for acquired experience to be sorted through and selectively applied (correspondence play) greater age is an advantage (at least to a certain point), whereas where quick grasp of the situation, high-speed recognition of patterns and rapid decision making are necessary (tournament play) youth is an advantage (relatively speaking).

Neglected capacities

The adolescence peak hypothesis does not take sufficient account of acquired 'cunning'. It also neglects factors like good sense in difficult situations, understanding of the way in which the events of life go together to form a consistent context, the ability to place events into perspective and a grasp of the fact that life is full of uncertainty. These are aspects of what can be called 'wisdom' (eg Baltes and Smith, 1990; Birren and Fisher, 1990) or 'sagacity' (Burt, 1970). Because of its diffuseness or 'fuzziness' this aspect of intellectual functioning has only begun to be emphasized in the last decade. More important for present purposes the studies whose findings underlie Figure 4.1 take little account of fantasy, innovation, daring, or unconventionality, aspects of mental ability that are particularly important for creativity.

What age-related deterioration really occurs?

Despite what has just been said Lindenberger (2000) concluded that increasing age really does bring genuine changes for the worse in intellectual functioning. However, these are relatively specific and do not justify drawing a general conclusion that people are finished at about 50 or perhaps a little later.

Cognitive changes

The weight of research findings suggests that there is deterioration in three areas:

- speed of information processing;
- the size and accessibility of working memory;
- the ability to apply attention selectively.

Lindenberger argued that memory and selective attention are really two aspects of a more general property – control of goal-directed behaviour – thus reducing to two the crucial dimensions on which substantial age-related deterioration occurs. Other properties persist until late in life. Of particular importance for the present discussion are findings such as those of Cornelius and Crespi (1987) and Perlmutter (1988), which show that characteristics important for creativity such as imagination do not disappear with increasing age.

Lindenberger demonstrated that the capacity to benefit from cognitive training (ie to acquire new knowledge and skills) is stable over the entire lifespan and does not show much deterioration with increasing age. Put plainly, people are capable of learning until very late in life. There is, however, a qualitative change that is important for the present discussion. Older adults tend to learn very specifically, acquiring new skills in relation to a specific task that makes sense to them and is of immediate importance, and making little generalization of new learning to situations other than the one in which the learning occurred. This means that they tend not to make remote associations, bisociate, or code broadly and flexibly (see Chapter 2). The result is a tendency for a reduction in novelty production.

Non-cognitive changes

The differences between adults and children and between older and younger adults are not purely cognitive in nature. To be sure they include deterioration in memory, thinking and learning strategies, in capacity for storage and recall of information and in speed of functioning. However, non-cognitive factors also play an important role, ie differences in interests and goals, changes in preferred working conditions, or alterations of the self-image, to give some examples. Recent discussions of learning in adults (eg Knapper and Cropley, 2000) argue that differences in intellectual performance at different ages may be due at least as much to differences in interests, motivation, social role and the like as to changes in ability. With increasing age adults possess more clearly developed personal goals, better articulated ideas about what constitutes worthwhile subject matter and a stronger desire to apply the results of their intellectual efforts in concrete situations that are important to them. This view is consistent with the finding mentioned in the discussion of cognitive aspects of ageing above, that older adults do not generalize new knowledge and skills to new situations.

Social factors

In addition, older adults are subjected to the effects of social factors such as fear of looking foolish. A senior manager or an older professor may resist change for fear of not being able to handle new ways and thus being exposed to others as no longer competent. This anxiety would be heightened by social stereotypes including the view that people over, let us say, 50 are inflexible and incapable of innovating. Increasing age is also associated with changed career roles, older people being expected to become guardians of advances already made and supervisors or mentors of the upcoming generation rather than risk takers and trailblazers. In work settings, older colleagues are often expected to leave the work at the cutting edge to the younger generation. The tendencies just described are effective in coping with specific, stable life conditions, especially where the senses and general physical vigour are fading. However, they militate against building broad categories, making unexpected associations, bisociating and similar forms of cognition identified in Chapter 2 as the foundation of creative thinking. They also discourage risk taking, flexibility, openness and similar non-cognitive factors in novelty production.

Application to creativity

The traditional position: the 40-year-old peak

What does this mean when applied to creativity? Focusing on people who actually became famous for their creative achievements (ie producers of 'acknowledged' novelty) the early classic study of Lehman (1953) reported that peak performances occurred most frequently between 30 and 40. This view is still widely supported (see Simonton, 1988a for a detailed analysis). Lehman's findings indicated that the age at which peak performances occur varies from discipline to discipline, mathematicians tending to become famous particularly early. None the less, there is agreement in the research literature (eg Cole, 1979; Dennis, 1966; Horner, Rushton and Vernon, 1986) that, allowing for differences in definitions and methodology, somewhere around 40 is the most productive age. (Despite this, it should be borne in mind that many famous creative individuals continued to produce until well into later life: Darwin, Freud and Einstein became famous in their 20s and remained active into their 70s – those who start youngest seem to continue longest.)

Methodological weaknesses

A major weakness of many case studies of age and acknowledged creativity is that they often include creative people who died young. Naturally such people made their creative achievements at an early age! The picture becomes somewhat different when people who lived into their 70s and longer are studied separately. Lindauer (1993) showed that the average age of peak performance of long-lived artists was not 35 but 50. There were also noticeable sex differences. Famous women artists produced more creative work in their 20s, men more in their 60s or even later, although both sexes experienced their peak years between 30 and 50. This suggests a social effect – in this case possibly sex role expectations – on the development of creativity. Focusing on individual people (ie adopting an ideographic approach), Lindauer (1993) reported substantial differences from person to person in patterns of creativity and age. In general, longer-lived famous artists maintained a high peak of creativity over a period of three decades usually in their 30s, 40s and 50s. Peak creativity was unusual in the 20s (although not non-existent) and fell off in the 60s and later although more common after 50 than before 30. A high level of creativity even in old age was quite common. Two members of the group of artists studied by Lindauer reached their peak in their 20s, to be sure, but six reached it in their 60s.

Crozier (1999) studied British novelists of the 20th century. The nomethetic approach showed the typical or characteristic pattern: for the group as a whole there was a rise to a peak of productivity followed by a decline over the last 20 years. When an ideographic approach was adopted, however, it was found among other things that the rise and fall curves were particularly steep for low productive writers and particularly flat for the highly productive. In other words productive writers worked up slowly to a peak and then declined slowly over many years, whereas less productive people peaked quickly and then declined equally rapidly. Gender did not play an important direct role in the relationship between age and creativity for these writers although occupational pattern (for instance being able to earn a living from writing or not), stability of family life and mental health did, especially in women writers.

In the field of music Simonton (1998) showed that among classical composers there is a steady increase in 'melodic originality' with increasing age until about 56, after which a degree of decline occurs, especially in the last few years before death. Simonton attributed this pattern of sustained increase in originality until quite late in life to a combination of, on the one hand, constant pressure on successful composers to continue producing novel works whose originality surpasses their previous efforts and, on the other, a growing boldness arising from greater experience, expertise and self-confidence. Late in their careers, not infrequently at age 60 or more, successful composers often show a reduction in originality accompanied, however, by an increase in productivity, as though the one is traded off for the other. Interestingly, these more numerous but less original compositions, which are often also shorter than earlier works, frequently enjoy widespread popularity.

Turning to scientists, Root-Bernstein, Bernstein and Garnier (1993) studied the productivity of 40 men who had all made enduring 'high impact' contributions in physics, chemistry, biochemistry and biology, including several Nobel Prize winners and a number of men who had been nominated for the Nobel Prize without actually winning it, some of them on more than one occasion. The contributions of these men were studied over a period of 20 years. The authors concluded that a fall-off in creativity after early achievements is common but by no means necessary: many of the people they studied went on producing into their 50s and 60s. It is interesting to notice that those who made a single achievement early and then ceased to be creative tended to have moved into management whereas those who continued to be creative avoided administrative work. Thus, changes in creativity with age may be more closely connected with career pattern rather than any inherent tendency for creativity to disappear as people get older. Making a similar point with a different group of creative workers, Dudek and Hall (1991) showed that architects who resisted retiring were creatively productive for many years more than those who retired early. Such findings suggest that the social convention of ceasing to work at about 60–65 may be a major causal factor in reduced creativity at older ages, not disappearance of the psychological potential for creativity.

Different kinds of creativity

A further possible explanation of conflicting findings on creativity and age is that there may be different kinds of creativity, the kind rather than the level of creativity being age-linked. Mumford and Gustafson (1988) made a distinction that is very useful in this regard. They differentiated between 'major' and 'minor' creativity. Significant breakthroughs (major creativity) may well tend to occur between about 30 and 40, broadening and consolidating (minor creativity) after that. Abra (1994) made a similar distinction between 'innovators' and 'perfectors'. (He also expressed this difference in an unkinder way by referring to 'visionaries' versus 'plodders'.) These arguments suggest that highly original ideas may tend to appear in youth (even if they are not fully thought out), perfecting of the breakthroughs coming later.

This conclusion can easily be related to the distinction made above between *mechanics* that peak in late adolescence or early adulthood and then fall off, and *pragmatics* that involve learnt knowledge and skills. Innovating in the sense of radical breakthroughs may be more a matter of speed, highly differentiated perception, ready formation of new categories, or independence and daring, which belong to the area of mechanics, whereas perfecting probably requires application of wisdom acquired during a long period of apprenticeship (ie pragmatics). Elshout (1990), for instance, showed that outstanding performance often requires about 20 years of preparation. The idea of different developmental curves for different aspects of creativity is also supported by studies of children's scores on creativity tests. For instance, sheer productivity (ability to produce a large *number* of ideas) seems to develop at a different rate from ability to produce *original* ideas (Burt, 1970; Guilford, 1967; Torrance, 1968).

Case studies of creative achievers such as Nobel Prize winners or persons rated as exceptionally creative by their peers (eg Simonton, 1988b; Weisberg, 1986) have been fruitful in this regard. Despite apparent exceptions such as Mozart, achieving recognition is often a very long process. Famous pianists and successful scientists, to take two examples, frequently require 15 or more years of intensive effort before their work is recognized as creative. If acquisition of the high technical skills necessary in many areas for polished creative products takes 15 or 20 years it is obvious that creativity in the form of consolidating, broadening and perfecting would be rare before the age of 40 or so. On the other hand the inspired shot in the dark or the sudden breakthrough, even if in an unpolished form, would be perfectly possible at younger ages or might even be facilitated by absence of fear of losing face, impulsiveness, rebelliousness, or other characteristics commonly associated with youth.

Developmental trends in 'ordinary' creativity

The findings reviewed above focus on acclaimed creativity. I turn now to everyday or ordinary creativity, especially in children.

'Slumps' in creativity

One of the earliest findings on the development of creativity in children was Torrance's (1968) identification of 'slumps' in creativity (measured by scores on tests) at the time children enter school and again during the fourth year of school (referred to as the 'fourth grade slump'). Krampen, Freilinger and Wilmes (1988) and Smith and Carlsson (1990) confirmed the slump at about age 6 and a later slump at between 10 and 16 years, depending on the individual and the society. In a recent study Camp (1994) reported a drop after the sixth grade. Urban (1991) found equivocal evidence although there was a slump at around 6 years of age. This was mainly attributable to a drop on one subtest of the creativity test he used (the TCT–DP – see Chapter 5) where a high score results from drawing outside the border printed around the test material (drawing fragments). Staying within the boundary of the page is one of the things children have to become accustomed to when they begin to learn to colour in and then write. Thus, Urban's findings support the point made by Torrance that the six-year-old slump may reflect the effects of school discipline on children's willingness to diverge. Shoumakova and Stetsenko (1993) in Russia and Heller (1994) in Germany reported a reduction in creativity with increasing schooling.

Other mechanisms that may contribute to slumps or surges in creativity at varying ages are increasing replacement of task-irrelevant private speech by task-solving speech in the sense of Vygotsky, increasing ability to distinguish between external reality and internal representations of it, and a related change from preoperational to operational thought in the sense of Piaget (see below). A similar Piagetian explanation is that thinking becomes less egocentric as children develop cognitively and more sociocentric (ie children pay more attention to social conventions and rules and less to uninhibited expression of their own ideas). The result is that production of ideas may move away from uninhibited expression towards accuracy and realism, with a consequent drop in novelty. Gardner (1982) emphasized the role of children's mastery of symbols in this increasing realism and consequent reduction in novelty. Before the age of about seven they make free use of symbols but as they become more aware of social conventions their representations of the world, for instance in drawings, become increasingly literal and thus less novel.

Findings on adults

Age-related dips are also visible in adults' production of everyday novelty. Various studies summarized by Runco and Charles (1997) suggest that there is a decline in test scores that may occur as early as between 30 and 40. On the other hand, some data indicate that scores are at their highest between 40 and 60. Once again there are differences in the developmental patterns for different abilities (eg originality vs flexibility) while there is the methodological problem that nearly all studies are cross-sectional. Runco and Charles also drew attention to the role of factors that are not directly part of creativity although related to age: older adults may be just as capable of originality as younger but be unable to produce responses fast enough on timed tests, they may be unaccustomed to tests and find them unmotivating, or be intimidated by the social stereotype of incompetence with increasing age. Test-based studies of adults are noticeably less optimistic than studies of sublime creativity (see above).

Differences between adults and children

Creativity and cognitive development

As people gain more experience and develop psychologically there is a switch in thinking away from focusing on the immediate and concrete properties of real physical objects to their general properties and then to their symbolic meaning. This is the core of the process of cognitive development. At the highest level operations can be carried out on symbols alone – the concrete object or experience is no longer necessary. For example, at the concrete level a dove is white, has feathers and can be seen in trees. An eagle is brown, also has feathers and lives high up in the crags. At a more general level a dove and an eagle are both birds. At a symbolic level a dove represents 'peace', an eagle 'war'. Finally, at the level of operations on symbols an eagle wearing a First World War spiked helmet pecking a dove with the head of the Statue of Liberty means war between Germany and the USA. When categories are based on simple, concrete information the category boundaries are clear cut and impermeable (boundary breaking is difficult or extremely stereotyped) and the networks at best rudimentary. The result is that production of novelty is difficult or is limited to simple departures from the usual codings. Categories based on abstract, complex properties, on the other hand, offer permeable category boundaries, readily permit bi- or trisociation and encourage the building of complex networks thus favouring production of effective novelty. Coding based on higher levels of generalization and abstraction offers increased chances of effective novelty.

What these considerations mean is that the production of effective novelty is facilitated by possession of higher-order cognitive systems. The emergence of higher-order cognition is the result of a systematic process of development that is linked to increasing experience with the external world. The stages in this orderly process of development are outlined below. Since adults are more cognitively mature than children differences would be expected between the two groups in production of novelty. The nature of these differences is also discussed below.

Stages in cognitive development

The best-known description of cognitive development is that of Piaget who identified four stages: the sensorimotor stage, the preoperational stage, the stage of concrete operations and the stage of formal operations. Case (1978) suggested that it is possible to identify a fifth stage involving recognition of second-order relations, while Sternberg and Dowing (1982) extended this to the third-order level (analogies between analogies). Commons, Richards and Kuhn (1982) also argued for a fifth stage, the stage of 'systematic operations', at which operations are carried out on classes to build systems. These authors also recognized a sixth stage of 'metasystematic operations' involving operations on systems. This differentiation of formal operational thinking offers promise for understanding the production of effective novelty and thus of creative giftedness. For instance, what Mumford and Gustafson (1988) called 'minor' creativity (the novel application of the already-known) could occur at the level of concrete operations, whereas 'major' creativity (development of new principles) seems to imply systematic or metasystematic operations.

Cognitive stages and creativity

Taylor (1975) suggested a classification system for creativity that is very helpful here. He identified several 'levels' of creativity. The lowest involves 'expressive spontaneity', which consists of unhindered productivity without regard to reality. It can occur on the basis of concrete or even prelogical thinking (ie no abstract principles are involved). In this case, the novelty involves observable behaviours or other concrete products, is probably novel only for the producer (and perhaps adoring parents or enthusiastic teachers) and is based on concrete, physical properties of real objects. Despite this, expressive spontaneity involves creativity of a sort. Indeed, as Tweney (1996) pointed out some forms of seeing and making combinations (one aspect of creativity – see Chapter 2), for instance pattern recognition, may be more effective via presymbolic processes.

The next level in Taylor's model, 'technical creativity', involves unusual mastery of knowledge, techniques or skills. It is apparent that the acquisition of such knowledge and skills is linked to age, children because of the brevity of their lives to date having had no opportunity of completing the necessary 'apprenticeship' (see also the discussion above). The next level, 'inventive creativity', makes use of the already-known in new ways. This would be greatly facilitated by the ability to see the abstract or symbolic 'meaning' of information, something that characteristically only begins to emerge at about 11 or 12 years of age (see below). However, both technical and inventive creativity produce novelty based on direct application of what already exists (in Piagetian terms 'concrete operations') and are bound by its structures and rules.

The final two levels are 'innovative creativity' (extension of existing ways of understanding and conceptualizing) and 'emergent creativity' (development of new forms of understanding), ie the novelty produced is at the level of classes or systems not concrete objects, although it is perfectly possible that innovative and emergent creativity could lead to concrete products. The crucial point is that creativity at these levels extends and changes existing ways of symbolizing an area of knowledge (innovative creativity) or creates new such systems (emergent creativity). The production of novelty at this level requires thinking at a level beyond the cognitive development of children, as will be discussed in greater detail below.

When thinking is based on simple, concrete information, creativity is limited to simple departures from the usual. Thinking based on abstract, complex properties, on the other hand, allows higher levels of generalization and abstraction and favours creativity. Minor or inventive creativity could occur at the level of concrete operations whereas major, innovative, or emergent creativity (development of new principles) requires possession of higher-order cognitive systems. If production of effective novelty requires a high level of cognitive development it is obvious that people who have not yet reached these levels could not be creative.

Children's creativity

It is customary to speak of children's 'creativity' even if the term is applied to rudimentary applications of fantasy such as unskilled drawings, simple, highly stereotyped stories or everyday pretend games (see the earlier reference to quasicreativity). In a certain sense even a crude, childish drawing does indeed produce novelty since prior to completion of the drawing the piece of paper on which it was drawn was blank. However, in the vast majority of cases this novelty is not effective in the sense spelt out in Chapter 1.

Characteristics of children's creativity

Rosenblatt and Winner (1988) distinguished three phases of children's creativity: the *preconventional phase* (up to the age of about 6–8 years), the *conventional phase* (from age 6–8 to about 10–12) and the *postconventional phase* (from about 12 years of age and extending into adulthood). Preconventional production of novelty displays spontaneity and emotional involvement and may lead to aesthetically pleasing products, but it is dominated by perception (especially visual) of the immediate concrete environment. As Runco, Okuda and Thurston (1991) put it, it is 'environmentally cued'.

Conventional (in the sense of Rosenblatt and Winner) production of novelty involves more highly developed thinking but becomes increasingly rule-bound as critical and evaluative skills develop, with the result that the novelty produced is stilted and conforms to external standards (ie it is not elegant or surprising). Postconventional novelty production involves abstract thinking and, with increasing cognitive development, working with classes and systems. It is enriched by, for instance, increased experience with the external world. The crucial element in postconventional production of novelty is that the individual takes account of external constraints and conventional values (necessary for effectiveness) but is able to produce novelty despite this. The difference between the preconventional phase and the postconventional can be stated rather baldly by saying that, in the main, children under about 10 are creative as a result of being ignorant of the constraints of the external world whereas people in the postconventional phase are familiar with these constraints but are able to transcend them. Ignorance of the external world is not conducive to effectiveness.

For some writers (eg Smith and Carlsson, 1983) this means that children under about 10 cannot be creative. However, according to Rosenblatt and Winner (1988) what is missing in the creativity of young children is not production of novelty but the regulatory element of (self-)evaluation. Their productions may be novel, spontaneous, uninhibited, even aesthetically pleasing but they often lack accuracy and adaptation to the constraints of reality. Vygotsky (see Ayman-Nolley, 1992) also emphasized that children lack *control* over the novelty they produce although this did not lead him to conclude that children cannot be creative. Taken together with their limited knowledge base, simpler interests and motives and less complex cognitions, this weakness of control functions leads according to Vygotsky to creativity that is 'less rich' than that of adults. Vygotsky emphasized the *subjective* nature of the creativity of children, which is egocentric and takes little account of the strict rules of reality or the social conventions. By contrast the creativity of adults is cognitively and socially more mature and pays more attention to the external world, ie it is *objective*. Adults' creativity combines subjective and objective elements and is thus enriched by their greater maturity and experience. This can be summarized by saying that children create for themselves whereas adults create both for themselves and for the external world.

Developmental stages of creativity

Urban (1991) identified six developmental stages of creativity in children based on originality, risk taking and unconventionality. He observed these stages in children's responses to the TCT–DP, a test that requires 'image production' via drawings based on fragments of drawings presented on the test sheet (Urban and Jellen, 1996 – for a more detailed discussion see Chapter 5). These stages include:

- *Autonomous scribbling/drawing.* Children scribble or draw independently of the fragments. They are not able to regulate their own behaviour in terms of the stimuli provided or the test instructions.
- *Imitation.* Children copy the fragments. They make use of the fragments but without any transformations.
- *Concluding/completing.* Children complete the fragments, producing more or less closed figures. These remain simple and concrete, eg circles, squares.
- *Isolated animation/objectivation.* Children interpret the figures and create more complex images although still as single, isolated and concrete objects.
- *Producing thematic relations.* Children use the fragments to create objects with an internal relationship or thematic structure. An intention to shape or form something becomes apparent.
- *Forming a holistic composition.* Children combine the fragments provided on the test sheet and integrate these with images that they themselves add to form a single, unified composition with a common theme. They express this theme in a holistic way, which is also visible in the formal quality of their drawings (regardless of level of technical skill in drawing).

These stages observed by Urban in the actual behaviour of children demonstrate a developmental progression in the way they produce novelty. *Autonomous scribbling* more or less ignores the constraints of the external world. In this sense it creates the appearance of originality, non-conformity and the like but is really the result of egocentricity and ignorance rather than creativity. At best it involves expressive spontaneity (see discussion of Taylor's 'levels' above). In the stage of *imitation* the children attend to the external world, it is true, but only to its concrete properties, and products are confined to the original stimuli. Thinking is preoperational and no novelty is produced. *Completing* involves some production of novelty but this is dominated by the stimulus materials and remains at a simple concrete level, although there is some evidence of imposition of the child's will or intention on the stimuli. In the case of *isolated animation* novelty is produced via *interpretation* of stimulus figures (ie for the first time they act as simple symbols) but products are units, and symbols remain isolated from each other. Elements of rudimentary inventive creativity are visible but these remain at a simple, concrete level. Constructing *thematic relations* means that categories begin to be produced as symbols are linked up with each other. This remains, however, at the level of concrete operational thinking. At the point where *holistic compositions* occur complexity and purpose become visible while fragments may be understood in terms of an abstract meaning assigned to them in the child's mind. This involves formal operations and permits products that are classes or even rudimentary systems.

Urban's description of the developmental stages of creativity documents a progression from 1) *egocentricism* (ignoring the external world) through 2) *domination by concrete immediately present stimuli* to a stage where 3) *the individual's will can be imposed on stimuli* rather than the reverse – stimuli acquire meanings assigned to them by the child rather than forced on the child via its focus on their immediate concrete properties. The principles on which this meaning is based become increasingly abstract and general and products move from isolated units to linked categories and classes. This progression provides conditions that ultimately permit the richer and more controlled creativity displayed by some adults.

Remaining creative in adulthood

Age differences in creative performance are not due to a general psychological deterioration after childhood and youth but to a combination of changes in both internal (psychological) and external (social) factors. In particular, there are striking differences between adults and children in experience, knowledge and self-evaluation skills on the one hand, self-image, motivation and similar factors on the other. External influences include social norms, career patterns and life roles. These latter factors often militate against creativity in adults. The findings suggest ways of maintaining creativity throughout childhood (for instance in schools), young adulthood (including higher education), during working life and in retirement.

A major social factor connecting creativity with age was discussed by Abra (1994). He showed that achieving breakthroughs often requires co-operation with others. This might take the form of brainstorming or similar kinds of interaction. Older people, especially those who have already achieved creative products, may find it more difficult to work with partners because they are accustomed either to working alone or to being the star of the show. In their study of creative scientists Root-Bernstein, Bernstein and Garnier (1993) found that a major difference between men who continued to be creative over a long period of time and those who made creative achievements early in life and then ceased to be creatively productive (although they were often active for many more years, producing, however, only 'plodding' work after the breakthrough) was that the lifespan creators frequently worked on several problems simultaneously or even switched areas of focus several times. They were willing to turn their attention to unfamiliar territory and go back to being beginners again. Root-Bernstein (1989) spoke of the 'novice effect' in this regard. Working in the same area over a long period of time leads to high levels of familiarity with the field but blunts the acuteness of the vision or inhibits openness to the spark of inspiration (Cropley, 1992a). The novice by contrast is not inhibited by the legacy of long years of work on narrow details. However, returning to novice status requires doing without the confidence in one's own power that arises from sovereignty in an area and without the status and respect from others that are part of being an acknowledged expert. Children are, by definition of course, novices.

Creative productivity is perfectly possible in adults, including older adults. However, certain psychological characteristics seem to be necessary – or at the very least favourable. These include:

- maintenance of sensitivity to problems;
- ability to avoid the strangulation of thought imposed by strict logic or knowledge acquired over a lifetime;
- continuing ability to accommodate to new knowledge (see earlier discussions of assimilation versus accommodation);
- conquering fear of the new and different (continuing openness to the novel);
- willingness to revert to beginner status, both cognitively and socially;
- willingness to recognize inadequacies in long-cherished knowledge and skills;
- toughness of the self-image (humility linked with self-confidence);
- ability to work with others without fear of losing face.

These requirements for remaining creative involve prerequisites that individuals can influence in themselves by a conscious act of will. They also apply both in private life as well as in a variety of occupational settings. They can be applied to both others and oneself. It is the presence (or absence) of such properties and not chronological age that determines continued capacity for producing novelty. They thus suggest principles for retaining the capacity to produce novelty throughout the lifespan such as:

- Remain sensitive to problems.
- Avoid being strangled by accumulated knowledge.
- Do not be afraid of the new.
- Consciously seek to accommodate to new experience.
- Be willing to revert to the status of beginner or novice.
- Consciously look for the inadequacies in what you know and can do.
- Have trust in yourself.
- Accept your weaknesses and do not regard revealing them as a sign of incompetence.

5

Measuring creativity: creative thinking

Csikszentmihalyi (1996) argued that creativity is essentially a term of praise in the minds of beholders not an objective characteristic of products. This raises a number of questions that will be dealt with in this chapter:

- Can observers recognize effective novelty when they see it?
- Are there indicators of creative potential that can be identified objectively?
- Can creative potential be quantified?
- How can characteristics of thinking like coding broadly, making transformations, or branching out be recognized?

Defining creativity

The need for a practical definition

There is no shortage of definitions of creativity in education, business, engineering and the arts as is apparent from Chapter 1, but most of these are theoretical in nature (Besemer, 1998). However, it is important that the term mean more or less the same to different people engaged in studying it. In addition to its usefulness for research this would greatly facilitate efforts to foster the development of creativity in applied settings such as education, government, business, or industry. At present a wide variety of procedures is justified on the grounds that they foster creativity although many of these have been criticized as being little more than unstructured busywork. Eisenberger and Armeli (1997) concluded that it is possible to foster creativity in practical settings but that this requires that the people involved know in concrete terms what is to be taught and what must be done differently in order to be more creative. Creativity tests offer a means for doing this and the present chapter explores their usefulness for this purpose.

Tests as a definition of creativity

In the case of intelligence, tests have already played their part in achieving an operational definition. Although Boring's famous comment that intelligence is that which intelligence tests test is often regarded as a piece of irony or cynicism, the point was in fact well taken: intelligence tests do define intelligence, at least for many practical purposes (eg research on abilities, clinical assessment, educational and vocational counselling). In a sense intelligence really does consist of whatever it is that leads to a high score on a relevant test. Repeated analyses in the last 100 years have shown what this is (large vocabulary, general and specific knowledge of things regarded as important in the society in question, socially valued skills, familiarity with social norms, good memory, rapid information processing, skill in applying conventional logic, resistance to distractions, willingness to follow instructions, etc). This operational definition has remained virtually unchanged for the last 80 years (Sternberg, 1997).

As early as about 40 years ago Thorndike (1963: 424) emphasized that 'it is imperative that we get a better understanding of what the different [creativity] tests... actually measure'. Of course a test-based definition of creativity introduces a revised version of Boring's maxim: 'Creativity is what creativity tests test'! The definition of creativity would be confined to what creativity theorists and test constructors put into the tests. Such a limitation raises problems of its own: for instance, properties that are difficult to express in numbers could be ignored. None the less, tests provide a way of meeting the need for more precision in defining creativity. Among other things such a definition would lead to more effective selection of contents of creativity programmes.

Using tests to assess people

It is more customary in psychology and education to think of tests as assessment or diagnostic instruments that determine people's standing on some measurable property than as a definition of a concept (such as creativity) or a source of indicators or markers for designing support programmes. The tests usually yield numerical scores on the various dimensions they measure and these permit differential diagnosis of test persons' strengths or weaknesses. Analyses of scores can be done *nomothetically* (a particular person's scores are compared with those of other similar people and rated, let us say, 'above average', 'average', or 'below average'). It can also be done *ideographically*: individuals are compared with themselves across domains and are said to have relative strengths or weaknesses in different areas regardless of how they compare with other people. In this case a given person could be above average in all domains when compared with other people but still be said to be weak in some specific areas, because scores in these are lower relative to his or her own overall standard. In the case of creativity tests there is something inherently contradictory in the idea of assessing novelty by looking in tables, so that there are often no standardized norms for tests or only rather rough norms. This suggests that ideographic use of creativity tests may be more appropriate. Of greater interest in the present chapter, however, is not the use of creativity tests to assess people but their usefulness in defining creativity. (Their ideographic use will be discussed in more detail in Chapter 6.)

Creativity of products

The main purpose of the present chapter is to focus on creative processes as these were outlined in Chapter 2. None the less the present section will start by looking briefly at the creativity of products. This helps in understanding more clearly what is meant by 'relevance' and 'effectiveness', two properties that were identified in Chapter 1 as crucial in creativity. Without a more concrete idea of what these mean a discussion of processes leading to production of effective novelty would be difficult.

Introducing novelty into a context

The properties of the creative product that have already been outlined (novelty, relevance and effectiveness) are all related to a specific context: 'novel' means previously unknown in a specified setting, 'relevant' means that the novelty refers to a specific context, and 'effective' means helping to deal with a particular problem, remembering that 'problem' can be understood in a general, abstract way. Thus, the novelty of a product can only be understood in terms of a context that is changed in surprising, effective ways by the product. Sternberg (1999) made this connection explicit by arguing that creative products 'propel a field' – a 'field' is some domain of knowledge or area of activity; it is part of what is meant here by 'context'. According to Sternberg, a creative product propels its field in seven ways:

1. *conceptual replication* (the product produces novelty by transferring what already exists more or less unchanged to a new field);

2. *redefinition* (the product produces novelty by seeing the known in a new way);
3. *forward incrementation* (it produces novelty by taking the known further in an existing direction);
4. *advance forward incrementation* (it not only extends the known in an existing direction but goes beyond what is currently tolerable);
5. *redirection* (it extends the known in a *new* direction);
6. *reconstruction and redirection* (it returns to an approach previously abandoned and breathes new life into that approach);
7. *re-initiation* (it begins at a radically different point from the current one and takes off in a new direction).

Internal and external effectiveness

Creativity has repeatedly been defined here as involving production of 'effective' novelty (for a recent summary see Cropley, 1999). One dimension of effectiveness is immediately apparent in the case of products: they should 'work'. This is what Jackson and Messick (1965) called 'external' effectiveness (relevance to a problem and effectiveness in solving it). These authors also emphasized a further aspect of effectiveness by giving weight to 'internal' criteria (harmony and pleasingness within the product itself regardless of how well it works) thus introducing what is essentially an aesthetic element. In practical settings these two forms of effectiveness can be regarded as hierarchically arranged. An engineer, for instance, would almost certainly give more weight to ensuring that a machine functioned or a bridge did not fall down (external effectiveness) before turning to the question of its beauty. Internal effectiveness might well be more in the nature of a bonus for such a person. On the other hand some artists might be prepared to sacrifice external effectiveness such as widespread public acceptance, popular admiration and high prices in order to achieve internal effectiveness as they understand it ('authenticity', harmony among the painting's elements, innovative use of colour). This suggests that the two may sometimes be traded off against each other according to the priorities of a particular creator.

On the other hand it is also possible that in some situations external and internal effectiveness may not compete with each other at all. As Miller (1992) showed, famous creative people such as Einstein referred to 'elegance' of a product as a major criterion of creativity. Einstein believed that the special effectiveness of a truly elegant solution is immediately apparent to knowledgeable observers, thus supporting the idea of the 'shock of recognition' caused by a creative product. He seemed to be implying that there may well be situations in which a number of 'merely' externally effective solutions exist, the creative moment consisting in recognizing the elegant (ie internally effective) one.

This instantaneous recognition of elegant solutions once someone else has produced them often produces the reaction: 'Why didn't I think of that?' or 'Of course! It's so obvious!' The effort involved in finding the solution (sometimes a lifetime of hard work) is in danger of going unrecognized, sometimes even by creators themselves as earlier comments on people like Poincaré and Housman have shown. Effectiveness of products thus needs to be judged in terms of both external and internal criteria.

The role of the observer

Recognizing these properties in concrete situations, however, has often proved difficult. This is largely because creativity as a property of products is a highly subjective notion that is strongly affected by the *Zeitgeist*. Csikszentmihalyi (1996) went so far as to suggest that 'creativity' may not be a distinct and separate property of products at all but simply a non-specific term of professional/aesthetic praise that observers apply to products they find good. In other words creativity may be no more than a general, ill-defined – although clearly positive – category of judgement in the minds of observers or even simply a non-specific positive term like 'Right on!' or 'Cool!' (although enjoying higher status than these). Applied to assessing creativity this would mean that when a number of observers say that something is creative then it is, regardless of what it was that led the raters to make this judgement. Creativity of a product would thus largely be in the eye of the beholder.

Among other creativity researchers Hennessey (1994) accepted at least part of this argument by emphasizing the method of 'consensual assessment'. She concluded that a product is creative when 'appropriate' judges label it in this way. The usefulness of this approach was demonstrated by studies in which groups of untrained undergraduates were asked to rate geometric designs or Picasso drawings on a seven-point scale according to *creativity of product* and *creativity of process*. The raters simply applied their own subjective understanding of these qualities. Hennessey reported reasonably high agreement among judges (inter-rater reliabilities of up to .93) and alpha reliabilities of the ratings of creativity ranging from .73 to .93. Other studies have confirmed that judging how effective, useful, or complex products are is not as difficult as might be supposed. Vosburg (1998) reported that untrained judges who rated products on seven-point scales such as 'very complex'–'not at all complex' or 'very understandable'–'not at all understandable', simply applying their own understanding of these terms, achieved inter-rater reliabilities of about .90. This means that different people's ratings of the same product were similar, despite the fact that they were not trained in any way to assess properties such as complexity or understandability.

Tests of the creativity of products

Researchers have developed formal scales for assessing the creativity of products. Taylor (1975) constructed the **Creative Product Inventory**, which measures seven dimensions: *generation*, *reformulation*, *originality*, *relevancy*, *hedonics*, *complexity* and *condensation*. Besemer and O'Quin (1987) developed the **Creative Product Semantic Scale**, which is based on three dimensions: *novelty* (the product is original, surprising and germinal), *resolution* (the product is valuable, logical, useful and understandable) and *elaboration and synthesis* (the product is organic, elegant, complex and well crafted). These dimensions are assessed by means of a semantic differential rating scale (eg 'surprising'–'unsurprising', 'logical'–'illogical', or 'elegant'–'inelegant') with 43 items in the latest version (Besemer and O'Quin, 1999). The assessors simply apply their own understanding of the meaning of these terms. In an empirical study using this procedure Besemer (1998) showed that the scale really did measure three dimensions. The ability of the scale to distinguish consistently among products (three chairs of quite different design) was also demonstrated, ie the ratings were shown to be a systematic response to properties of the chairs. Ratings on the three dimensions had reliabilities ranging from .69 to .87 (alpha coefficients) with the majority of coefficients being in excess of .80. In other words the ratings would not fluctuate wildly if the same chairs were reassessed at a later time by the same raters.

The answer to the fundamental questions of this section (What is meant by novelty, relevance and effectiveness of a product? How can these properties be recognized in real life?) is that they are far less difficult to define in practice than theory suggests should be the case. Apparently, intelligent observers already possess at least a rough understanding of what is meant by the terms in question, acquired perhaps via latent learning (see Chapter 2). The observers can apply this understanding with reasonable levels of consistency and with a high level of agreement between themselves and other observers. The scales outlined in the previous paragraphs offer promise for operationalizing effectiveness (as against sheer novelty or surprisingness) in terms of both external criteria (workability and usefulness) and also internal ones (complexity, condensation, logic, understandability and well-craftedness).

Creative processes

A large number of procedures exist that are said to measure creativity. Torrance and Goff (1989) identified no fewer than 255. Other fairly recent reviews are to be found in the 1989 *Mental Measurements Yearbook* (Kramer and Conoley, 1989) as well as in Sweetland and Keyser (1991). Despite the profusion of tests Seitz (1997: 347) recently concluded that 'our knowledge of what psychological processes underlie creative achievement is still in a rudimentary stage of development'. Following sections will focus on tests related to these processes. Tests of creative personality, motivation and social influences will be discussed in the next chapter. The purpose of the review that follows is to identify in more or less operational terms the processes involved in production of effective novelty. Some tests of creative processes strongly resemble conventional abilities tests in certain respects although there are also striking differences, as will become apparent in the course of this section.

Creative thinking

The best-known procedures for testing creativity focus on thinking itself. These instruments are the longest established and most widely used of the modern creativity era and have come close to pre-empting the term 'creativity test'. Most have in common that they are based on the seminal work of Guilford (1950), even where this is not specifically acknowledged. He distinguished between thinking that aims at finding the single best, correct answer (convergent thinking) and thinking that seeks to generate new, unexpected answers (divergent thinking). Divergent thinking tests typically consist of open-ended, relatively unstructured tasks (eg 'Suggest as many uses as you can think of for a tin can', or 'Complete the incomplete drawing below in any way you wish') whose function is to promote production of many and varied answers rather than recall or discovery of the single, best answer that already exists and is to be found in the test manual.

Scoring tests of creative thinking

Although it may seem odd to discuss scoring of tests of creative thinking before describing the tests themselves this will be done here because such a discussion makes it possible to introduce and explain several important concepts in the area of creative thinking. The most widely applied approach to scoring the tests focuses on three aspects of divergent thinking: *fluency* (quantity of answers), *flexibility* (variability of idea categories in the answers) and *originality* (uncommonness of answers). Fluency requires mere counting of answers. Flexibility and originality, however, focus on the quality or style of answers. Flexibility involves the number of separate categories (in the sense of Bruner – see Chapter 2) in the answers, while originality assesses the uncommonness or surprisingness of individual answers. Some tests extend scoring by including dimensions such as *elaboration* (complexity and completeness of answers) or *effectiveness* (link to the constraints of the real world – see above).

To illustrate in a concrete way these dimensions of scoring consider the following example. As a response to the test item, 'Write down as many uses as you can think of for a tin can', the four answers 'saucepan', 'billy can', 'kettle' and 'suit of armour for a mouse to give it a fair chance in a fight with a cat' would each score one point for *fluency*, yielding a total of four. (It is merely necessary to count the number of answers.) However, there are two basic idea categories in the four answers: 'container' on the one hand (saucepan, billy can, kettle), 'protective covering' on the other (suit of armour). Thus, the four answers would score two points for *flexibility*. Turning to originality, the answers 'saucepan', 'billy can' and 'kettle' are commonplace and would score nothing, whereas 'suit of armour for a mouse to give it a fair chance in a fight with a cat' is uncommon and would score several points, exactly how many depending on the particular scoring method used (eg two points using Torrance's approach (1999), four points according to Cropley (1967)). The 'suit of armour' answer is also obviously far more elaborate than 'kettle' or 'saucepan' and would score highly if this dimension were applied. Its effectiveness remains to be tested!

Scoring for originality can be very laborious. Obviously, there is something inherently self-contradictory about having pre-existing lists of novel answers, since the essence of novelty is that an answer is new. Thus, scoring by consulting a test manual seems to be inappropriate. Despite this Torrance (1999) gives lists of common answers for his tests (Torrance's tests are discussed in more detail below). Common answers receive no points. He also gives lists of fairly uncommon answers that receive some recognition (one point). All other answers that do not appear in the manual are regarded as original and worth two points. However, although this approach makes scoring for originality less tedious it limits the usefulness of the tests in cultures other than the one where the word lists were compiled. To take a simple example, an Australian boy in a Canadian school made the extraordinarily unusual (for that country) suggestion for a use for a tin can, 'Use it as the wicket for a game of cricket.' Unsurprisingly, this was not included in the test manual's list of common answers and received two points. However, in Australia (at least this was the case 50 years ago) a 4-gallon kerosene (paraffin) tin is a highly favoured wicket for a street game because it makes an unmistakable sound when the batsman is bowled, and thus prevents arguments about whether he is out.

It is possible to deal with this cultural relevance of answers by explicitly incorporating it into the scoring procedures (eg Cropley, 1967). This is done by calculating the relative frequency of each answer to a given item in a specific group – 'saucepan', for instance, might appear on 30 per cent of protocols, 'armour for a mouse' by contrast on perhaps 0.1 per cent. Answers given by only a few members of the group (such as 'armour') are regarded as original. It is possible to score answers in a more differentiated way by assigning different values to them according to their relative frequency/infrequency, for instance zero for answers occurring on more than 15 per cent of tests, one point for answers on from 7 per cent to 14 per cent of tests, two points for 3–6 per cent, three points for 1–2 per cent and four points for less than 1 per cent. These values correspond approximately to the proportions lying beyond half standard deviation intervals along the X-axis of a normally distributed trait – approximately 15 per cent of scores lie beyond one standard deviation (SD) away from the mean, approximately 7 per cent beyond one and a half SDs, approximately 3 per cent beyond two SDs and so on. In this way originality is defined in the specific context of a particular group via a statistical procedure. The percentages for a given answer may be quite different in different groups. In an Australian sample, for instance, the 'wicket' answer might be given by 20 per cent of children and receive zero points, whereas in a Canadian group it might occur in less than 1 per cent and receive four points. Thus, the originality score of a particular answer given by a specific child depends on the answers of the rest of the group.

This procedure is laborious and time-consuming since each protocol has to be assessed twice, once to tally the relative frequency of each suggestion for each item, a second time to assign the values calculated via the first step for the particular item in the particular group. These values would obviously change from group to group and have to be recalculated every time. This approach has the disadvantage that it cannot be used to score a small number of tests since calculating the relative frequencies of answers requires a substantial number of participants. A second disadvantage is that the values assigned to answers are dependent on the make-up of the group tested and cannot be transferred to other groups unless they closely resemble the first one. On the other hand the scores reflect the unusualness of answers *in a specific context* and thus take account of the fact that the context is one of the determining factors in the creativity of a product. The scoring system is also based on a model of the distribution of novelty (it assumes that novelty is normally distributed) and differentiates between answers that have been shown empirically to be not at all novel, mildly novel, rather novel, very novel, or absolutely astonishing.

Although scores for the other dimensions tend to correlate substantially with fluency it was demonstrated quite early (Cropley, 1972a) that the various dimensions are not the same. Some schoolchildren produce only a small total number of answers on divergent thinking tests of which many are highly original (low fluency but high originality). Other children produce large numbers of answers of which few or none are original (high fluency, low originality). Still others produce a consistently high proportion of original answers throughout a large number of answers (high on both fluency and originality) or a consistently low level of originality in a small number of answers (low on both).

Tests of divergent production

Guilford (1976) himself published the **Creativity Tests for Children**, which is based on his Structure of Intellect (SI) model of intelligence. The SI model is a comprehensive system for analysing intellectual functioning that integrates functions traditionally associated with conventional intelligence and those nowadays associated with creativity. It classifies intellectual functioning according to three dimensions: *operations*, *contents* and *products*. Among the operations are 'convergent production' (comparable with convergent thinking – see above) and 'divergent production' (related to divergent thinking). Suitable for grades 4–6, the Guilford scale involves 10 divergent production tests from either the semantic (verbal) or the visual and figural (non-verbal) content areas. Examples are 'names for stories', 'different letter groups', or 'making objects'. These tests qualify as creativity tests because they focus on the *operation* of divergent production although all six kinds of *product* are involved (units, classes, relations, systems, transformations, implications). Scoring of the tests concentrates on free production of a large number of ideas (fluency), not on originality or effectiveness.

The test manual reports reliabilities ranging from .42 to .97, mostly however between .70 and .85. Test scores correlate only 'moderately' with teacher ratings of creativity and at a low level (-.06 to .35) with the nowadays better-known Torrance Tests (see below). However, in a recent large-scale study Mumford *et al* (1998) administered the Guilford Consequences test (Christensen, Merrifield and Guilford, 1953) to over 1800 US Army officers of both sexes and correlated scores with problem-solving capacity as assessed by the officers' responses to four theoretical problem situations, to each of which they had to formulate a plan of action (eg organize a massive transfer of military aid to an ally that had requested assistance). The solutions were rated by judges according to originality and quality and inter-rater reliabilities in excess of .90 achieved. The originality scores on the Consequences test correlated about .50 with the rated originality of the problem solutions. Integrating these findings with ratings of the officers' real-life achievements obtained by self-reports, Mumford and his colleagues concluded that originality as measured by the test made a substantial contribution not only to the officers' ability to solve paper-and-pencil problems (ie construct validity) but also to their ability to solve real-life problems (predictive validity).

Based on the SI model, the **Structure of the Intellect Learning Abilities Test: Evaluation, Leadership and Creative Thinking** (**SOI: ELCT**) (Meeker, 1985) measures eight cognitive activities connected with creativity, all of them involving divergent production: *divergent symbolic relations*, *divergent symbolic units*, *divergent figural units*, *divergent semantic units*, *divergent semantic relations*, *divergent semantic transformations*, *divergent figural relations* and *divergent figural transformations*. Factor analytic studies support the construct validity of this test and inter-rater reliabilities are often very high (up to .99). Although the test does not seem to have enjoyed widespread use outside a circle of SOI specialists it is of great interest because it makes concrete the concept of divergent thinking in terms of dimensions introduced by Guilford himself.

Torrance's tests of divergent thinking

The best known and most widely used of the tests based on divergent thinking, however, are the **Torrance Tests of Creative Thinking** (**TTCT**). This test battery was initially published in 1966 and since revised several times including a very recent updating (Torrance, 1999). It has established itself on a worldwide basis among practitioners as well as researchers and its role in defining creativity in the sense of Boring's aphorism can scarcely be overestimated.

The test materials include a verbal section, 'thinking creatively with words', and a non-verbal or figural section, 'thinking creatively with pictures', both of them having two forms – A and B. There are six verbal 'activities' (*asking*, *guessing causes*, *guessing consequences*, *product improvement*, *unusual uses* and *just suppose*) and three figural 'activities' (*picture construction*, *picture completion* and *lines*). The verbal activities yield scores on the three 'classical' scoring dimensions outlined below (*fluency*, *flexibility* and *originality*: referred to by Torrance as 'mental characteristics'). The non-verbal activities yield scores for five mental characteristics: *fluency*, *flexibility*, *elaboration*, *abstractness of titles* and *resistance to premature closure*. In addition, however, the figural tests can be scored for 13 'creative strengths'. Of these nearly all are related to thinking (ie cognition) including *storytelling articulateness*, *synthesis of incomplete figures* and *fantasy*, although *emotional expressiveness* goes some way beyond cognition in the direction of affect.

The test manual (Torrance, 1999) reports a median inter-rater reliability for the TTCT of .97 derived from a number of relevant studies. Other research (see for instance Sweetland and Keyser, 1991) indicates that the figure is commonly greater than .90. According to Treffinger (1985) test–retest reliabilities of the various subdimensions commonly lie between .60 and .70. In the case of validity Plucker (1999) concluded that verbal scores on the TTCT (but not the figural) accounted for about 50 per cent of the variance of scores on two real-life criteria of creativity: publicly recognized creative achievements and participation in creative activities. This corresponds to a validity coefficient of about .7. A substantial number of studies of the TTCT's predictive validity (for summaries see, for instance, Torrance, 1999 and Plucker, 1999) indicate that its scores differentiate between students who subsequently go on to achieve public acclaim as creative and those who do not.

The Wallach and Kogan test

Another influential creativity test to appear during this period was that of Wallach and Kogan (1965). Their major contribution was perhaps their emphasis on a gamelike atmosphere and the absence of time limits in the testing procedure. This test contains three verbal subtests (*instances*, *alternate uses* and *similarities*) and two subtests consisting of ambiguous figural stimuli (*pattern meanings*, *line meanings*). Perhaps the most widely applied subtest is *alternate uses*, which as the name suggests asks respondents to give as many unusual uses as they can for various common items (eg newspaper, knife, car tyre, button, shoe, key). Originally the test was scored by counting the number of responses (fluency) and by identifying responses that were unique to a specific person within the group being tested (uniqueness). Nowadays some users also score the test for flexibility, originality (statistical uncommonness) and usefulness (practicality and relevance to reality). Fluency and flexibility require merely counting but originality and usefulness involve rating answers on a seven-point scale ('not original'–'very original', 'not useful'–'very useful'). (As was pointed out above raters seem to be able to make such ratings with a substantial degree of consensus and reliability.) Kogan (1983) listed many studies supporting the validity and reliability of this test. More recently Vosburg (1998) reported inter-rater reliabilities of .92 for originality ratings and .83 for usefulness. An overall alpha (internal consistency) reliability of .86 was reported by the same author. Hocevar and Bachelor (1989) conducted a multivariate analysis of subtests of the TTCT and the Wallach–Kogan Test and concluded that despite shortcomings both measure verbal fluency in a psychometrically acceptable way.

Remote Associates Test

A further frequently cited 'creativity' test of the foundation period in the 1960s was the **Remote Associates Test** (**RAT** – Mednick, 1962). This test is no longer obtainable but is described here because of its historical importance. It is based on the fact that each person learns a number of different more or less 'successful' responses to recurring situations in life as a result of frequent exposure to them. Some of the responses are paired with the stimulus in question frequently, others less frequently or seldom. As a result each person possesses several alternative possibilities for reacting to recurring situations. These are organized in a hierarchy, the ones frequently used with success in the past standing high in the hierarchy, the ones seldom used low in it. When a known stimulus recurs in a new situation people draw from this hierarchy to find a response. It is possible to pair the stimulus with an unusual (seldom used) response but most people select a response high in the hierarchy and thus common. However, some people consistently select responses low in the hierarchy – ie they favour remote associates – and thus produce uncommon responses. As a result they are judged to be creative.

Each item of the RAT consists of several distinct words such as 'moon', 'grass' and 'cheese' that do not seem to be connected. The task is to find a fourth word that links these words. Successfully doing this requires making a remote association with at least one of the words. In the case of the example just given, 'blue' could be the solution: blue moon, blue grass, blue cheese. The test has 30 items for which 40 minutes are allowed. The score is the number of solutions found. Mednick reported internal consistency coefficients of .91 and .92 respectively when the test was administered to samples of male and female undergraduates. The correlation with instructors' ratings on a university-level design course was .70 and the scale distinguished significantly between psychology students rated as creative researchers and those rated as low on creativity. Scores on the RAT also distinguished between students with liberal social attitudes and those with conservative attitudes, as well as between those with artistic and those with mechanical–agricultural vocational interests. However, the validity of the RAT was questioned almost from its first appearance. As Kasof (1997) summarized the findings, the RAT has not shown more than moderate correlations with creative behaviour in non-test situations.

Two-track tests

An important advance in creativity testing in recent years derives from increasing recognition that actual creative production does not depend on divergent thinking alone but also requires convergent thinking (eg Brophy, 1998; Facaoaru, 1985; Rickards, 1994). Rickards argued that the process of producing novelty needs both kinds of thinking in order to be 'complete'. Facaoaru called for a 'two-track' testing procedure that assesses the area of overlap between the two kinds of thinking. She developed the **Divergent–Convergent Problem Solving Processes Scale** (Facaoaru and Bittner, 1987), which assesses among other things 'goal-directed divergent thinking', 'flexibility' and 'task commitment'.

Sternberg's **Triarchic Abilities Test** (for a brief introduction, see Sternberg, 1997) also emphasizes the idea that intellectual ability can be better understood in terms of several 'facets', in this case *analytical ability*, *practical ability* and – of particular interest for the present discussion – *creative ability*. So far, the test includes material for two age levels: 8–10 years and 15 years and up. The creativity test involves both multiple choice items and an essay, as well as requiring novel numerical operations. According to Sternberg (1997) this procedure is reliable, displays construct validity – creativity scores correlate only moderately with those on the other two dimensions – and possesses predictive validity in that test scores correlate with grades in university courses that emphasize creativity.

Image production

Urban and Jellen's (1996) **Test of Creative Thinking (Divergent Production) (TCT–DP)** takes a different approach from those of the procedures described above. It is based on a theory of creativity derived from Gestalt psychology and emphasizing what the authors call 'image production'. Although respondents are asked to complete incomplete figures as in several other tests, scores are not obtained by ascertaining the statistical frequency or uncommonness of the figures produced – calculated essentially by counting – but by rating the figures on various dimensions yielded by the theory of creativity. Thus, a particular figure is creative or not regardless of how many people drew similar figures. The test yields scores on 14 dimensions including *boundary breaking*, *new elements*, *unconventionality* and *humour and affectivity*. The test has two forms, A and B, on each of which the people taking it are presented with a sheet of paper containing incomplete figures. Respondents have the task of making a drawing containing the fragments in any way they wish. Form B is simply the mirror image of Form A and the authors regard the two as equivalent. The test can be used with people of a wide range of ages – according to the manual from 9 to 95! In my own practical experience I have used it with someone as young as 4½, applying precisely the same scoring procedure as with members of a group of managers in a seminar for adults held at the same time. The boy in question scored 34, about the same as most of the adults in the seminar. This was despite the marked difference in sophistication of the images created, and shows that the test's scores are not based on artistic skill or particular life experiences but on personal characteristics that can be observed even in young children.

Studies in a number of different countries indicate that the inter-rater reliability of the test is above .90 while test–retest reliability is about .70–.75 (in Australia, Cropley and Cropley (2000) obtained an inter-rater reliability of .94 and a test–retest reliability of .75 for university students). Validity coefficients show a typical pattern: low but often statistically significant correlations with IQ scores, mixed but generally higher correlations with other creativity tests and correlations of up to .82 with teacher ratings of creativity. Correlations with real-life criteria show that TCT–DP scores distinguish between, for instance, people who follow acknowledged 'creative' pursuits such as music and those who do not. The test's subtests relate to creative performance in life in a differentiated way, thus increasing its diagnostic value. For instance *completions*, *boundary breaking* and *unconventionality* are related to creativity in music whereas *new elements*, *emotional quality* and *thematic connections* are related to sport. This supports the authors' view that the test can be used as a screening instrument. They suggest that it is particularly helpful for use with people in whom creativity might otherwise go undetected with the result that they might suffer as a result of lack of stimulation or of opportunity.

Problem solving

Early in the modern era, Newell, Shaw and Simon (1962) defined creativity as a special form of problem solving. Other writers too have distinguished between simple problem solving and 'creative' problem solving (eg Getzels and Csikszentmihalyi, 1976). Brophy (1998) concluded that finding, identifying and clarifying problems are the aspects of problem solving that lead to innovative, novel solutions (ie creativity).

Adapting vs innovating

Kirton's (1989) **Adaptation–Innovation Inventory** (**KAI**) does not mention creativity in its title, it is true, but it is very frequently cited in creativity research. This test distinguishes between people who, when confronted with a problem, seek to solve it by making use of what they already know and can do (adaptors) and people who try to reorganize and restructure the problem (innovators). Kirton's view is that adaptors and innovators can score equally well on some creativity tests (eg tests of verbal fluency) and that both adapting and innovating are involved in creative problem solving. The difference is thus not one of level but of style although the innovative style, which is accompanied by greater motivation to be creative, higher levels of risk taking and greater self-confidence, leads to higher productivity. (See discussions of non-cognitive factors in creativity below.)

The scale consists of 32 items (eg 'will always think of something when stuck', 'is methodical and systematic', 'often risks doing things differently') on which respondents rate themselves indicating how difficult it would be for them to be like this on a five-point scale ranging from 'very easy' to 'very hard'. The procedure yields an *overall* score (high scores (over 96) = innovator) and scores on three subscales: *originality*, *conformity* and *efficiency*. Kirton himself reported KR_{20} reliabilities of from .76 to .82 for the subscales and .88 for the total score, and test–retest reliability over seven months of .82 for the total score. In a recent application of the scale Puccio, Treffinger and Talbot (1995) reported alpha reliabilities for the total score of .86–.88 and from .61 to .83 for the subscales. The same authors reported relatively low correlations of KAI subtests with creative performance, ranging from about .25 to .47 for the subscale *originality* with the rated originality of products. Puccio, Treffinger and Talbot concluded that the innovator–adaptor dimension is not related in a global way to creativity but to specific aspects whose precise nature is not yet clear.

Cognitive processing skills

Mumford and co-workers (for a recent summary see Mumford *et al*, 1997) have made a more differentiated analysis of the cognitive processing skills that are decisive in creative problem solving. They identified dimensions such as *problem construction*, *information encoding*, *category selection* and *category combination and reorganization* and constructed tests of these processes. The tests are of considerable interest since they derive from a theory of creative problem solving and help to define creativity operationally. The *category combination* test, for instance, involves 'problems' consisting of sets of four exemplars of each of three categories. To take an example in the style of Mumford *et al* (1997), a problem could consist of the following three sets of exemplars: table, chair, lamp, bed; banana, pineapple, orange, peach; telephone book, search warrant, marriage certificate, map. These are given without naming the categories defined by the exemplars. The respondents' task is: 1) to identify the categories defined by the exemplars; 2) to combine these categories to create a new, superordinate category; 3) to provide a label for the new category and write a brief, one-sentence description of it; 4) to list as many additional exemplars of the supercategory as possible; 5) to list additional features linking the exemplars combined in the new category. To continue with the above example, a respondent might identify the three subordinate categories as 'furniture', 'fruit' and 'printed documents' and might then combine these to form the supercategory of 'forest products', supporting this with the explanatory sentence 'All the furniture could be made of wood, all the documents of paper (which is made from wood), and fruit and wood come from trees, which grow in a forest.'

In Mumford *et al*'s study, five judges rated the respondents' products on a five-point scale for quality and originality of solutions. After a brief discussion to iron out discrepancies inter-rater reliabilities of .84 and .81 were achieved for quality and originality respectively. When *category combination* scores were compared with a criterion consisting of originality of solutions to simulated management and advertising problems (construct validity) correlations of .32 and .40 were achieved. Similar coefficients were obtained for *problem construction*, *information encoding* and *category selection* with the same criteria. These coefficients contrast with correlations of -.01 to .28 for Total SAT (Scholastic

Aptitude Test – an instrument widely used in the United States for selection of students for postgraduate studies) and College GPA (undergraduate average) with originality of solutions to the management and advertising problems. When *problem construction*, *information encoding*, *category selection* and *category combination* scores were combined in a regression approach the multiple correlations with originality of the solutions to the advertising task was .45, with originality of the management task .61.

Inductive thinking

A problem-solving test that adopts a novel approach is the **Creative Reasoning Test** (Doolittle, 1990). This test has two levels, Level A for grades 3–6 and Level B for college level. There are two forms of each level (Form 1 and Form 2). A novel aspect of this test is that the problems to be solved are presented in the form of *riddles*. At Level A these take the form of four-line rhymes in which some animal or object gives clues to its identity. Respondents must work out what the animal or object is. An example in the style of this test would be: I grow in the park,/where I stand tall and green./For birds I am home./When the wind blows I lean. Respondents are required to find the correct answer and a scoring key is provided that contains these answers. According to Doolittle the test, which is in some ways reminiscent of the RAT (see above), requires associative, inductive and divergent thinking. Since answers are specified in the scoring key inter-rater, reliability is not an issue. The author reported reliabilities of .63–.99 and validity (correlations with scores on the RAT) of .70, the latter scarcely surprising in view of the similarity of contents.

Real-life problems

The **Creative Imagination Test** (Schubert, Wagner and Schubert, 1988) presents respondents with real-life problems and requires them to suggest solutions, which are evaluated according to their number and quality. This approach is reminiscent of the Creative Problem Solving procedure (CPS) that has become popular in some school-based programmes for fostering creativity. The problems presented for solving in this procedure are often vast in nature (eg eliminating hunger from the world) and the 'solutions' offered appropriately sublime (eg teach people to share). Milgram (1990) called for 'stringent' assessment criteria that take account of reality and reported that these show higher validity than 'lenient' approaches that encourage vast flights of fancy with little immediate relevance to the real world.

Overview

The test procedures that have been reviewed in this chapter indicate that a number of characteristics of creative products and creative processes can be quantified – see Table 5.1.

Table 5.1 Measurable aspects of products and processes

Qualities of Products	Qualities of Processes
originality	'uncensored' perception and coding of information
relevance	fluency of ideas (large number of ideas)
usefulness	problem recognition and construction
complexity	unusual combinations of ideas (remote associates)
understandability	combining of categories (boundary breaking)
surprisingness	construction of broad categories (accommodating)
elegance/well-craftedness	recognizing solutions (category selection)
germinality	transforming and restructuring ideas seeing implications elaborating and extending ideas self-directed evaluation of ideas

These properties can be regarded as measurable dimensions of creativity. Furthermore, raters can agree on the level of these dimensions on a particular test protocol and their ratings are stable, ie they would give similar ratings to a given protocol if they rated it a second time. The people taking the tests tend to behave consistently within a test and to obtain similar scores if they do a given test a second time. The tests also correlate moderately well with other creativity tests, with ratings of creativity and with real-life criteria of creativity (ie they are valid). Table 6.2 (see p 125) summarizes data for reliability and validity of both tests of thinking and non-cognitive tests. Chapter 6 also compares this data with those for a widely used and much admired intelligence test (the WISC–R) in order to give an idea of their level of respectability.

6

Measuring creativity: personal properties

Creativity can also be studied by looking at psychological properties of creative people. These involve:

- personality traits;
- patterns of motivation;
- attitudes and values.

The practical facilitation of creativity has as much need of clear conceptualization of these non-cognitive aspects as of the cognitive dimensions discussed in the previous chapter. Tests offer guidelines for the necessary operationalization and will be discussed from that point of view in this chapter. In particular the tests indicate more concretely what is meant by terms like 'showing pervasive and enduring enthusiasm' or 'having an aesthetic orientation' since their items often give examples of concrete behaviours defining these dimensions.

Personal properties

There are two major approaches to measuring the personal properties involved in creativity: *biographical inventories* on the one hand, *personality tests* on the other. Biographical inventories collect information on people's life history (eg family experiences, hobbies and interests, education, career, life achievements).

Personality tests assess personal properties such as flexibility, extraversion, aggressiveness, emotionality, tolerance, as well as attitudes, values and feelings. An important general distinction cutting across content areas is between tests whose content is factual (for instance whether or not respondents or their parents play a musical instrument) and those involving opinions, subjective preferences, life goals and the like. In general, biographical inventories focus more on objective, factual information, although respondents' answers are not free from errors of recollection, wishful thinking, or selective perception. Personality scales give greater emphasis to subjective material such as preferences, feelings, or opinions and are thus more subject to the effects of factors such as day-to-day fluctuations in mood.

Life experience and creativity

An early biographical inventory developed by Schaefer and Anastasi (1968) consists of 165 items, some of them in multiple choice format, some involving selecting from alternatives and some open-ended. The scale focuses on factual information and measures five areas: 'family background' (eg educational level of parents, degree of public recognition of parents or siblings), 'intellectual and cultural orientation' (eg interests and hobbies, level of availability of demanding literature, frequency of visits to museums or art galleries), motivation – referred to by Schaefer and Anastasi as 'pervasive and continuing enthusiasm' – (possession and use of special equipment such as a microscope, willingness to skip meals to work on a project, taking summer jobs in a field of interest), 'breadth of interest' (number of hobbies pursued, number of 'favourite' school subjects) and 'drive towards novelty and diversity' (level of interest in unusual art forms, extent of unconventional collections).

Two scoring keys are available, one yielding a score for *artistic creativity*, the other for *scientific creativity*. In a study of students in the last three years of high school the authors reported that the scale discriminated significantly between creative adolescents and members of matched control groups, the criterion of creativity being teachers' ratings of products produced by the students. The test correctly identified 96 per cent of the students whose products were rated by teachers as artistically creative, although 34 per cent of the students rated as non-creative by teachers were also identified by the test (false positives). By contrast, the test selected only 46 per cent of the scientifically creative, with 10 per cent false positives. The resulting validity coefficient for the artistic creativity subscale of .64 is within the acceptable range, but the figure of .35 for scientific creativity is very low.

A study of electrical engineers by Michael and Colson (1979) was successful in identifying technical–scientific creativity via a biographical inventory, at least in adults. They administered the **Life Experience Inventory (LEI)** to 100 electrical engineers who had been classified as creative or non-creative on the basis of whether or not they held patents. The 100-item inventory concentrates on factual information (eg number of changes of address in childhood, composition of family, education, hobbies and recreation). As the authors pointed out, this approach enhances reliability. In the initial study 49 items differentiated between creative and non-creative engineers. An intuitive grouping of these items by the authors indicated that they cover four areas: 'self-striving or self-improvement' (eg enjoying competition, displaying curiosity, being committed to an area of interest), 'parental striving' (parental emphasis on getting ahead, perceived need to do well in order to satisfy parents), 'social participation and social experience' (membership of organizations, helping other students with their schoolwork) and 'independence training' (being allowed as children to choose their own friends, being allowed to set their own standards in judging their own accomplishments). In a cross-validation study with 98 engineers, a validity coefficient of .62 was obtained (criterion = possession or not of patents). No fewer than 83 per cent of the engineers above the cut-off point on the inventory were indeed creative according to the criterion (ie correctly identified), although 29 per cent of those not identified were actually creative (false negatives).

The low validity coefficient obtained by Schaefer and Anastasi for scientific creativity may be contrasted with the more encouraging figures for the LEI. This difference reflects two factors. The first is the difficulty by contrast with artistic creativity of establishing a criterion of scientific creativity in schoolchildren. After all, not many children or adolescents make patentable breakthroughs, but substantial numbers act in plays, play in orchestras, or write for the school magazine. The second is the probable later emergence of creative behaviour in science (as against art) as a result of the need for a long period of study and training in this area: unlike art there is no societal acclaim of 'naïve' science, which is usually regarded as ignorant or at best misguided. Where a 'rigorous' (Milgram, 1990) criterion of effective novelty exists – such as possession or not of patents – production of effective novelty in science refers almost automatically to adults. In their case the validity of inventories for identifying scientific creativity may well reach acceptable levels. However, differentiation of creativity into artistic vs scientific does not seem to be warranted with schoolchildren, at least when using life inventories.

Interests and activities

Wallach and Wing (1969) introduced the concept of 'non-academic talented accomplishments' as a measure of real-life creativity and Hocevar (1981) later concluded that assessment of children's degree of participation in their non-school lives in creative activities is the most defensible form of assessment of their creativity. Building on Hocevar's work Runco (1987) developed the **Creative Activities Checklist**, suitable for use with children in grades 5 to 8. The test simply asks participants to indicate how frequently they have participated in recent times in real-life activities in six areas: literature, music, drama, arts, crafts and science (these areas are highly reminiscent of Wallach and Wing's study). Scoring can be carried out by simply adding the number of instances of participation in relevant activities in the last year (eg writing a story or poem, playing at a school, church or club concert, acting in a school play, participating in a science fair). In some studies respondents merely list their three most creative achievements to date. Runco (1987) reported inter-rater reliabilities in excess of .90 for the checklist. Very recently Russ, Robins and Christiano (1999) obtained alpha coefficients of about .90 for reliability of the total scale of the Creative Activities Checklist and from about .50 to .85 for the various areas. In the case of validity it was shown as early as 1972 (Cropley, 1972b) that non-academic talented accomplishments listed by high-school children correlated significantly with divergent thinking scores obtained five years earlier (canonical correlation of .51 for boys), thus showing a certain degree of predictive validity of such tests.

Milgram developed a self-description inventory that investigated participation in challenging out-of-school activities. Although her scale, the **Tel-Aviv Activities and Accomplishment Inventory (TAAI)**, does not use 'creativity' in its title Milgram refers to it as 'a measure of specific creative talent' (Milgram and Hong, 1999). The adolescent version of this scale consists of 61 items on which participants indicate by answering 'Yes' or 'No' whether they have engaged in challenging out-of-school activities in areas such as science, dance, music, art, creative writing, or drama. Examples of items include publishing an article or poem, giving a dance performance, or receiving a science award. Milgram and Hong summarized the results of a number of studies in several countries and concluded that the scale has high discriminant validity (ie it measures something different from intelligence tests or school grades) and that this is a better predictor of career accomplishments than IQ or school grades, at least in the case of able students.

Special personal characteristics

A further approach to the study of the creative person involves identifying special personal characteristics whose presence is thought (often on the basis of studies of the personalities of acknowledged creatives) to increase the likelihood of creativity or even to be essential for its appearance (see the more detailed discussion in Chapter 3).

The dimension of *preference for complexity* has already been mentioned (see Chapter 3). The **Visual Aesthetic Sensitivity Test** (Götz, 1985) has been used in a number of settings to measure individual differences on this trait and it has been shown that it is stable and can be measured reliably. Gestalt psychologists also emphasized preference for complexity and Barron and Welsh (eg Welsh, 1975) designed the **Barron–Welsh Art Scale** and the **Figure Preference Test** on the basis of this approach. These tests contain figures of different degrees of complexity and varying levels of symmetry. People taking the test are asked to indicate which figures they prefer. Shaughnessy and Manz (1991) reported a substantial number of studies that supported the validity of these tests by showing that preference for high complexity and asymmetry is an indicator of creativity.

The **Creativity Checklist** (Johnson, 1979) also assesses preference for complexity, although it is broader in content and measures additional characteristics. It can be used for rating people at all age levels including adults in work settings. Using a five-point scale ranging from 'never' to 'consistently' observers rate the behaviour of the people being assessed on eight dimensions: among these are *ingenuity*, *resourcefulness*, *independence*, *positive self-referencing* and *preference for complexity*. Inter-rater reliabilities ranged from .70 to .80 and the test correlated between .51 (RAT) and .56 (TTCT) with other tests.

The **Creative Behavior Inventory** (Kirschenbaum, 1989) has two forms, the first intended for grades 1–6 (elementary school level), the second for 7–12 (secondary level). The test contains 10 items on which teachers rate children on a scale ranging from 1–10 according to the frequency with which the child behaves in the way indicated, eg 'This child notices and remembers details.' The ratings yield scores on five dimensions: *contact*, *consciousness*, *interest*, *fantasy* and *total score*. The first four are thought to be vital in the phase of preparation in the process of creative thinking (see the expanded phase model in Chapter 3). The author reported a reliability of .93 for the test and showed that it distinguished well between children who produced creative products in the course of an enrichment programme and those who did not.

The tests just described involved children being rated by other people such as teachers. However, Kumar, Kemmler and Holman (1997) emphasized that *self-rating* scales have greater phenomenological authenticity (validity) since the people being tested describe themselves. An early example of a self-rating scale is the **Group Inventory for Finding Creative Talent** (**GIFT**), which the authors (Rimm and Davis, 1980) described as measuring attitudes involved in creativity. There are three levels of the scale: a 32-item scale for kindergarten to grade 2, a 34-item scale for grades 3–4 and a 33-item scale for grades 5–6. As the name implies, the test can be administered in a group setting. Children taking the test answer 'Yes' or 'No' to statements about themselves such as, 'I like to make up my own songs', or 'Easy puzzles are the most fun.' This test yields scores for traits like *curiosity* or *originality*. Rimm and Davis reported internal consistencies of .80–.88. In various studies validity was measured by correlating test scores with teacher ratings, judged creativity of drawings and judged creativity of stories. The resulting coefficients were sometimes as low as .07 but were in the main in the area .30–.40. Extensions upwards of GIFT for junior and senior secondary school exist: the **Group Inventory for Finding Interests** (**GIFF I** and **GIFF II**; Davis and Rimm, 1982). As far as their psychological contents are concerned these scales do not differ markedly from GIFT.

Kumar, Kemmler and Holman's (1997) **Creativity Styles Questionnaire** (**CSQ**) measures seven dimensions: *belief in unconscious processes*, *use of techniques*, *use of other people*, *final product orientation*, *environmental control*, *superstition* and *use of senses*. Using a five-point scale ranging from 'strongly agree' to 'strongly disagree' participants rate themselves on 76 items (eg 'Creative ideas occur to me without even thinking about them', 'When I get a new idea, I get completely absorbed by it', or 'I typically create new ideas by combining existing ideas'). Kumar, Kemmler and Holman reported alpha coefficients for the seven subscales ranging from .45 to .83. Their research has shown that creative students rate themselves as more 'possessed' by new ideas, as working on many ideas simultaneously, as having lots of ideas, as being willing to show their creative products to other people and as enjoying creating even when there is no tangible result. They are also characterized by using a large number of techniques to be creative and being less dominated by the need to produce a concrete product.

Another recent self-rating scale is the **Abedi–Schumacher Creativity Test** (O'Neil, Abedi and Spielberger, 1994), a multiple choice test on which students rate themselves on a three-point scale on 60 questions regarded as indicators for fluency, flexibility, originality, or elaboration (eg 'How do you approach a complex task?'). Auzmendi, Villa and Abedi (1996) reported internal reliabilities of .61 to .75 (average =.66) for the four subscales when the test was administered to over 2200 Spanish children. Scores on the subscales correlated only between .02 and .32 with teachers' ratings of creativity (average correlation =.24) and scores on the TTCT (average correlation =.11). These were mainly statistically significant but do not offer convincing evidence of the validity of the test. The reliabilities also fell short of customary levels. Despite this Auzmendi, Villa and Abedi concluded that further refinement of the scale would 'easily' deal with this shortcoming. These authors also reported data on a further self-rating scale, the **Villa and Auzmendi Creativity Test**, which consists of a list of 20 adjectives such as 'imaginative' or 'flexible' on which students rate themselves using a five-point scale ranging from 'very' to 'not at all'. This test also yields scores for fluency, flexibility, originality and elaboration. Internal consistencies for the subscales ranged from .14 to.69 (average =.41). Subscale scores correlated between .20 and .55 with subscales of the Abedi–Schumacher test.

Colangelo *et al* (1992) initially developed the **Iowa Inventiveness Inventory** by studying inventors who held industrial or agricultural patents. On the basis of interviews with these people a pool of 200 self-descriptive statements was established and tried out with other groups (eg 'Whenever I look at a machine, I can see how to change it'). Respondents indicate agreement on a five-point scale. The final instrument consists of 61 statements that distinguished significantly between acknowledged creative individuals and other people, for instance sorting into the expected order acknowledged inventors, 'young inventors' rated as inventive by teachers and non-inventive academically talented adolescents. The test–retest reliability of the inventiveness score reported by Colangelo *et al* was .66 and internal consistency was .70.

Adopting a psychoanalytic approach the Swedish psychologist Smith (see Ryhammer and Smith, 1999; Smith and Fäldt, 1999) developed the **Creative Functioning Test** (**CFT**). This test regards creativity as dependent upon the ability to communicate with one's own subconscious and admit subconscious associations into consciousness. It involves gradually prolonged tachistoscopic exposure of a still-life painting until it is correctly identified. After this the painting is again exposed, this time with decreasing length of exposure ('inverted series'). People taking the test are not specifically informed that the same picture is being shown throughout. At some point in the inverted series, as the identity of the picture becomes less and less clear-cut because of very short exposure time, creative participants switch from what they have already correctly identified the stimulus as being to a new identification based on subjective impressions gained in the fleeting glimpses they receive. They may switch identification on two or more occasions despite the fact that it is the same stimulus and that its true identity is known to them. Less creative observers stick to their original identification – according to Smith and Fäldt (1999) they are 'bound by the constraints of correctness'. People who make a new interpretation more readily are adjudged to be less constrained and thus potentially more creative.

Smith and Fäldt reported that CFT scores correlated significantly with how attractive participants found creative personality traits (eg fantasy, inventiveness) when describing themselves. Ryhammer and Smith reported reliabilities (correlations with a parallel form of the test) of .71 for young people and .84 for adults. Correlations with other tests of creative traits (construct validity) such as originality, richness of ideas, creative interests and creative ideas ranged from .64 to .83.

Procedures based on the Adjective Check List

Various researchers have developed creativity subscales of the well-known **Adjective Check List** (**ACL**) (Gough and Heilbrun, 1983). The checklist can be used for both self-ratings and also for ratings by observers. Smith and Schaefer (1969) developed a 27-item subset of adjectives that, when used as a self-rating scale, discriminated significantly between high-school students judged by their teachers to be more or less creative. It also discriminated between scientists and engineers judged on the basis of a biographical inventory to be creative and others judged to be less creative. This scale also possessed a certain degree of construct validity, the scores of business undergraduates correlating .63 with the originality subscale of Kirton's Adaptor–Innovator Scale (see above), .41 with self-ratings of creativity and .48 with colleagues' ratings. Domino developed a 59-item subscale of the ACL, the **Domino Creativity Scale**, which also discriminated between several groups of more and less creative college students when used by instructors to rate the students (Domino, 1994). The criterion of creativity involved either instructors' ratings or choice of a creative course (eg dance, music, cinematography) versus choice of a less creative course. The scale also discriminated significantly between inventors and non-inventors. Other assessments of validity yielded values of up to .65 (correlations with other creativity scales), .63 (self-ratings of creativity), .55 (colleagues' ratings), or .34 (instructors' ratings). The Schaefer and Domino scales correlate about .90 with each other, scarcely surprising when it is borne in mind that they have 19 common items. Domino reported internal reliability of .88–.91 for his scale.

Gough himself developed the 30-item **Creative Personality Scale** (**CPS**) (Gough and Heilbrun, 1983), largely because despite their usefulness with schoolchildren and college students both the Schaefer and Domino scales showed little or no correlation with the rated creativity of mature scientists. This subscale, which has become a routine element of the scoring of the ACL, involves 18 adjectives that receive a positive weight (eg 'clever', 'wide interests', 'original') and 12 that receive a negative weight (eg 'sincere', 'conventional', 'commonplace'). Its scores differentiate between creative and less creative adults in many, but not all studies. Reported reliability coefficients for the CPS are often about .80) although Gough and Heilbrun themselves reported an internal consistency coefficient of .63 and test–retest reliabilities of about .70, depending on gender. It correlates moderately with scores on Guilford tests of divergent thinking (about .25) and with measures of openness as well as with self-assessments (.41) and peer assessments (.48) of creativity, while correlations with creativity at work, in university studies (as rated by faculty members) and in biographical inventories are about .40.

Motivation

Some researchers have concentrated on the role of motivation in creativity (eg Motamedi, 1982; Necka, 1986). Studies of people who enjoyed acclaim as highly creative have demonstrated the importance of dedication almost to the point of obsession in their creative careers. Examples are Biermann's (1985) study of mathematicians and Csikszentmihalyi's (1988) study of musicians. Lehwald's (1985) scale for diagnosing *Erkenntnisstreben* (thirst for knowledge) measures aspects of motivation relevant to the present discussion.

Directly related to the role of motivation in creativity is Williams's (1972) **How Do You Really Feel About Yourself?** Test, which measures curiosity, imagination, risk taking and preference for complexity. This test has been used with schoolchildren in years 6 to 12. More recent is the same author's (1980) **Creativity Assessment Packet**. This scale is designed for use with children in grades 3–12. It includes 12 partially complete figures that are completed by the child and scored for fluency, flexibility, originality and elaboration. These are flanked by a self-rating scale involving 50 multiple choice items that are scored for 'divergent feelings' (curiosity, risk taking, desire for complexity and imagination). There is also a rating scale for use by parents or teachers on which they rate the frequency of behaviours indicating the presence of the traits just mentioned. The test manual reports test–retest reliabilities in the .60s and validity coefficients of .71–.76. Apparently the internal consistency of this test is considerably higher than its test–retest reliability. Otherwise the validity coefficients reported would be mathematically impossible since a test cannot correlate higher with other tests than it does with itself.

The **Creatrix Inventory** (Byrd, 1986) is of considerable interest because it integrates both cognitive (thinking) and non-cognitive (motivation) dimensions of creativity. It is based on the concept of 'idea production', creativity being regarded as the result of an interaction between creative thinking and the motivational dimension of risk taking. The test consists of 56 self-rating statements, 28 measuring creative thinking and 28 risk taking. These are answered with the help of a nine-point scale ranging from complete disagreement to complete agreement (eg 'Day-dreaming is a useful activity'). Scores on the items of each dimension are summed and the total score for the dimension rated as high, medium, or low. Each person's scores are then plotted on a two-dimensional matrix (creativity versus risk taking) and the person assigned to one of eight 'styles': *reproducer, modifier, challenger, practicalizer, innovator, synthesizer, dreamer* and *planner*. The innovator is high on both creative thinking and risk taking, the reproducer low on both, the challenger high on risk taking but not creativity, the dreamer high on creativity but not risk taking and so on. Byrd reported a test–retest reliability of .72 for this scale.

Basadur and Hausdorf (1996) emphasized a somewhat different aspect of the personal correlates of creativity: *attitudes* favourable to creativity (eg placing a high value on new ideas, belief that creative thinking is/is not bizarre). They constructed tests for measuring such attitudes. The 24-item **Basadur Preference Scale** consists of statements with which respondents express their degree of agreement/disagreement on a five-point scale ranging from strong agreement to strong disagreement. Items include 'Creative people generally seem to have scrambled minds', 'New ideas seldom work out', or 'Ideas are only important if they impact on major projects.' Factor analysis yielded three dimensions when the scale was administered to university students and young adults working in business settings: *valuing new ideas, creative individual stereotypes* and *too busy for new ideas*. Test–retest reliabilities of the three dimensions ranged from .58 to .63 while alpha coefficients ranged from .58 to .76. Basadur and Hausdorf reported even lower validity coefficients involving correlations of about .25 with other creativity tests.

The **Creativity Attitude Survey** (Schaefer, 1971) also focuses on attitudes. It consists of 30 self-rating items answered by selecting 'Yes' or 'No' and is suitable for use with grades 4–6. It measures the dimensions 'confidence in one's own ideas', 'appreciation of fantasy', 'theoretical and aesthetic orientation', 'openness to impulse expression' and 'desire for novelty'. According to the manual this test possesses a split-half reliability of .81–.75 and test–retest reliability of .61.

Overview

Dimensions of creativity

Non-cognitive facets of creativity measured by the tests discussed in the present chapter are listed below in Table 6.1. Taken together with the analysis in the previous chapter (see Table 5.1), Table 6.1 shows that tests define creativity in a multifaceted way (products, processes, motivation, personality, interests), albeit with differing degrees of stringency. This point will be discussed more fully below.

Table 6.1 Test-defined properties of the creative person

Motivation	Personality
goal-directedness	active imagination
fascination for a task or area	flexibility
resistance to premature closure	curiosity
risk taking	independence
preference for asymmetry	acceptance of own differentness
preference for complexity	tolerance for ambiguity
willingness to ask many (unusual) questions	trust in own senses
willingness to display results	openness to subconscious material
willingness to consult other people (but not simply to carry out orders)	ability to work on several ideas simultaneously
desire to go beyond the conventional	ability to restructure problems
	ability to abstract from the concrete

Table 6.2 summarizes the data on reliability and validity of both cognitive and non-cognitive tests. Thus, it brings together material from both this chapter and the previous one. For ease of reading, the coefficients cited in the table have been rounded up or down by placing only 0 or 5 in the second decimal place, as well as being bunched by omitting occasional outlier values that distort the general picture. The table does not take account of statements in some studies indicating that creativity tests are 'good' predictors of adult creativity where these were not supported by numerical data.

Table 6.2 Psychometric properties of creativity tests

	Reliability		Validity			
Aspect of Creativity	**Internal**	**Test–Retest**	**Inter-rater**	**Ratings**	**Other Tests**	**Real Life**
Creative Products	.70–.90+	–	.70–.90+	–	–	–
Creative Thinking	.70–.90+	.60–.75	.65–.90+	.25–.70	up to .70	.30–.70
The Creative Person						
–biographical data	.50–.90	–	.90	–	–	.60
–personal properties	.45–.90+	.55–.80+	.70–.90	.20–.70	.20–.60	.30–.40
–motivation, attitudes	.60–.80+	.60–.80	.75+	.60–.70	.20–.55	.25–.50
Adjective Check Lists	.65–.90	.70	–	.30–.50	.25–.65	.40–.50

Reliability

In the case of inter-rater reliability, coefficients in excess of .90 are regularly reported. This means that the dimensions measured by the tests can be assessed with high agreement among different raters: scores of individual people are not dependent upon who scores their test. Problems of defining scoring dimensions like effectiveness or originality in such a way that different raters understand them in a similar way and agree with each other are thus more apparent than real. Internal reliabilities (usually alpha coefficients) commonly reach .80 and are often higher while test–retest reliabilities range from .60 to .80. These findings can be summarized by saying that people taking the tests behave in a consistent manner within a single testing while their scores are also reasonably stable over time. A comparison with data for the highly respected Wechsler intelligence scales shows that the figures for creativity tests are better than some critics have suggested. For the subtests of the WISC–R, Sattler (1992) listed split-half reliabilities (these are usually higher than test–retest coefficients) ranging from .70 to .86 (median =.77).

Validity

Validity coefficients are generally speaking lower than those for reliability, a common state of affairs with psychological tests. Not surprisingly the highest inter-test correlations (construct validity) were found among divergent thinking tests (up to .70), which focus on a single aspect of creativity and are thus fairly unitary in their approach. Measures of personal properties correlate about .50 with each other. The lower coefficients for tests in this area are not surprising since Table 6.1 shows that individual tests focus on differing aspects of creativity. Because of this diversity of test content Davis and Rimm (1998) recommended that assessments of creativity should be based on several different tests. None the less, these construct validity coefficients can be compared with corresponding coefficients (correlations with other intelligence tests) for WISC–R Verbal and Performance IQs reported by Sattler. These range from .26 to .75 (median =.61). The IQs are composites obtained by summing six subtests so that the validity coefficients are enhanced by combining information from several sources. The lowest validity coefficients (.40–.50) involve creativity tests' ability to predict achievements in real life, sometimes years later. These coefficients are usually about .50. By contrast, IQs frequently correlate about .70 with school grades, although much lower with gifted achievements in adult life (eg Gibson and Light, 1967).

Stocktaking

The usefulness of creativity tests

Some writers have suggested that there is no need for a separate concept 'creativity test' at all. Wallach (1976) concluded that 'tests tell us little about talent' and Carroll (1993) argued that cognitive tests do not measure a separate ability but 'broad retrieval (fluency)'. However, despite the relatively low predictive validity coefficients discussed above various authors both early (eg Cropley, 1972b) and more recently (eg Milgram and Hong, 1999; Plucker, 1999) have concluded that creativity test scores are better predictors of creative life achievements than IQs or school grades. Plucker used sophisticated statistical procedures to reanalyse 20-year longitudinal data on predictive validity originally collected by Torrance. He concluded that composite verbal (but not figural) creativity scores on the TTCT (obtained by averaging scores on three testings) accounted for about 50 per cent of the variance of scores on the criterion of publicly recognized creative achievements and participation in creative activities obtained several years later, and predicted about three times as much of the criterion variance as IQs. This corresponds to a predictive validity coefficient of about .7.

Helson's (1996, 1999) study that has repeatedly been cited is also informative here. Her findings are particularly important because: 1) they are longitudinal, stretching over more than 30 years; 2) they use a criterion of creativity derived from real-life behaviour, indeed behaviour related to earning a living, rather than a criterion such as another 'creativity' test or self- or observer ratings. She showed that almost all 'creativity' scores obtained from female college students aged 21 at the time of testing correlated with ratings of the degree of creativity of their occupations at age 52. These ratings differentiated between: 1) 'conventional' and 'realistic' occupations (lowest level of creativity – one point); 2) 'social' occupations (an intermediate level – two points); and 3) 'artistic' and 'investigative' occupations (highest level – three points). People in an artistic or investigative occupation who had achieved substantial recognition as creative (socio-cultural validation of acclaimed creativity) were placed in a higher category, receiving four or five points according to the level of acclaim. Examples include writers, artists, dancers and musicians. She reported correlations of .38–.48 with the occupational ratings for measures of personality (eg originality) on the one hand and self-ratings of interests on the other obtained no less than 30 years earlier.

One possible explanation for the relatively low predictive validity of creativity tests is that they do not resemble real-life creative tasks (questionable face validity) whereas IQ tests resemble school tasks quite closely. Related to this is the fact that *achievement* requires more than simply the psychological potential called in this book 'creativity'. Other factors also play a major role when it comes to real-life achievements, some of them psychological (diligence, technical skill, or knowledge of a field, presumably acquired via convergent thinking), some as mundane as sheer luck or opportunity, or even something as apparently simple as good timing (see Treffinger's (1995) discussion of 'assisters' – Chapter 1). It also seems that other aspects of personality over and above creative traits play a role in real-life creative achievement. In her study Helson (1999) showed that youthful openness and unconventionality (typical characteristics emphasized in creativity tests) are strongly predictive of adult creative achievement only when they are associated with depth, commitment and self-discipline. When accompanied by unresolved identity problems, lack of persistence and self-defeating behaviour they are not. Helson distinguished between creative *potential* and creative *productivity*: personality tests can only measure the former with any confidence. Consequently a number of authors (eg Helson, 1999; Kitto, Lok and Rudowicz, 1994) have suggested that creativity tests are best thought of as tests of *creative potential* not of creativity.

Among tests of creative thinking the TCT–DP has much to recommend it. It is based on a more general theory of creativity than the relatively *ad hoc* test-derived models centring on divergent thinking (Torrance) or divergent production (Guilford) and encompasses both thinking and personality. My own experience confirms that it is also suitable for administration to people over a very wide age range, is readily accepted by respondents, is easy to administer and score, and can be used for counselling purposes (see for instance Cropley and Cropley, 2000). The scores can be used either at the differentiated level of the 13 dimensions suggested in the handbook (Urban and Jellen, 1996) or by combining subtest scores to form the three more complex dimensions 'productivity', 'novelty' and 'unconventionality' that have been demonstrated factor analytically (eg Cropley and Cropley, 2000).

A differentiated approach to fostering creativity

A focus on a multidimensional concept of creativity, on development of potential and on differentiated counselling suggests that creativity tests can make a substantial contribution to promoting the emergence of creative potential. In particular they provide the basis for an individualized approach to this task by making it possible to look in a differentiated way, on the one hand at the different psychological components of creativity, on the other at the individual psychological profiles of different people. This application of tests is quite different from the gatekeeper role they often play through their use as the basis for selection (and its mirror image, exclusion).

Differentiation among personal factors

The desire to develop people's creative potential raises the question of the extent to which the necessary properties really can be changed by educational experiences. It is not difficult to imagine that knowledge, skills and abilities (ie cognitive properties) can be affected positively by training. Indeed the assumption that this is the case is at the heart of all educational procedures and institutions and it would be absurd to challenge it. However, the core of the concept of personality is that it consists of traits that develop early as a result of interactions between biological predispositions and a particular set of environmental conditions, stabilize, and then regulate later interactions with that environment. In the absence of pathological processes personality is not amenable to rapid change. Thus, although the practical question of how to foster the growth of properties favourable for novelty production is examined in more detail in Chapter 7 it is necessary to look first at the fundamental question of the amenability of personal properties to change.

Experience in the classroom suggests that some aspects of personality and motivation are relatively easy to influence in a positive way (eg short-term interest in a specific topic, hope of success in a particular activity) whereas others are difficult to affect (eg inner directedness, tolerance of ambiguity). Properties of the latter kind are more general, cutting across many fields, are affected by events outside the classroom (eg in the home) and may have developed over years, including the pre-school years. It is possible to develop a tentative classification of personal properties that are favourable for production of effective novelty according to the ease with which they can be influenced by educational measures. As an aid to such a classification, Figure 6.1 divides personal properties into two groups that are placed at opposite ends of the vertical axis. Characteristics that are easy to modify are placed at the upper pole of the axis, those that are difficult to modify at the lower. The degree of difficulty assigned to various properties is based on an intuitive analysis only – it is not derived from formal empirical evidence. On the horizontal axis properties are divided into assisters (their presence is favourable for novelty production and fostering creativity involves strengthening them) and blockers (their presence inhibits novelty production and fostering creativity involves weakening them). Both dimensions are treated as bipolar: properties regarded as favourable are not differentiated according to degree of helpfulness but are simply classified as 'assisters', all negative factors as 'blockers'. In a similar way, characteristics are simply regarded as 'easy' or 'difficult' to encourage or eliminate, with intermediate positions on the Y-axis having no significance. This means, of course, that the information in Figure 6.1 is schematic only. Its purpose is merely to introduce the basic idea that personal properties need to be looked at in a differentiated way when considering how to foster the emergence of creativity.

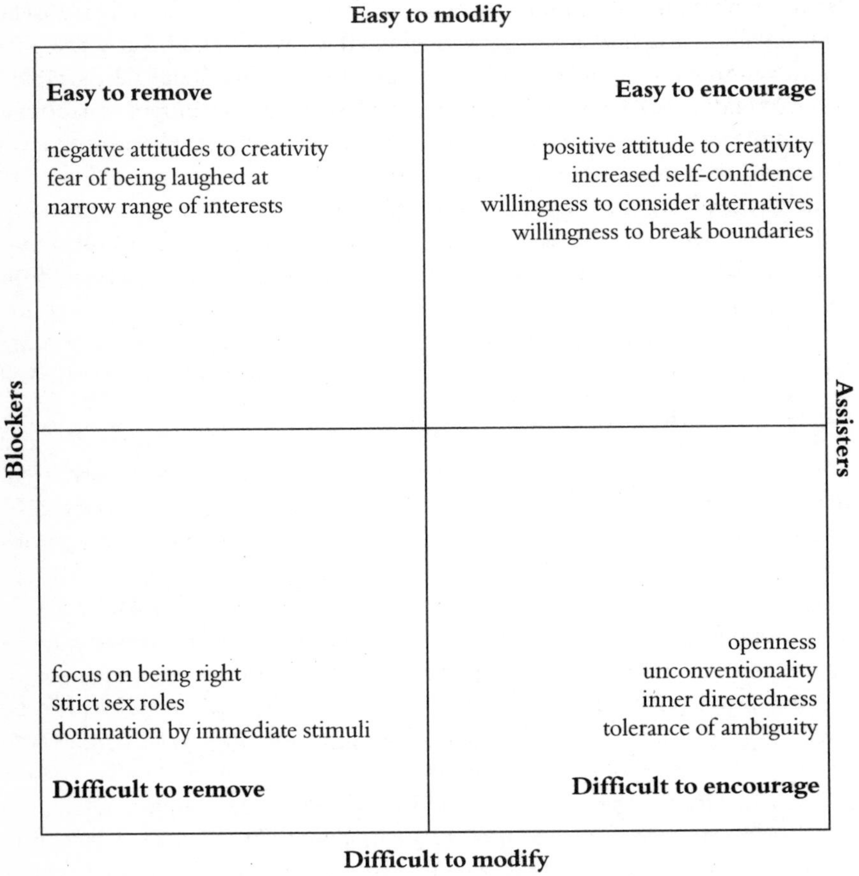

Easy to modify

Blockers	Assisters
Easy to remove negative attitudes to creativity fear of being laughed at narrow range of interests	**Easy to encourage** positive attitude to creativity increased self-confidence willingness to consider alternatives willingness to break boundaries
focus on being right strict sex roles domination by immediate stimuli **Difficult to remove**	openness unconventionality inner directedness tolerance of ambiguity **Difficult to encourage**

Difficult to modify

Figure 6.1 Ease and difficulty of fostering assisters and blockers

A differentiation between assisters and blockers accompanied by consideration of the ease or difficulty of affecting the factor in question in the desired way would provide the foundation for more efficient approaches to fostering the development of creativity.

An individualized approach to the person

It is also possible with the help of tests to adopt a more differentiated, individualized approach to each particular person. A framework for doing this is presented in Table 6.3, where the psychological components of creativity are divided into four areas: 1) general and specific knowledge; 2) thinking skills related to creativity; 3) motivation; 4) personal properties. For simplicity's sake these are looked at dichotomously only, ie as though there were only two possible levels in each case: favourable for creativity or unfavourable. In the table a plus sign indicates a favourable state, a minus sign an unfavourable one. It has repeatedly been emphasized in earlier chapters and will be emphasized again in Chapter 7 that the various areas interact with each other. None the less, in Table 6.3 the four dimensions are depicted as though they function independently. This is done simply for ease of discussion. The table shows all 16 combinations that are theoretically possible with two levels of each of four dimensions.

Table 6.3 Possible combinations of psychological prerequisites for creativity

	Possible Combinations															
	1	2	3	4	5	6	7	8	9	10	11	12	13	14	15	16
Knowledge	+	+	+	+	–	–	–	–	+	+	+	+	–	–	–	–
Thinking Skills	+	+	+	–	+	+	–	–	–	–	–	+	+	+	–	–
Motivation	+	+	–	+	+	–	+	–	–	+	–	–	+	–	+	–
Personality	+	–	+	+	+	+	+	+	–	–	+	–	–	–	–	–

Column 1 depicts a child in whom all four elements are favourably developed and represents 'fully realized' creativity. Column 2 describes a child in whom only the personal properties are unfavourable ('stifled' creativity), Column 3 a child in whom only motivation is missing ('abandoned' creativity) and Column 4 a child with the desire and the personal properties but without the necessary thinking skills ('frustrated' creativity). Finally, Column 5 involves a case in which everything except the necessary knowledge and skills is present. This person would exemplify 'pseudocreativity', mere daubing or clanging or verbalizing without reference to standards or norms. This kind of creativity was common in universities in the 1960s when many students and some staff assumed that simply wanting to diverge and giving rein to this urge by producing blindly – without the tedious and time-consuming need for knowing or being able – was sufficient for creativity.

Individual people could be 'diagnosed' using this four-dimensional system and a relatively individualized approach to fostering creativity adopted. People displaying let us say abandoned creativity (lack of motivation) would need a different kind of 'treatment' to foster their creativity from those displaying frustrated creativity (lack of thinking skills). Procedures appropriate for frustrated creativity such as exercises to develop divergent thinking might well simply bore those who have abandoned their creative potentials, thus strengthening their lack of motivation. To take a second example, procedures for releasing stifled creativity such as developing positive attitudes might increase the frustration of people with favourable personal properties but lacking skills. Thus, in addition to their role in defining creativity, creativity tests offer prospects for developing differentiated approaches to fostering creativity that indicate to individual people where their weaknesses lie and what they need to do differently. In this sense they are seen as counselling instruments.

7

Fostering creativity in educational settings

From early in the modern creativity era the discussion emphasized education rather than aesthetics or other areas that everyday thinking typically associates with creativity. Several ideas became prominent:

- Creativity is necessary for economic and social progress.
- Despite this there is a lack of creativity in society.
- The lack is an educational problem.
- It is possible to reform educational practice so that it promotes creativity.

The present chapter is concerned with examining these issues and especially with providing guidelines on how the educational reform can be achieved. Its purpose is not to provide a catalogue of standard techniques that can be learnt by heart and reapplied in an automatized way but to develop general guidelines that can assist educators in planning their own procedures.

Creativity and education

One-sidedness in educational thinking

Earlier approaches to the study of intellectual ability in schools – partly as a result of the influence of Binet and Terman in popularizing the idea of intelligence – treated it as mainly a matter of efficient acquisition of socially relevant and valued information (successful learning of facts), rapid and accurate recall of this upon demand (well-organized and rapid memory) and clever application of the most appropriate elements of the already known in life (recognition of the familiar in new situations, application of logic, familiarity with the 'right' way of doing things). Even prior to the modern Guilford era some educational thinkers were aware of this approach's limitations, but it had proved very useful in predicting many aspects of school and life performance and had come to dominate educational and psychological thinking. In his famous address Guilford (1950) called for more emphasis on branching out, generating alternatives and making unusual associations, which he called 'divergent thinking'. No doubt partly because of the title Guilford gave his paper ('Creativity') divergent thinking was quickly equated with creativity and interest focused on 'creativity' *versus* intelligence (see for instance Getzels and Jackson, 1962), as though the two were antagonistic. It seemed that educational institutions were concentrating on the former to the near exclusion of the latter, and the call went up for schools to redress the imbalance and foster creativity.

Shortly after this the Sputnik shock already referred to led to concern in the United States that the nation's educational system was producing large numbers of graduates but that most of these were trained simply to apply the already known in conventional ways. The perceived need was for people capable of inventiveness and originality. The post-Guilford educational discussion of the need for more emphasis on creativity was already in progress and the two streams of thought merged in the idea that creativity should be fostered in the classroom in order to promote national security. Ironically, the initial legislation emphasizing creativity in schools in the United States was the National Defense Education Act. This linking of creativity, national survival and education led to a massive surge of interest in the topic of school and creativity, a surge that was not confined to the United States but also took place in other Western European and North American societies.

Goals of fostering creativity

Despite the increase in interest just outlined the desire of some educators to emphasize creativity in the classroom initially aroused controversy and opposition. It was argued among other things that creativity is by its very nature mysterious and unknowable and thus incapable of being promoted or fostered by mere mortals. A second argument was that since creativity is a special property found in only a few individuals its promotion would lead to elitism. Finally there was fear that fostering creativity would lead to the forcing of children, who would become victims of creativity fanaticism among teachers and parents. At a more everyday level many teachers and parents were uneasy about emphasizing creativity in school because this might mean encouraging unruly, disobedient, careless, imprecise, or just plain naughty behaviour. Others saw the call for creativity in the classroom as meaning that basic skills and standards or even fundamental principles such as correct–incorrect would be abandoned.

Indeed some studies (eg Colangelo and Dettman, 1983) have shown that children identified as creatively talented really have been forced by ambitious parents into long hours of practice on, for instance, a musical instrument, in the hope that they would develop into creative musicians on the world stage. Their creativity training took most of their time or turned their parents into slave-drivers intent on living out their own frustrated ambitions through their children. In some cases an unremitting focus on the children forced them into a dominant role in which they had to behave like mothers and fathers to their own parents. Such children have sometimes complained of, among other things, being robbed of their childhood or having had their family life destroyed.

This cannot be the aim of efforts to foster creativity in the classroom. Most educational researchers and theorists interested in promoting creativity reject the elitist view and concentrate on aspects of creativity that they believe are present at least as potentials in everybody. The need to foster creativity is then seen as deriving from the responsibility of schools to foster the fullest development of all positive aspects of the personality of all children, even where this means acknowledging and accepting a diversity of abilities and talents. This is a humanistic goal that has been given great prominence in educational philosophy for hundreds of years. It is assumed in this book that appropriate learning conditions can promote at least some elements of creativity in many if not all children. The central focus of fostering creativity in the classroom is thus not production of creative geniuses and it is not necessary for teachers interested in fostering creativity to set their sights on achieving scientific, technological, literary, artistic or other revolutions. Of course teachers may sometimes make a contribution in this direction by sowing the seeds. Research (eg Bloom, 1985) has shown that teachers have sometimes played a key role in the emergence, even years later, of widely acclaimed creative talents. None the less, teachers need not regard this intimidating goal as defining their primary responsibility in the classroom.

The value of creativity in the classroom

Probably the dominant characteristic of modern life is that it is subject to unprecedentedly rapid change (for a fuller discussion see Chapter 8). At the level of the individual it is evident that knowledge and skills have ever diminishing half-lives (the period of time within which 50 per cent of what a person knows or can do will become obsolete). The knowledge and skills needed in the future may not even be known at the time a person attends school or university. As a result, these institutions cannot limit themselves to the transmission of set contents, techniques and values, since these will soon be useless or even detrimental to living a full life, but must also promote flexibility, openness for the new, the ability to adapt or see new ways of doing things, and courage in the face of the unexpected. These properties are becoming increasingly necessary if people are to adapt to a changing world and will probably continue to be important throughout each person's lifetime, whereas specific skills and knowledge rapidly become obsolete. The psychological definition of creativity emphasizes adaptability and the like, so that fostering creativity can be seen as part of the preparation of children to engage in a process of lifelong flexibility and adaptation rather than of clinging to the already obsolescent. Finally, creativity helps people cope with the challenges of life and resulting personal stresses and strains and is thus closely connected with mental health (Cropley, 1990). These considerations mean that the fostering of creativity in the classroom is part of educational efforts aimed at the development of individuals capable of maximizing their own self-fulfilment.

It is also important to note that fostering creativity is not inconsistent with traditional school goals such as acquisition of knowledge and skills. Ai (1999) pointed out that beginning with the seminal study of Getzels and Jackson (1962) many empirical studies have shown a connection between creativity and school grades. As was shown in Chapter 1, creativity seems to supplement conventional intelligence in promoting good performance, with the result that it has largely been accepted in modern thinking as part of giftedness (Cropley, 1994; Sternberg and Lubart, 1995). None the less, this relationship is not universally supported. Some researchers (see for instance Ai, 1999) have argued that creativity only contributes to academic achievement in cases where the criterion of achievement emphasizes production of novelty. Despite this, as was pointed out earlier, comprehensive analyses such as that of Plucker (1999) indicate that creativity scores are indeed connected with later creative behaviour and predict creative achievement better than intelligence tests (eg Milgram and Hong, 1999).

Turning to teaching methods it has been shown that learning activities that emphasize branching out, finding out, or inventing such as discovery learning, learning under playlike conditions and learning with the help of fantasy can be more effective than traditional methods such as face-to-face lecturing or rote learning (Cropley, 1992b). Teaching and learning methods that emphasize creativity can also have strongly beneficial effects on pupils' motivation as well as their attitudes to school and their self-image. This has been known since early research such as that of Suchman (1961) who showed that children taught by 'inquiry methods', in which teachers confine themselves to answering 'Yes' or 'No' to questions posed by pupils, acquired as much knowledge of physics as those taught by conventional methods and were significantly more curious about science. More recently, Langer *et al* (1989) and Yager (1989) obtained similar findings about discovery methods and acquisition of facts while also demonstrating greater motivation to learn and increased intrinsic motivation among the children in question.

The position of teachers

Surveys have shown that in theory at least teachers overwhelmingly support creativity as something that should be fostered in the classroom – Feldhusen and Treffinger (1975) reported that 96 per cent of them expressed this view. However, in actual classroom practice they often frown upon traits associated with creativity or even actively dislike characteristics such as boldness, desire for novelty or originality. From almost the beginning of relevant research (eg Torrance, 1965) it has been shown that teachers prefer courteousness, punctuality, obedience and receptiveness to other people's (the teacher's) ideas. In the area of thinking, high skill in memorization and accurate recall are often preferred to critical thinking or independent decision making. This teacher bias has also been demonstrated in countries outside the USA such as Australia (Howieson, 1984), Nigeria (Obuche, 1986), or Turkey (Oral and Guncer, 1993). Empirical findings (Stone, 1980) have shown that even in grade 2 (ie at a level where it might be expected that a certain amount of divergence from everyday norms would be tolerated) children who scored highest on tests of creativity were the ones most often in trouble with teachers.

Findings of this kind have continued to be reported despite great emphasis on creativity over the last 30–40 years. In more recent studies Oral and Guncer (1993) reported that highly creative children were seen by Turkish teachers as being belligerent and defiant, and Westby and Dawson (1995) found that teachers described creative children as being similar to the kind of child they liked least. Scott (1999) summarized a number of relevant recent studies that supported this view and in addition showed in her own research that US elementary school teachers rated creative pupils as more disruptive than less creative youngsters. It is not being suggested here that undisciplined, disruptive, defiant, ignorant, aggressive, or humiliating behaviour should be accepted in the name of fostering creativity. Punctuality, obedience and consideration for others on the one hand, or good memory, speed and accuracy on the other, are obviously important characteristics both for school and for life itself. However, when such properties are overemphasized and discovering, branching out, speculating, experimenting or innovating are rejected it can be said that teaching has become excessively one-sided. What teachers need is guidelines on what is meant by creativity in the classroom and on what to do in order to foster its further development.

Creativity-fostering teachers

Some teachers are particularly good at promoting students' creativity (Cropley, 1992b). They provide a model of creative behaviour, reinforce such behaviour when pupils display it, protect creative pupils from conformity pressure and establish a classroom climate that permits alternative solutions, tolerates constructive errors, encourages effective surprise and does not isolate non-conformers. Clark's (1996) research on teachers who had been rated as particularly successful with gifted children made a direct link between giftedness and creativity. These teachers, among other things, emphasized 'creative production', showed 'flexibility', accepted 'alternative suggestions', encouraged 'expression of ideas' and tolerated 'humour'. They were themselves creative and had stronger personal contacts with their students. Summarizing the literature, it can be said that creativity-fostering teachers are those who:

- encourage students to learn independently;
- have a co-operative, socially integrative style of teaching;
- do not neglect mastery of factual knowledge;
- tolerate 'sensible' or bold errors;
- promote self-evaluation;
- take questions seriously;
- offer opportunities to work with varied materials under different conditions;
- help students learn to cope with frustration and failure;
- reward courage as much as being right.

Programmes and procedures

Idea-getting techniques

Some procedures for fostering creativity consist of specific techniques that can be learnt and then applied in many different situations, usually in order to get ideas (eg *brainstorming*, *synectics*, *creative problem solving*, *morphological methods*, *bionics*, *imagery training*, *mind maps*, the *KJ Method*, or the *NM Method*). Most of these are described by Torrance (1992) or Michalko (1998). Although they are suitable for use with schoolchildren they are often also applied in business, for instance in product development or in advertising.

Probably the best known of all these is brainstorming (Osborn, 1953), which has become the prototype for a number of related techniques. Classical brainstorming is a group activity in which each member of the group is encouraged to put forward ideas without any constraints, no matter how implausible. Criticism is not permitted, because of its inhibitory effect, especially so-called 'killer phrases' such as 'But how would you get that to work', 'You'll never get management to buy that', or 'Where will the money come from?' Quantity of ideas is important rather than quality and 'hitch-hiking' by attaching one's ideas to those of others is encouraged. There are various procedures for selecting, recording, testing and otherwise ultimately relating ideas to reality such as appointing a 'scribe' who writes down ideas and later presents them to the group. More recently, brainstorming has been used as an individual procedure or in 'quasi group' settings. In the latter case a number of people are simultaneously present so that at a formal level a group exists. However, individual people go through the idea production procedures alone and do not interact with the other members of the group until they reach an advanced stage in the process (eg each person has already brainstormed an individual solution).

In the KJ Method, individual members of the group initially write on cards their ideas for defining the core of the problem at hand (one idea per card). The cards are then sorted by the group into sets containing conceptually similar statements on the nature of the problem and the different sets given labels that summarize the essence of the concept underlying the set of cards. For instance, a group applying the method to designing a revolutionary new form of public transport might come up with statements of the problem that are sorted into the categories 'How could it be financed?' 'What energy source could be used?' 'How should routes be planned?' 'How could safety levels be raised?' and 'What special staff training would be needed?' In the second phase sets of solutions are constructed in a similar way.

Some procedures retain the central principle of unhindered production of ideas but go beyond simple blind generation of ideas. In Mind Maps, for instance, the central theme is written down and then a 'spray' of associations recorded, each association functioning as the beginning of a new spray of further associations. To continue with the example above, the theme 'public transport' might produce a spray of associations including 'passengers', 'schedules', 'vehicles'. Among the associations to 'passengers' might be 'complaints', 'peak hour masses', 'fare evasion' and 'security'. 'Schedules' might evoke among others 'frequency', 'reliability' and 'routes', and associations to 'vehicles' might include 'comfort', 'safety' and 'power source'. Solutions are found by identifying patterns or threads found in the masses of associations. One thread running through these (entirely fictitious) sprays of associations is

'Increase numbers of passengers by providing frequent services in comfortable vehicles using socially acceptable sources of energy and running frequent schedules on high-density routes.' (This 'solution' is banal, of course, but it was constructed here purely to illustrate the nature of the procedure.)

The *Hierarchical Method* (eg Butler and Kline, 1998) involves an even stronger element of organization and structure. Although the element of generating large numbers of possible solutions is retained, this approach is based on the idea that a hierarchical organization of ideas (rather than simple masses of ideas or associational chains) produces solutions of better quality. Suggested solutions are sorted into classes on the basis of common content, as in other techniques already mentioned. Subsequently, hierarchies are formed by combining lower-level classes into superordinate classes, or by contrast by breaking down higher-order classes into lower-level categories. In the public transport example already introduced, a higher-order category might be 'energy source'. This might be broken down into 'forms of energy' and 'methods of harnessing'. The category 'forms of energy' could have subcategories lower in the hierarchy that would be applied to each form identified in the previous step such as 'cost', 'availability', 'environmental impact' and 'practicability'. At a still lower level, 'cost' could have categories such as 'impact on passenger numbers', 'impact on national economy' and 'alternative ways of covering'.

Creative Problem Solving (CPS) is based on Wallas's stage model (see Chapter 3). In its 'classical' form (Parnes, 1981) it involves five steps, which can be applied in a systematic way to finding, investigating and solving problems. Treffinger and colleagues (eg Treffinger, Isaksen and Dorval, 1995) have added a preliminary stage at the very beginning, with the result that CPS is nowadays understood as having six steps: mess finding; fact finding; problem finding; idea finding; solution finding; acceptance finding. In his book, Parnes (1981) goes through a large number of problems with readers in order to make the steps automatic so that they can be reapplied over and over again with new problems. Treffinger (1995) extended understanding of CPS by emphasizing that it is not a purely cognitive exercise: he drew attention to the role of other people in the acceptance finding phase, both assisters and resisters. A children's version of CPS has been published by Eberle and Standish (1985) and this is included in Table 7.1 below.

Instructional approaches to fostering creativity

Treffinger, Sortore and Cross (1993) reported in excess of 250 published sets of materials that can be regarded as instructional resources for fostering creativity. Huczynski's (1983) encyclopaedia of methods listed dozens that could be applied to nurturing creativity in schoolchildren including 'buzz groups', 'flexastudy', 'lateral thinking' and 'mathetics'. Some resources consist of simple, specific games, such as 'bridge building', 'idea production', or 'creative connections' (Cropley, 1992b). Others involve mental techniques that can be learnt quickly and then applied in a wide variety of settings as general ways of getting ideas, such as the *SCAMPER* procedure, originally developed by Osborn. This approach assumes that production of novelty simply involves changing what already exists and includes seven change techniques: **s**ubstituting, **c**ombining, **a**dapting, **m**agnifying, **p**utting to a different use, **e**liminating and **r**earranging/reversing.

Many of the instructional resources now available involve programmes – often based on a model of creativity, and sometimes with substantial special materials – that are used systematically over a period of at least several weeks (for instance, a school term or year) with the intention of inculcating a general disposition to be creative. (Such programmes often include training in various techniques.) The United States Patent and Trademark Office (1990) listed about 25 such packages, and Treffinger, Sortore and Cross briefly (1993) described several. A number of examples of such programmes are summarized in Table 7.1.

Popular and commercial programmes

In addition to more scientific works on fostering creativity there is a substantial number of semi-scientific or popular publications with essentially commercial goals aimed at organizations (business/commerce, the armed forces, government) and individuals (adults interested in self-help, teachers, parents). Many of these were developed by practitioners, not necessarily researchers or even traditional educators. Probably the best known are deBono's publications in which he has elaborated the concept of 'lateral thinking' (eg deBono, 1970). Originally a medical practitioner, he has developed not only a graphic and picturesque terminology (eg 'water' and 'rock' logic), but has also published the *CoRT Thinking Program* (deBono, 1978), a set of strategies for creative thinking that has been widely applied in business and education. Michalko (eg 1996, 1998), a former officer in the US Army, has recently become prominent in the USA with programmes such as *Thinkertoys* (aimed at nurturing business creativity), or *Cracking Creativity* (self-training).

'able 7.1 Main characteristics of well-known creativity programmes

Programme	Level	Materials	Aimed at Promoting
Imagi/Craft	elementary school	dramatized recordings of great moments in the lives of famous inventors and discoverers	the feeling that their own ideas are important widened horizons career aspirations of a creative kind
Purdue Creative Thinking Program	fourth grade	audio tapes and accompanying printed exercises	verbal and figural fluency, flexibility, originality and elaboration
Productive Thinking Program	fifth and sixth grades	booklets containing cartoons – uses principles of programmed instruction	problem-solving strategies attitudes to problem solving
Myers-Torrance Idea Books	elementary school	workbooks containing exercises	perceptual and cognitive abilities needed for creativity
Creative Problem Solving	all levels	no special materials – makes great use of brainstorming	finding problems collecting data finding ideas finding solutions implementing solutions
Talents Unlimited	all levels	workbooks based on idea of 'inventive thinking', aimed at problem solving emphasis on brainstorming	thinking productively communicating planning making decisions forecasting

Table 7.1 Main characteristics of well-known creativity programmes *(continued)*

Khatena Training Method	adults and children	no special materials simple teacher-made aids	breaking away from the obvious transposing ideas seeing analogies restructuring information synthesizing ideas
Osborn–Parnes Program	high school and college level	no special materials primary emphasis on brainstorming	getting many ideas separating idea generation and idea evaluation
Clapham–Schuster Program	college level	no special materials relaxation exercises definition of creativity as involving combining ideas brainstorming, synectics, etc	getting ideas understanding creativity using metacognitive techniques (setting goals, expecting success, coping with failure)
Creative Dramatics	all school levels	exercises involving touching, listening to and smelling common items pantomime activities such as removing things from an imaginary box play-making – acting out stories	imagination discovery sensory awareness control of emotions self-confidence humour

Such books are often based on scholarly findings even if the connection is sometimes loose. They are frequently technically well produced, extremely readable, easy to understand and plausible. In addition they often contain sensible and humane advice with which very few people would disagree and many of them are undoubtedly capable of bringing benefits. However, there are problems with much of this popular literature and these were summarized by Hruby (1999) – he was reviewing a specific book, but his comments are very pertinent and can be applied here in a more general way. He complained that enthusiasm for educational reform can 'run away with itself'. Among other weaknesses he identified: presenting speculations, conjectures and hypotheses as established facts; confusing correlations with causal relationships; making unjustified sweeping generalizations that are either not unequivocally supported by research or are even contradicted by some findings; drawing unwarranted conclusions about the implications of research findings for practice; failing to understand the factors that inhibit conversion of admirable recommendations into practice. Some popular books proclaim incompletely digested research findings as containing a 'revolutionary' panacea that can be applied in a set way in any and all situations without taking account of the individuals involved, the special characteristics of the situation, or the personal or structural factors facilitating or impeding implementation of good practice. Moderation, flexibility and sensitivity are recommended in their use.

The holistic approach

The need to consider all factors

Although later programmes of the kind listed in Table 7.1 go beyond knowledge, problem solving and decision making they still concentrate on the cognitive aspects of creativity even if factors such as self-concept or positive attitudes to problem solving are sometimes considered. A narrow conceptualization of creativity is inherent in the programmes whereas what is needed is an integrative, holistic approach (Cropley, 1997b; Urban, 1997). Treffinger, Sortore and Cross also stressed the importance of what they called the 'full "ecological system" of creativity' (1993). This involves recognition of the fact that creativity arises from an interaction among a number of elements including:

- the individual's creative potential;
- other psychological properties of the individual;
- aspects of the creative process such as divergent thinking;
- aspects of the environment such as the degree of risk that it will accept;

- special characteristics of the task itself such as its degree of definition;
- the nature of the desired solution such as the level of novelty that will be tolerated.

It should be noted that all but the first three of these are aspects of the task, the setting or the solution, not of the person or the process. In other words fostering creativity cannot be achieved by focusing on the individual person alone. Treffinger, Sortore and Cross (1993) concluded that it is possible to foster creativity in the 'ecological' or 'interactionist' sense but that the full range of factors just mentioned must be specified. A simple school-based example can be seen by looking at the effect that examinations have on creativity. Where these demand reproduction of set facts in a setting where only low levels of risk can be accepted (eg where failure would be catastrophic) the task itself (rejection of novelty or ambiguity) and the setting (intolerance of risk) militate strongly against creativity. (This should not be seen as an argument against either exams or factual knowledge. It is perfectly possible to construct exams or to test factual knowledge in ways that do not block creativity.)

In order to base programmes on the full ecological system of creativity it is necessary to specify: 1) the factors that are involved in the development of children's capacity to be creative (for instance, abilities, motivation and personal properties); 2) the components of the creative process; 3) the characteristics of the creativity-facilitating environment; 4) the nature of the interactions among these factors. The analysis needs to be capable of integrating research findings showing the simultaneous importance of conflicting factors such as divergent and convergent thinking, intrinsic and extrinsic motivation, or apparently contradictory personality characteristics. An appropriate model is presented in following sections.

The person: the componential model

Urban (1990) analysed the interactions leading to creativity by distinguishing a number of 'components' that work together. These focus on the person but also look at the relationships among characteristics of the learner and of the setting. The model is based on six components, each with a set of subcomponents that work together for and in the creative process within a framework of environmental conditions (see Figure 7.1). The first three components that are cognitive in nature are:

1. general knowledge and a thinking base;
2. a specific knowledge base and area-specific skills;
3. divergent thinking and acting.

The other three components representing personal properties of the individual are:

4. focusing and task commitment;
5. motivation and motives;
6. openness and tolerance of ambiguity.

The model (for more detail see Urban, 1990, 1994, 1995a, 1997, 2000) emphasizes that the elements of creativity form an interacting, mutually dependent system. No single component alone is sufficient or responsible for the whole creative process that leads to a creative product. The (sub)components are used for, participate in, or determine the creative process to differing degrees and work with differing subcomponents or combinations of subcomponents. Each (sub)component plays its role at a certain stage or phase of the creative process at a certain level, or in a certain situation. Each component is a prerequisite for, and at the same time a result of, others. A simple example is that divergent, associational thinking is facilitated by possession of deep domain-specific knowledge, broad, open perception and networking in the processing and storing of information (see for instance Chapter 2). Other related subcomponents are the resistance to group pressure that is necessary for non-conformist behaviour and autonomy of thinking, at least at certain times and in certain settings (such as the classroom). Making remote associations is easier for people who are ready to take risks, playfulness and willingness to experiment encourage numerous and varied answers, and passionate interest leads to tolerance of ambiguity.

The interactionistic or holistic approach shows that the optimum conditions for creativity exist when all dimensions (eg the properties of the person, the situation, the task and the solution) are favourable. Where this is not the case (probably the usual state of affairs) different combinations of favourable and unfavourable circumstances would hinder or facilitate creativity in different ways. For instance, the measures needed to promote creativity in people who possessed the necessary personal properties but found themselves in an unfavourable environment where a novel solution would not be accepted would differ from those needed for people in a favourable setting who, however, lacked the will to produce novelty. As was pointed out in Chapter 6, what is needed in order to work out how to promote creativity in a particular individual is thus a 'differential diagnosis' of creativity in that person. The different kinds of creativity tests that are now emerging could provide the tools for this (see Chapters 5 and 6). The dimensions of such an analysis were presented in Table 6.3 (see p 131).

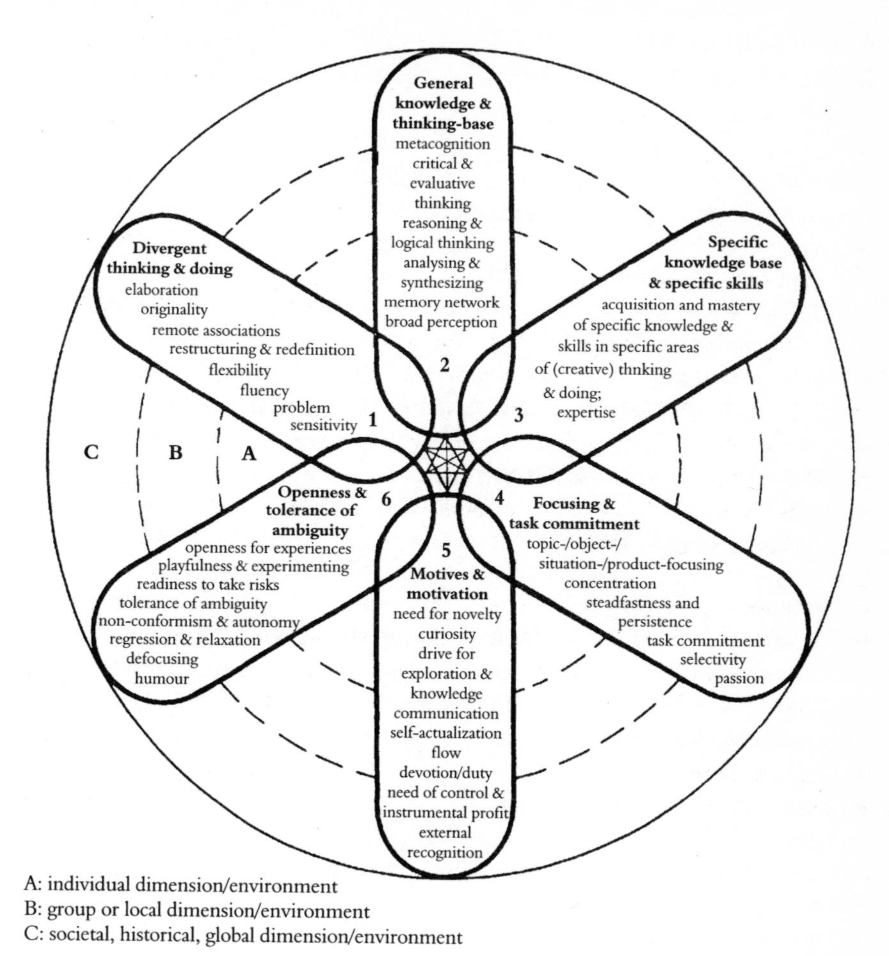

Figure 7.1 The componential model of ceativity

Fostering creativity in the classroom

What needs to be fostered?

The analyses in preceding sections make it possible to indicate in general terms some of the things that need to be fostered in the classroom. Following Urban's model these are divided here – in the case of the properties of the individual – into cognitive, personal and motivational properties.

Cognitive aspects

Looking first at the cognitive domain, fostering creativity in schoolchildren would require promotion of:

- rich and varied experience in many different settings;
- a fund of general knowledge;
- specialized knowledge;
- analysing and synthesizing skills;
- skill at seeing connections, overlaps, similarities and logical implications (convergent thinking);
- skill at making remote associations, linking apparently separate fields (bisociating) and forming new gestalts (divergent thinking);
- preference for accommodating rather than assimilating;
- ability to recognize and define problems;
- ability to plan one's own learning and evaluate progress (executive or metacognitive abilities).

Personality

In the case of personality, creativity requires promotion in children of:

- openness to new ideas and experiences;
- adventurousness;
- autonomy;
- ego strength;
- positive self-evaluation and high self-esteem;
- acceptance of all (even contradictory) aspects of one's own self;
- preference for complexity;
- tolerance for ambiguity.

Motivation

Turning to motivation the findings, especially those presented in Chapter 3, suggest that teachers should seek to foster in students:

- a concept of creativity and a positive attitude to it;
- curiosity;
- willingness to risk being wrong;
- drive to experiment;
- task commitment, persistence and determination;
- willingness to try difficult tasks;
- desire for novelty;
- freedom from domination by external rewards (intrinsic motivation);

- readiness to accept a challenge;
- readiness for risk taking.

Interaction with the environment

The dynamics and mechanics of the componential functional system are not, however, fully determined by the personal aspects. They are highly dependent on the discouraging/inhibiting versus nurturing/stimulating/inspiring/cultivating influences of the various environmental systems in which creative individuals become active. These may be classified in a threefold way:

1. the individual, subjective dimension, with the direct, situational, material and social environment;
2. the group or local dimension with family, peer group, school and local educational system (the micro-environment);
3. the societal, historical, global dimension with the cultural, political and scientific conditions (the macro- and meta-environment).

A product must be communicated to other people and at least tolerated by them ('socio-cultural validation') if it is to be acclaimed as creative. What Csikszentmihalyi (1996) called a 'congenial' environment is vital. Thus the macro- and meta-environments are clearly not irrelevant but they will not be considered in detail here since, as has already been emphasized in several places, the goal is not to produce acclaimed creative geniuses but individuals who can get ideas, try something new, take a risk and so on in the micro-environment of the home or the classroom.

The most obvious effect of these settings is that they inhibit creativity. For instance when teachers and classmates are intolerant of differentness, reject novelty or surprisingness, or impose sanctions against even 'inspired' failures, the effect is to dampen pupils' willingness to depart from the safe and conventional. This means that creativity requires on the part of the creator:

- independence and non-conformity;
- knowledge of the social rules and willingness to operate within them (if close to the edge);
- courage to risk being wrong or laughed at;
- ability to communicate in a way others can understand and accept.

On the part of the social environment, creativity requires:

- acceptance of differentness;
- openness and tolerance of variability;

- absence of rigid sanctions against (harmless) mistakes;
- provision of a 'creativogenic' climate.

The sections that follow give guidelines on how the requirements spelt out in this section can be implemented.

Facilitatory classroom practice

Introducing open learning

The pedagogical concept of *open teaching and learning* seems to provide essential conditions for fostering creativity (Urban, 1995b, 1996). When adopted by highly competent teachers open learning and instruction mean:

- offering meaningful enrichment of the children's perceptual horizons;
- enabling self-directed work, allowing a high degree of initiative, spontaneity and experimentation without fear of sanctions against incorrect solutions, errors, or mistakes;
- encouraging and accepting constructive non-conformist behaviour;
- encouraging and accepting original ideas;
- providing for challenging and stimulating learning materials;
- creating organizational and structural conditions that allow open and reversible distribution of roles, themes and problems, as well as sharing of activities;
- providing support and positive feedback for questioning and exploring behaviour and problem finding and not just problem solving;
- fostering identification of the child with school (learning) activities by allowing self-determination and joint responsibility;
- supporting development of positive self-assessment and a favourable self-concept;
- increasing autonomy in/of learning by recognition and self-evaluation of progress;
- making it possible for children to experience social creativity and the 'creative plus' during group interactions and through joint projects with self-selected partners;
- reducing stress on achievement and avoiding negative stress by introducing playful activities;
- fostering intense concentration and task commitment through high motivation and interest in self-selected topics;
- creating an atmosphere free from anxiety and time pressure without abandoning sense of responsibility;
- establishing psychological security, openness and freedom;
- nurturing sensibility, flexibility and divergent thinking.

This kind of concept implies a changed and enriched role of the educator or teacher who is no longer just instructor, evaluator, censor and authority but stimulator, elicitor, moderator, stabilizer, helper, mediator, counsellor, friend, participating observer, initiator, partner, instructor, organizer, expert, mentor and model (Urban, 1996).

Stimulating creativity

Fostering creativity is an integral part of education and should be a guiding principle for teaching *all* children. It should not be reduced to a collection of set exercises carried out at fixed times as part of a 'creativity programme' as the discussion of special techniques and programmes above may seem to suggest. The desire to foster creativity is at the heart of a philosophy or principle that should underlie *all* teaching and learning in all subject areas and at all times. This section contains a number of relatively general recommendations for teachers who wish to implement relevant 'best practice' in their classrooms. Although formulated for teachers in school the recommendations could in principle also be implemented in other educational institutions as well as in settings such as the workplace, wherever there is a felt need for creative productivity or innovation. These recommendations are based on Urban (1996; see, too, Cropley and Urban, 2000):

1. Stimulate and maintain a creative group atmosphere that allows learners to speak, think and work free of stress and anxiety and without fear of sanctions.
2. Avoid group pressure and factors such as envy associated with competition but allow and support a co-operative climate.
3. Try to avoid and prevent negative reactions or sanctions by classmates.
4. Provide for adequate alternation of periods of activity and relaxation that foster reflection.
5. Demonstrate and appreciate humour.
6. Stimulate and support free play and manipulation of objects and ideas (eg 'What if...?').
7. Support self-initiated questioning and learning.
8. Provoke and provide for situations challenging, stimulating, or requiring creative behaviour.
9. Be careful with/hold back (excessively) rapid feedback promoting rigid or stereotyped patterns of behaviour or solutions.
10. Act as a model for and support constructive questioning of rules or seemingly indispensable facts or patterns.
11. Try to avoid as much as possible 'suggestive' questions or questions that require a simple 'yes/no' answer.

12. Instead of questions, try to formulate statements that may stimulate or provoke questions by the students.
13. Do not provide strategies for finding solutions too quickly but instead give hints step by step in order to stimulate independent thinking.
14. Allow errors and mistakes (as long as they are not physically or psychologically harmful to the child or to others).
15. Interpret errors as signs of individual and constructive effort towards a self-detected solution.
16. Try to discover the strategy that led to an error (qualitative error analysis).
17. Try to make students sensitive to stimuli from different aspects of the environment (material, symbolic, social).
18. Support interest in and acquisition of knowledge in a broad variety of different areas.
19. Give stimulation and examples for systematic investigating, redefining, altering of ideas, stories, statements, presentations, etc.
20. Demonstrate tolerance and appreciation of unusual thoughts, original ideas, or creative products.
21. Teach students to accept, acknowledge and appreciate their own creative thinking behaviour and production as well as that of others.
22. Provide manifold and stimulating material for the elaboration of ideas.
23. Support and attach importance to the full elaboration or realization (of all implications) of creative ideas.
24. Develop and demonstrate constructive criticism not just criticism.
25. Make students sensitive to possible implications and consequences of solutions.

Some idea of what these processes would mean in everyday practice can be gained from the following examples. Contents could be drawn from students' experiences outside school, for instance during camping trips, out-of-school projects, hobby activities, or even shopping ('Introducing open learning: offering meaningful enrichment of the child's perceptual horizon'). The teacher could also go beyond setting tests on which answers can be scored either 'correct' or 'incorrect' and even include items that are insoluble. Students could be required to describe and evaluate the thinking that led to the best answer they could find to such questions, and grades could be based on this evaluation regardless of formal correctness (or not) of the actual answer ('Introducing open learning: increasing autonomy and self-evaluation'). Students could be assigned problems in any content area to solve in groups and be required to submit reports on the way in which the group facilitated or inhibited problem solving ('Introducing open learning: making it possible for children to experience social creativity').

To turn to specific subjects, in *history* instead of asking for a list of the causes of the American War of Independence a teacher could ask students to describe what the modern world would be like if the British had granted the North American colonies representation in the House of Commons. In *woodwork* or *metalwork* students could be given the task of building a novel device such as a car driven by the energy stored in a mousetrap or a device for moving an uncooked egg from a 2-metre-high platform to the ground without breaking it. In *mathematics* students could be asked to indicate the consequences for geometry, engineering or real life if it were found that the sum of the angles of a triangle is not 180° but 200°. In *modern languages* (German, French or Russian) they could be given the assignment of explaining what problems of expressing meaning would arise if reflexive verbs suddenly ceased to exist in the language in question, or of showing the means by which a language without widespread use of reflexive verbs (such as English) solves the problem of communicating meaning created by their absence.

These examples cover only a minute corner of the full spectrum of disciplines and levels that exists in primary, secondary and tertiary education. They are presented here merely as illustrations that give some idea of what is meant in practice by the guidelines spelt out above. It is worth emphasizing that these examples are not intended to legitimize ignorance under the pretext of being creative. This involves what is rather vulgarly but very appropriately expressed in German as *Gedankenrulpzen* (belching ideas) or at best quasicreativity (containing novelty but without a close link to facts). The answers would aim at combining production of novelty and production of orthodoxy, a process that is seen in this book as being at the heart of creative behaviour.

Relevant and effective answers to the examples suggested above would require solid knowledge of the field in question in addition to production of novelty. Someone who for instance did not know what reflexive verbs are could not apply fantasy to analysing their importance in specifying meaning. Turning to the question about the American War of Independence, the answer, 'The word "carpetbagger" would not exist in the English language because the Civil War would not have taken place, since the abolition of slavery in Britain in 1833 would have applied in the American colonies too,' shows historical and linguistic knowledge as well as broad coding. By contrast, 'The USA would have had King Bill, Queen Hillary and Princess Chelsea' involves a novel idea, it is true, but without any depth of historical knowledge or understanding or even plausibility (only quasicreativity), while 'Democracy and the greatness of the human spirit would soon triumph once again over the forces of oppression and reaction' is simply a fine sounding catch cry that could have been applied to any one of thousands of questions (quasicreativity).

A framework for stocktaking

Creativity is not simply a matter of helping children get better at having as many ideas as possible in the shortest possible time. On the contrary it involves both the whole person and all aspects of personal development as well as all phases of the creative process. Teachers need guidelines that help them to review their own practices in order to evaluate how far their teaching is fostering development of children's creative thinking, learning and acting. The questions below provide such guidelines. They are organized according to the components model set out above and refer to classroom instruction at all levels. Their intention is to provide a framework for teachers to evaluate their own classroom practices. By asking themselves the questions, teachers can evaluate how far they have moved towards becoming 'creativity-fostering' teachers. In each case the answer that indicates creativity-fostering practice should be obvious from the material presented above. The section is based on the work of Urban (1996; see, too, Cropley and Urban, 2000).

Component 1: divergent thinking

- Is asking questions allowed and appreciated?
- Is the teacher open and sensitive to problems raised by students?
- Does the teacher try to make children aware of open questions, sensitive to their environment and willing to use all their senses?
- Are problems simply presented, or (to the maximum degree possible) discovered?
- Are pre-existing answers simply presented?
- Do time and organization allow more than one attempt at finding a solution?
- Are objects and topics considered from different aspects?
- Are phases or ways and/or goals/products kept open or shaped openly?
- Are students encouraged not always to be satisfied with the first correct solution?
- Is a 'deviant' method or solution – originality – expected and appreciated?
- In general, does anything happen (in school) that could be called 'divergent thinking', or is learning nothing more than regurgitation of accumulated knowledge that has been obtained from textbooks or teachers?

Component 2: general knowledge and thinking base

- Do learning tasks require and promote broad and differentiated perception or do they restrict focus?

- Does learning use different sensory channels and varying methods so that experiences and knowledge may be anchored and accessible in memory storage in various ways?
- Is the structure of learning objects/subjects analysed?
- Is there a focus on the learning process not simply on the result?
- Are solution methods questioned or optimized?
- Are 'why?' questions asked and answered so that cause–effect relations can be studied?
- Is there instruction on systematic analysing and synthesizing of problems, topics, facts, situations, etc?
- Are there challenges requiring both inductive and deductive reasoning?
- Is evaluation asked for and desired?
- Is the learning process made explicit and reflected upon with students so that metacognitive thinking is initiated and furthered?

Component 3: specific knowledge base and specific skills

- Is the development of special interests encouraged, for example by additive or extra-curricular provision, mentor systems, competitions, etc?
- Are individual interests brought into or built into schoolwork?
- Are there opportunities/possibilities for students to obtain experience via in-depth studies?
- Is both experts' and children's expertise appreciated?

Component 4: focusing and task commitment

- Is sustained occupation with a special activity allowed or supported (for example research work on a project carried on for the entire school year)?
- Do the timetable and school organization support such activities?
- Is task commitment rewarded?
- Is there an expectation that tasks have to be fulfilled and brought to an end?
- Are children supported in recognizing and avoiding distractions?
- What is the role of self-evaluation and external reward?

Component 5: motives and motivation

- Are children's questions accepted and expanded upon?
- Is the curiosity of the children stimulated and supported?
- Are there opportunities for self-directed learning and discovery learning in order to support and promote intrinsic motivation?
- Are individual interests appreciated and supported?
- Is unnecessary repetition avoided?
- Can children identify with their work?

Component 6: openness and tolerance of ambiguity

- Is school not only a place for traditional instruction, but a place of living, of fun, of (mental) adventure?
- Does instruction bring the real world into school? Does instruction reach out into reality?
- Is school a place for fantasy and imagination?
- Is school a place for eu-stress (good stress) and relaxation?
- Is there a place for laughter (not at the expense of others) and appreciation of humour?
- Is the teacher able to accept an open result for an instructional unit?
- Are there opportunities to explore and investigate objects in a playful and experimental way?
- Are errors allowed or are quick and correct results demanded?
- Is the individuality and uniqueness of each person appreciated or is conformist behaviour demanded?

It is hoped that by repeatedly asking themselves the questions above teachers will be able to evaluate their own teaching practice and modify it in order to become more supportive and facilitative of creativity. Appropriately modified, the guidelines for self-evaluation can be applied to all levels of education and even to management practices. Finally, they can also be applied by parents to their behaviour in raising their own children.

8

Creativity in higher education

Creativity is not something for the family and school-level education alone, but is also an urgent need in post-school education. This chapter looks at the following questions:

1. Why is creativity important in higher education?
2. To what extent is higher education fostering creativity?
3. What factors in higher education inhibit creativity?
4. How can things be done differently?

The pressure for reform

Dealing with a changing world

Economic change

Globalization and competition have produced new challenges for business. One of the reactions is that many corporations have 'discovered' creativity. According to Munroe (1995) 70 per cent of the cost of a product is determined by its design, so that creative design can lead to substantial savings. As a result, creativity training for employees is becoming widespread (Clapham, 1997; Thakray, 1995). According to the 1995 US Industry Report, corporations are now budgeting billions of US dollars for creativity training programmes. Demand for training is said to be outstripping the supply of trainers (Hequet,

1995). This means that considerations of the global marketplace and the skills needed for a successful career are reinforcing the importance of fostering creativity in higher education (eg Steiner, 1998). At their meeting in Cologne in June 1999 the members of the Group of Eight (Britain, Canada, France, Germany, Italy, Japan, Russia and the United States) – essentially the world's biggest economies – identified 'entrepreneurship' as the key property that needs to be developed in students.

Change and the individual

Problem solving, independent and critical thinking and similar properties are not important solely because of their role in economic development of the nation, increased profit for firms and career advancement for individuals. In addition to changes in economics and the work world, societies are experiencing demographic, social and cultural change. These pose threats to survival of a civil society, maintenance of mental health, resistance to alienation and similar social and psychological aspects of life. Obviously, change is not necessarily a bad thing in itself. There may well be aspects of life and areas of the globe where more rapid change is desirable. However, the present cycle of change has two special features that are potentially destructive. The first is its rapidity. In the past change has always been slow relative to the life expectancy of a single human being so that people could adapt to a set of conditions that remained more or less constant during their lifetime (Knowles, 1975). The present set of changes, by contrast, is occurring so rapidly that the cycle may repeat itself several times within a single lifetime. The second feature of change in the modern world is that it is global. It transcends regional and national boundaries.

Change and education

The connection between change and education has received considerable attention in recent years. Neice and Murray (1997) called for a 'pedagogical ethic' oriented towards coping with change. The European Union (European Commission, 1996) also took change as a key idea, especially scientific and technological change, and identified the need for appropriate 'advances in methods of knowledge acquisition'. The crucial point for the present discussion is that people need to be able to adjust to change that is both rapid and sweeping, both for their own well-being and for that of the societies in which they live. This means that education will need to foster flexibility, openness, ability to produce novelty, ability to tolerate uncertainty and similar properties – in other words, creativity. Mezirow, one of the most prominent thinkers in modern discussions of post-school education and particularly adult education, made a similar point (Mezirow *et al*, 1990) and endorsed the earlier call by

Botkin, Elmandjra and Malitza (1979) for tertiary education 'that can bring change, renewal, restructuring...'

Focus on higher education

The challenges that have just been outlined also have important implications for schools. However, the present chapter focuses on higher education. This phase of education merits special study because of its particular importance in educational systems. This importance derives from the prestige and influence of universities and colleges within the educational systems of most countries and from their role in developing theory and conducting research. What universities teach, investigate and promote influences knowledge, attitudes, values and practices in many areas of society. Tertiary institutions educate the people who will later shape the development of society. They also play a major role in the training of teachers, where they provide not only knowledge, but also a system of values (such as belief in the importance of openness and flexibility). In addition, university teachers themselves serve as important role models and can demonstrate the kinds of properties outlined in Chapter 7 as characteristics of the creativity-facilitating teacher. Higher education is what Williams (1977) called the 'dominant force' in education. As a result, it seems plausible that learners' experiences in higher education will have important effects on the practice of teaching and learning at other levels.

Lack of creativity in higher education

At least since the Sputnik shock of 1957 higher education has widely been regarded as indifferent or even hostile to creativity. Empirical studies have supported this view. In the specific case of engineering, Snyder (1967) showed that students at a US university who preferred trying new solutions dropped out of engineering courses three times more frequently than those who preferred conventional solutions. Gluskinos (1971) found no correlation between creativity as measured by a creativity test and GPAs in engineering courses. Despite this, the literature over the years demonstrates the existence of a continuing interest in universities in fostering creativity (eg Masi, 1989). However, a recent survey (Government of Australia, 1999) suggests that universities are not providing the necessary training. According to employers in the survey three-quarters of all new graduates in Australia, regardless of discipline, are 'unsuitable' for employment because of 'skill deficiencies' in creativity, problem solving, and independent and critical thinking.

Various other writers in recent years have criticized higher education in terms familiar to advocates of creativity. In Britain the General Medical Council recognized that medical education is overloaded with factual material (Exley and Dennick, 1996) that discourages higher-order cognitive functions such as evaluation, synthesis and problem solving, and engenders an attitude of passivity. Exley and Dennick recommended recognition that students must learn to cope with rapid change and new discoveries. Turning to engineering education various writers including Steiner (1998) have emphasized the importance of the kind of skills, abilities, attitudes, values and motives described in Chapters 2 and 3 (eg ability to think autonomously, to solve problems, to cope with the unexpected). These are seen as crucial for innovation, which is itself regarded as a key but neglected element of engineering curricula.

Shortcomings in higher education

One-sidedness

Conventional education systems often hinder the development of skills, attitudes and motives necessary for production of novelty. Among other things they frequently perpetuate the idea that there is always a single best answer to every problem and that this can readily be ascertained by correct application of set techniques and conventional logic that need to be learnt and then reapplied over and over again. It is believed that teachers know all the answers and that their duty is to pass these on to their students at the appropriate time. By doing this teachers save learners the effort of seeking answers for themselves as well as the uncertainty associated with not knowing in advance that what they are doing is correct. As a result students acquire only the skills needed to produce orthodoxy (see Chapter 2) and the associated attitudes, values, motives, self-image and the like.

According to Gardner (1983) there are seven 'intelligences': linguistic, musical, logical-mathematical, spatial, bodily-kinaesthetic, intuitive and personal. When excessive emphasis is placed on some intelligences to the neglect of others intellectual development is one-sided. For example, it can be argued that traditional education favours linguistic and logical-mathematical intelligence but neglects what Gardner calls 'intuitive' intelligence.

Existing education is also one-sided in another sense: it stresses some forms of learning but not others. To take an example, most schools and even universities still emphasize other-directed, face-to-face learning, while neglecting self-directed and independent learning. These weaknesses limit the abilities, values, attitudes and self-image that learners develop and thus have unfavourable consequences that are particularly problematic for production of novelty. The Flinders University of South Australia recently decided to introduce special measures to assist students to develop *independent learning skills*. Supporting the proposal the President of the Students' Union said that high-school graduates come to university seriously lacking in such skills and this causes them substantial problems, especially when they find themselves in situations where they have to learn without the nurturing influence of a group.

Inappropriate concept of knowledge

The most obvious result of learning is acquisition of *knowledge*. It is not being suggested here that in the interest of fostering creativity, knowledge should cease to be valued as a result of university studies. However, it is possible to conceptualize knowledge in a more 'creativity-friendly' way than is traditionally the case. Anderson's (1993) definition is helpful here. He emphasized not possession of discrete pieces of information (factual knowledge) but 1) generalized schemas or master plans for making sense out of new events and 2) effective tactics for dealing with these events. Candy, Crebert and O'Leary (1994) stressed the importance of not only domain-specific information but also 'generic knowledge' – knowledge about the interconnectedness of fields. These in turn lead to what they labelled 'helicopter vision'. Frederiksen and Collins (1996) referred to 'flexible knowledge': not just facts that can be applied profitably to new variants of familiar situations but also knowledge that allows people to respond effectively when exposed to novelty and change. Botkin, Elmandjra and Malitza (1979) had much the same idea in mind when they wrote about the importance of 'anticipatory learning': learning that promotes the ability to solve novel problems that have not been seen before by either learners or their teachers. Anticipatory knowledge is precisely what is needed for creativity.

Lack of emphasis on creative thinking skills

In discussing learning in adults Mezirow (1990) emphasized the importance of making 'a new or revised interpretation of an experience', more or less what is meant in this book by the term 'producing novelty'. The problem is that as a result of experience people possess 'habits of perceiving, thinking, remembering, problem solving'. These habits provide *frames of reference* that make it possible to categorize and interpret new events. Although such habits or frames are extremely useful because they make it easy to interpret experience they are also limiting and restricting because they 'constrain' meaning by encouraging people to see the new in terms of the past, and thus inhibit production of novelty. Mezirow called for provision of learning experiences that emancipate people from dealing with the present as simply a repetition of the past. He called the necessary approach 'transformative learning'. For the present purposes transformative learning would enable people to break away from seeing the new in terms of the past and always dealing with it in the same way as previously, and would thus facilitate production of novelty.

Resnick (1987) focused on thinking, especially *higher-order thinking*. This has the following characteristics: 1) it is non-algorithmic (the pathway to the required solution is not specified in advance); 2) it is complex; 3) it often yields multiple solutions; 4) it requires 'nuanced judgment' from the learners (there are choice points where the learners must take the next step on the basis of experience or even intuition); 5) it involves multiple criteria; 6) it entails uncertainty; 7) it requires self-regulation; 8) it demands that learners impose a meaning of their own on apparent disorder rather than discover a pre-existing meaning; and lastly 9) it requires effort. These characteristics can be contrasted with those of thinking that focuses on acquisition of set knowledge followed by reapplication of this knowledge in the future, ie production not of novelty but of orthodoxy (see Chapter 2). Higher-order thinking, by contrast, which encompasses complexity, uncertainty and multiple solutions, favours production of novelty.

Resnick also emphasized the 'executive processes' necessary for higher-order thinking. These encompass what are often called metacognitive aspects of learning: the ability to reflect on one's own learning processes and change them as necessary. They include:

- keeping track of one's own understanding of the issue under consideration;
- organizing one's attention;
- organizing the available resources;
- reviewing one's own progress with the learning task.

To these can be added (Frederiksen and Collins, 1996): effective strategies for representing and solving problems; strategies for choosing more promising approaches; insight into how systems work; skills for applying this understanding. The ability of students to articulate their own metacognitions is of considerable importance here. Articulation permits conscious self-reflection, highly specific feedback (correction) by teachers and communication with other learners to compare methods, identify different approaches and make improvements.

Fostering creativity in higher education

The creative learner

Although they were not specifically discussing creativity, Candy, Crebert and O'Leary (1994) summed up the characteristics of the idealized creative learner as conceptualized in this book. According to them, such people have:

- an inquiring mind characterized by a love of learning, curiosity, a critical spirit and self-monitoring of their own learning;
- helicopter vision involving mastery of a particular field paired with broad vision and a sense of the interconnectedness of different fields;
- information literacy including skill in locating, retrieving, decoding (from different sources, such as words, charts or diagrams), evaluating, managing and using information;
- learning skills focused on 'deep' learning (deduction of general principles underlying specific knowledge that can be applied in novel situations not just situations identical to the one in which the learning occurred; deep learning is to be contrasted with 'surface' learning that consists essentially of acquisition of facts);
- a sense of 'personal urgency' deriving from a favourable self-concept, self-organizing skills and a positive attitude to learning.

Training students to be creative

Attempts to train university students to be more creative have produced mixed results. Rubinstein (1980) and Woods (1983) reported some success in training engineering students in problem solving. More recently, in a pre-test–post-test study Basadur, Graen and Scandura (1986) showed that a programme emphasizing divergent thinking increased the preference of manufacturing engineering students for generating new solutions although the study did not report any changes in actual performance. Clapham and Schuster (1992) administered creativity tests to students from a variety of majors. About half of them then received creativity training that emphasized deferment of judgement, brainstorming, incubation and idea-getting techniques while the remainder acted as controls. The statistical analysis showed that the test scores of the trained students had increased significantly more than those of the controls.

Despite earlier scepticism about the effectiveness of creativity training (eg Mansfield, Busse and Krepelka, 1978), Feldhusen and Goh (1995) concluded that it is possible to enhance creativity in students by teaching them to seek new ideas, recognize novel approaches when they see them and assess the effectiveness of novel solutions. Clapham (1997) reviewed possible mechanisms through which beneficial effects of creativity training in higher education occur and concluded that they can be attributed to programmes' ability to foster: 1) development of appropriate thinking skills; 2) acquisition of positive attitudes to creativity and creative performance; 3) motivation to be creative; 4) perception of oneself as capable of being creative; 5) reduction of anxiety about creativity; 6) experience of positive mood in problem-solving situations. It is apparent that this list goes beyond simply thinking skills and encompasses attitudes, motivation, self-image and similar factors.

Fostering creativity in engineers: a brief case study

Some aspects of breaking out of the straitjacket imposed by traditional university instruction can be seen in a project involving a psychology professor and an engineering instructor (Cropley and Cropley, 2000). They introduced a class on engineering innovation in an electronic engineering degree programme. Second-year students received lectures on creativity emphasizing its importance for engineering practice and developing a practical definition (introduction of effective novelty). This material was made concrete with the help of case studies of famous innovations. As part of their assessment students were required to design and build a wheeled vehicle powered by the energy stored in a mousetrap. Although a minimum passing grade was guaranteed if the vehicle proved to be capable of moving under its own power, assessment emphasized the importance of novelty, elegance and germinality (all of which had been explained to the students) for obtaining a high mark. In addition, students were required to submit individual reports analysing the way their own thinking, motivation and personality characteristics, as well as social factors, influenced their approach to the task.

Almost all participants succeeded in constructing a vehicle that met the minimum formal requirements (it had wheels and was capable of moving itself). Several of the resulting models were elegantly designed and well finished. However, most students assumed that the vehicle had to be four-wheeled and had to run on the ground like a car or truck. In addition, most focused on the energy stored in the trap's spring as the source of power as well as consciously opting for a vehicle that was *effective* in the sense that it could cover well over a metre, and was *socially acceptable* in that it looked like existing vehicles. Only a few were able to break away from conventional thinking. One group constructed an aeroplane launched by a catapult powered by the mousetrap's spring (the plane had wheels and easily covered a metre), thus expanding the concept 'wheeled vehicle', in the sense of Sternberg's 'propulsion' model of creativity (see Chapter 5). Another group built a large hollow wheel set rolling by a weight mounted in its interior and wound into position by the trap's spring, thus expanding the meaning of 'wheeled'.

Even more novelty was produced by a group that set fire to the mousetrap and used the heat generated by the flames to fire up the boiler of a steam locomotive, thus using the chemical energy stored in the wood, whereas almost all others focused on the mechanical energy of the spring. Finally one group offered the most radical solution: a wheeled cart attached to the mousetrap by a string. When the mousetrap was thrown off the table on which the vehicle stood its weight pulled the cart along as the trap fell to the floor, thus using the gravitational force acting on the mousetrap's mass as the source of energy. The only limit on the distance this method could propel the vehicle was the height of the surface from which the mousetrap was thrown.

Comparisons of the trained students with a control group suggested that the cross-disciplinary (psychological) contents had had some positive effects although it was apparent that a single course was not sufficient to achieve real change in the direction of creativity. The students' logs of their own thinking while designing their vehicles showed that many of them consciously opted for a 'safe' solution, preferring to produce orthodoxy rather than risky novelty despite the fact that they knew production of novelty was necessary for a high grade. These people elected to build a model of a conventional car or truck that they were certain would run a metre and would not strike others as odd or 'way out', preferring this to trying to be original because of the risk of building a vehicle that did not work. (An example is a group whose members thought of using the mousetrap's spring to compress a bellows, which would inflate a balloon, which would then deflate violently and drive the vehicle by its jet action. However, they abandoned this novel approach as too risky, since it might not have worked!) A few students, by contrast, indicated that they went all out for novelty, accepting the risk of a fiasco. The protocols suggested that risk takers were highly motivated by the task, whereas it intimidated risk avoiders.

Necessary changes in higher education

Changed admission criteria

One area where universities may have been acting against creativity is that of admission procedures. In Germany the press periodically reports cases of applicants being refused admission to university despite substantial creative achievements, such as published research with a high level of novelty, because their overall secondary school grades are not high enough. (Many such students eventually attend universities in the USA.) In Australia the University of Adelaide no longer selects medical students solely on the basis of school grades but since 1996 makes use of a combination of academic standing, an aptitude test (the Undergraduate Medicine and Health Sciences Admission Test) and interviews. The last two procedures attempt to identify an applicant's personal qualities such as compassion, empathy, or dedication, as well as *problem-solving ability*, *communication skills* and *ability to work in teams*. It is argued that these and not sheer academic brilliance are crucial for success in the real-life practice of medicine, although candidates must still achieve grades in the top 10 per cent of all matriculants. Although academic staff have observed no drop in performance of students there has been a storm of protest from the parents of more conventionally gifted candidates, including appeals to the South Australian ombudsman (who ruled that the procedure was permissible). Thus, public willingness to accept changed criteria may be low.

Appropriate teaching methods

A second area where practice may militate against production of novelty is teaching methods, especially the predominance of the lecture, which is still the most common teaching method in universities (Bligh, 1998). Lectures involve passive learning that is largely out of the control of the student. Bligh concluded that the lecture is as effective as other methods such as classroom discussions for transmitting information but that for achieving higher-level conceptual skills most lectures are not as effective as active learning approaches. Lectures are also relatively ineffective for changing attitudes or fostering personal or social adjustment in students. From the point of view of promoting creativity Bligh's conclusion that lectures do not promote learning to solve problems is of particular interest.

However, getting faculty to change from the lecture method (either by adapting it to allow for more student interaction or by replacing it with other, more active teaching methods) often meets with considerable resistance. It is often argued that the lecture is inexpensive since it rarely involves equipment costs and allows a single teacher to address large numbers of students simultaneously. The lecture also makes fewer demands on the instructor's time, both in terms of interacting with students and in preparation for teaching, compared to, say, project-based learning. It seems likely, however, that the lecture has retained its prominence simply because it is the method that university teachers were themselves exposed to as students. Since the great majority of university lecturers receive no instruction in methods of teaching and learning it is hardly surprising that they use the only role models available to them from their own higher education.

While most concern about traditional teaching methods in higher education has focused upon the lecture, the formal laboratory too is not without its critics. Elton (1983) summarized the dissatisfaction with the method that has been expressed on both sides of the Atlantic. A major concern here is that student work in the laboratory frequently gives a false impression of how science is carried out, how problems are solved and discoveries made. This is thought to be because of the artificial constraints within the laboratory – the need for students to work on set exercises within limited time periods. All too often undue emphasis is placed upon the importance of getting the correct result as opposed to the process of investigation, and the impression is given that science is a neat, cut-and-dried means of arriving at elegant, single, best solutions.

Hazel and Baillie (1998) summarized the problems with traditional labs, especially as they relate to learning goals and outcomes:

- Learning goals for the lab are often not made explicit to students and are sometimes not even clear to the teacher.
- Goals are often too diffuse, while some goals are not exclusive to labs and could be attained more efficiently elsewhere.
- Labs and the way they are assessed often emphasize low-level learning and discourage understanding of links between methods and theory.
- Assessment of labs often fails to test whether goals have been attained (and some students do well without even attending the lab!).
- Students often find 'cookbook' labs tedious and do not take them seriously.

To this might be added the criticism that feedback to students on effective performance in labs is often lacking and hence there is little chance for reflection and improvement in the problem-solving skills that laboratory work is supposed to encourage. Hazel and Baillie went on to offer suggestions for improving the quality of learning in laboratories, many of which are consistent with the idea of fostering production of novelty: learning by introducing projects that require students to work more autonomously and in collaborative teams; use of peer assessment, learning portfolios and reflective journals.

Reduction in excessive specialization

A different aspect of university and college teaching that relates to fostering creativity is the question of specialization and fragmentation of content. This militates against integrating insights from a variety of disciplines via wide coding, unexpected associations and the like. Candy, Crebert and O'Leary (1994) gave great weight to the importance of 'deep' learning, especially the acquisition of transferable knowledge and skills. None the less, they saw this as resting upon a foundation of domain-specific knowledge. Thus, they did not reject out of hand the idea of individual disciplines as some earlier protagonists of interdisciplinary studies had done. Their model of the undergraduate curriculum defines a hierarchical relationship between elements including among other things: 1) domain-specific knowledge and skills; 2) 'contextual' elements; 3) generic or transferable knowledge and skills. They had no difficulty with emphasis on domain-specific knowledge but rather with the hierarchical organization of knowledge. At present teaching and learning are often preoccupied almost exclusively with discipline-specific content while generic knowledge and skills are at best a hoped-for, more or less incidental outcome derived from the process of acquiring the material of the discipline.

Some universities have introduced interdisciplinary studies, including the Faculty of Medicine at McMaster University, Ontario, Roskilde University in Denmark and Evergreen College in Washington State. Many of the successful experiments include a curriculum that involves students in tackling problems rather than mastering traditional bodies of subject matter from particular disciplines. Other approaches of a more limited nature include a requirement that students take part in an interdisciplinary course or courses (often at the beginning of their programme of study) but within the context of an otherwise traditional institution and discipline-based programme. One example of this type was the University of Keele's foundation year (just abandoned after 49 years) in which first-year students worked on a set of issues or problems that, by their nature, transcended disciplinary boundaries. A similar approach is exemplified by the University Foundation Units offered at Murdoch University in Western Australia, required for all beginning students and intended to ensure all undergraduates have an experience of interdisciplinary study.

Changing the role of instructors

Achieving radical changes in teaching and learning activities would depend to a considerable degree upon acceptance of an altered role for instructors in colleges and universities. For example, in a system oriented towards production of novelty teachers would be seen more as guides or helpers than as authoritative sources of all knowledge. Staff are thus important not only because they specify content and teaching and learning strategies as well as assessing students' work, but also because on the one hand they establish what Candy, Crebert and O'Leary (1994) called the 'climate' and on the other they act as models. This means among other things that it is important that they show curiosity and passion, and are themselves obviously involved in production of novelty. One possibility is that instructors and students could work together in areas where neither are expert. This was the basis of Keele's foundation year, mentioned above, in which small groups of staff and students explored topics that lay outside the teacher's own expertise. This approach has been adopted in other British universities, as well as in universities elsewhere in the Commonwealth, such as Zambia. Equally important, if university teachers are to function effectively as models they themselves would have to engage in the process of novelty production. Of course many university teachers already do this in their role as scholars and researchers where updating knowledge and skills is an essential part of remaining current in the field.

Barr and Tagg (1995) called for a paradigm shift away from an *instruction* (eg through teaching that is largely based on lectures conveying traditional content) to a *learning* paradigm. Here the emphasis is not on transferring existing knowledge (without denying its importance) but on assisting students to *discover* and *construct* knowledge for themselves and to solve problems. Barr and Tagg's paper has provoked considerable debate in North American higher education and the authors admit that there are formidable institutional and attitudinal barriers to change in the direction they recommend.

Changing assessment

The credentialling function is a familiar one in institutions of higher education. While teaching is perhaps their major activity an equally important related task involves the certification that learning has taken place. The credentialling role of higher education is of major importance for society at large since it serves as a screening mechanism for a very wide variety of occupations. In effect it is assessment methods rather than stated course objectives that drive learning: students study what they need to pass tests and if this requires rote learning then this will take priority over more lofty goals such as creativity. Students are often extremely adept at pinpointing what is *really* required to do well in a course, based upon subtle cues from the instructors when they talk about assessment procedures, on inspection of previously used tests, conversations with former students and so on.

Students' success at disentangling the hidden curriculum may be reflected in high marks but these grades may be a poor reflection of the problem-solving, critical thinking, divergent skills of novelty production. Hence it is not surprising that academic grades are poor predictors of success and satisfaction in many careers (eg Heath, 1977). This raises serious questions about customary methods of teaching and assessing student performance in higher education. Dissatisfaction with assessment practices has continued to the present, and the past 10 years have seen increasing calls for 'alternative assessment' approaches that include performance-based assessment, portfolio assessment and 'authentic' assessment (Anderson, 1998). The latter emphasizes concrete experience in settings resembling real life and examinations testing properties closely related to the real-life practice of the discipline in question.

Creativity-facilitating approaches to learning

Independent learning

Approaches that stress developing students' problem-solving ability, decision-making skills and creativity frequently use teaching strategies that aim at promoting effective self-directed or independent learning – the precise terminology employed is less important than the underlying learning processes involved. In a discussion of project-based learning Morgan (1983) suggested two components that are vital in learning oriented towards promoting novelty production: the first is students' responsibility for designing their own learning activities and the second is active student involvement in the solution of real-life problems.

One approach that stresses these two components is 'guided design' (Wales, Nardi and Stager, 1993). The underlying philosophy of guided design is that effective problem solving or decision making is best learnt by confronting students with carefully designed but open-ended problems. Each problem is planned in such a way that to arrive at a solution students must make use of the discipline-based subject matter they are learning. At the same time, decision making and problem solving are seen as skills in their own right and are taught explicitly, guided by printed materials prepared by the teacher that break down the problem-solving process and allow students to gain insight into their own intellectual approach to decision making. According to its originators guided design is intended to be used where some type of professional training is involved that includes decision making as a central component, where there is an established body of information on which students can draw to help them make their decisions and where the decisions made by professionals frequently have to be implemented by others. Hence the teaching of guided design actually models the approach of a professional working in the real world. For example, it emphasizes learning from a wide variety of sources, working with open-ended problems and concentration on issues that are drawn from real life.

Students work in teams of five or six on problems formulated by the instructor. They must identify the 'real issue' and set goals for their work as well as list underlying constraints; they are then required to generate possible solutions, choose a most likely solution, analyse and evaluate it and report their results. A key feature of the approach is the provision of feedback to students at each step along the way. It is also emphasized that there is no one correct solution and that the actual process of decision making and problem solving is more important than the particular solution arrived at. In fact, the guided design method requires students to examine closely the way in which they made their group decisions and to try to learn from this experience and from the expertise of others in the team and the class. Wales and Stager claimed that learners not only acquire relevant knowledge in this way but also develop an ability to learn independently, solve problems logically yet creatively, gather information from a variety of sources, make appropriate value judgements, work as part of a team and communicate their ideas to others.

Problem-based learning

Another promising approach is the problem-based learning approach pioneered by the medical school at McMaster University in Hamilton, Ontario, which has served as the basis for a number of similar innovations in various parts of the world. The McMaster programme has the specific aim of producing self-directed learners who can recognize their own personal educational needs, select appropriate learning resources and evaluate their own progress in studying (Ferrier, Marrin and Seidman, 1988). The curriculum adopts an interdisciplinary problem-based approach in which students work in a sequence of small groups for three years. Students have to direct their own learning and accept responsibility for the progress of the entire group in terms of objectives that are specified for the programme as a whole and for the individual segments.

In each segment students work in a tutorial group of five plus a tutor and the group must decide on the methods and strategies for learning to be employed. Groups are confronted with sets of problems, clinical experiences and a variety of additional resources. They are also encouraged to identify further problems, find other resources and even specify new objectives. The goals for the various segments laid down by the programme administrators stress general skills and concepts rather than acquisition of facts. Final responsibility for evaluation rests with the tutor but self- and peer evaluation form an additional important component. Problem-based learning is now dominant in Canadian medical education and has spread to medical schools in Europe (eg the University of Dundee), Australia (Newcastle University) and the USA (Harvard). It has also been adopted for professional education in many other fields including engineering and law.

Learning via electronic media

Information technology links together the computer with its immense capacity for storing and handling information and electronic communication systems that enable the information to be sent over great distances and to numerous reception points, virtually instantaneously. The most common manifestations today are the Internet and the World Wide Web. The new technologies have considerable implications for educational practice – not only in providing new ways of delivering learning materials (eg increasing access through distance learning) but also in facilitating communication among learners and changing the ways in which instructional resources might be organized and presented. Even more than that, technology is now an all-pervasive aspect of people's everyday lives (Green, 1999). It offers prospects of catering to individual differences between learners, making learning more flexible, active, integrative and relevant to real-life issues and promoting more collaborative, self-directed and reflective learning.

One very promising use of computer-based instruction involves *simulation* of some task or situation that would normally be difficult to bring into the classroom or home. The effectiveness of simulations to teach complicated skills has been known for some time – for example flight simulators used in pilot training. The simulated reality of the computer provides conditions with a number of the advantages offered by play that were discussed in Chapter 3: an opportunity to produce novelty without risk since a simulation can be reversed at will. Computers are no longer limited to presenting text but can also show videos, play sounds, even provide a virtual reality that includes sensation of touch, movement, all in three dimensions. These applications involve both active learning and individualization – in the sense that the learner controls the interaction with the program. There are many examples of computer simulations for teaching in higher education. The most successful from the point of view of learning seem to be ones where a computer interface would be used in the real-life situation (manipulating financial information, controlling an oil refinery) rather than those where other essential non-computing skills are involved – for example, medical diagnosis (Tannenbaum, 1999).

Distance learning

Educational technology also offers opportunities to individualize learning by breaking away from face-to-face teaching. This is typically seen as in the domain of distance education, which is often regarded as an inferior substitute for 'real' face-to-face learning. However, Cropley and Kahl (1983, 1986) gave several examples of organizational aspects of distance learning that – despite often being viewed as shortcomings – can, in fact, have beneficial consequences for learning.

- Distance learners do not have their time on task organized and supervised by an expert (a teacher). As a result, they must take at least partial responsibility for planning and organizing their own learning.
- They do not receive regular and immediate feedback during a learning task. As a result, they must themselves assess their own progress, decide on new approaches, etc.
- They do not learn in a group. As a result, they must develop skill in learning alone.
- Learning outside settings specifically designed to foster it requires *special psychological components* of which motivation is possibly the most obvious. In particular learners outside the traditional system must be largely self- or intrinsically motivated.

The value of such psychological properties is, of course, not confined to distance learning. The ability to plan, organize and evaluate one's own learning, for instance, is desirable in all learning settings. Cropley and Kahl (1983, 1986) emphasized this point by arguing that rather than trying to make distance learning more like face-to-face learning many elements that lead to effective learning outside the classroom should be incorporated into face-to-face learning. However, in practice many packaged distance courses tend to be extremely prescriptive, perhaps out of a conviction that conventional forms of learning are the best and that less traditional teaching/learning strategies are 'back door' forms of higher education. Thus programmes may try to minimize students' autonomy in planning and guiding their own study.

Distance educators not uncommonly strive to replicate face-to-face instruction to the maximum degree possible: by insisting that the same syllabus and examinations be used as in the face-to-face version of the course, using a standard textbook and sending out packages of highly structured lecture notes derived from the 'live' class. This is done in the interests of maintaining common standards between distance courses and those given in the more traditional manner. In doing this, however, distance educators may sacrifice the opportunity of challenging students to take more responsibility for their own learning instead of just relying on the authority of teacher and textbook writer. The communications technologies now used increasingly in distance education offer the potential for much more flexible, interactive and student-centred learning. Yet the great majority of distance courses continue to rely heavily on print-based materials that are conceptually little different from the old correspondence courses and often stress mastery of information rather than production of novelty.

As Knapper and Cropley (2000) emphasized there are substantial barriers to achieving change in higher education, and a reorientation towards production of novelty that goes beyond lip service may prove very difficult to achieve. At the risk of ending on a pessimistic note problems include the fact that many students will have to unlearn previous study habits and attitudes to education. In particular, there will be a need to communicate new values – for example that students' own learning is more important than blind respect for authority, or that active learning is more useful than passive learning, even though it may be initially more difficult.

Epilogue: a brief stocktaking

In closing this book it is worth asking whether the 50 years of the Guilford era have really had an impact on educational practice. The first thing that must be emphasized is that the *idea* of creativity has become widespread in educational circles. Its importance is often mentioned in preambles to school curricula and in speeches by school principals, education officials, policy makers and politicians. Research already cited earlier indicates that almost all teachers express their approval of fostering creativity as an educational goal. However, a great deal of this verbiage is little more than lip service. After all, who is against creativity? The danger is that the call for creativity has become simply a catch cry that is not really regarded as having any serious implications for actual practice! A prime example of this phenomenon is to be seen in a speech made at an educational conference in Belgium about 20 years ago. An official of the repressive, totalitarian regime of East Germany – where nothing could be published until it had been vetted by the state, budding university teachers were denied the highest degree (the *Habilitation*) if they were adjudged to be politically unsound (regardless of the creativity of their research) and where applying for a visa to visit West Germany (ie wanting to be exposed to different social norms) was a crime often punished by internment – spoke glibly of his government's commitment to fostering creativity as a major cornerstone of the educational system! Who indeed is against creativity?

Two issues need to be made clear here. First, people interested in fostering creativity should take pains to distinguish between pseudocreativity and quasicreativity on the one hand, and production of effective novelty on the other. Only the latter should be taken seriously. Second, creativity is not an add-on via a dedicated lesson or two per week but a general principle that should inform all instruction. How this can be done was outlined in Chapter 7.

In responding to the first point above, it may be argued that production of effective novelty is beyond children or indeed anyone without the 15-year apprenticeship already discussed. However, a basic principle of this book is that it is possible to work out concepts of effective novelty that can be applied at all age and ability levels (see earlier discussions, including Chapter 7).

Acceptance of pseudo- and quasicreativity may even allow creativity to degenerate into simply an alibi for enjoying an easy life – for both pupils and teachers.

As far as the second point is concerned, there is no doubt that orienting their own teaching towards fostering creativity presents teachers with difficult challenges that require more rather than less effort on their part, as well as demanding that they activate their own creativity. Learning via creativity exposes students and teachers to uncertainty, one of the states that people seem to like least, as I have already argued. An apocryphal story illustrates this point. A man was facing the firing squad. Seconds before he was to die he was offered a choice: he could be shot at once or released unarmed into a forest full of savage beasts that might or might not catch and eat him. If he got through the forest he would be safe and his sentence repealed. After thinking it over the man elected to be shot: after all, instant death was safe and secure and would not leave him worrying about his future, whereas running the gauntlet in the park would expose him to all the terrors of an uncertain fate!

In earlier chapters repeated reference was made to the need for a *congenial environment* if production of effective novelty is to flourish. Turning to higher education it is pertinent to ask here if universities in the European–North American tradition offer such an environment. In Chapter 3 (p 67) four central properties of the environment were listed: openness, positive attitude to novelty, acceptance of personal differentness and willingness to reward divergence. Do universities typically possess these properties? The answer is that the institutions themselves, as institutions, show limited openness to and suspicion of novelty. By and large traditional approaches still prevail in selection, teaching and examining of students and in selecting and promoting teachers. Personal differentness is tolerated in an almost *laissez-faire* atmosphere, it is true, but this tolerance is largely taken advantage of by producers of pseudocreativity – at best gadflies or even opportunists. The combination of deep knowledge and personal differentness is, unfortunately, uncommon. The 'different' student is viewed with suspicion and the conventional individual is preferred for PhD scholarships and the like, with the result that the next generation of teachers is selected for production of orthodoxy, not novelty. Thus, divergence tends not only not to be rewarded, but even to be punished.

To be fair, the institutions and the teachers are in a difficult position. With a few exceptions they receive large amounts of public funding and are expected to use this responsibly, ie to avoid risk and stick to the tried and trusted. Furthermore, higher education is the gateway to high-status professions and well-paid jobs, so that the level of risk is high for students and their parents – as well as high-school students and their parents – if the system becomes fluid and less predictable. Public tolerance for uncertainty is low and this is easily understandable. The public outcry over the University of Adelaide's change in admission procedures for medical school is a good example (p 165). Although the idea of ability to empathize or to work in teams as an additional qualification for budding doctors is very attractive, a change in the rules for gaining admission to medical school poses an alarming threat for high-school students part-way through the process of acquiring what they thought were the necessary qualifications.

Turning to the people rather than the institutions, both staff and students are also exposed to great risk when production of effective novelty is emphasized. Once again, proven ways of operating that produce high levels of certainty are questioned. Since the essence of novelty is that it was previously unknown, it is impossible to say in advance what will be successful and what not. To avoid this problem funding agencies almost seem to require that research applications specify in advance what will be discovered, thus guaranteeing that there will be no novelty produced! As Hans Selye once told me, he found it necessary to finance his creative research by disguising it as part of plodding projects where it was obvious what would emerge. When he discovered the general adaptation syndrome, for instance, he was working on something quite different and did not know that his pursuit of something that piqued his curiosity would eventually lead to the general adaptation syndrome. How could he, since no one had ever heard of it because it was novel? Selye first had to discover the problem (a specific biological reaction to stressors, regardless of their nature – infection or other illness; physical mishandling; hunger, etc; prolonged mental strain such as anxiety or chronic anger) and then solve it.

The answer might be provision of untied funds to researchers to make it possible for them to produce effective novelty by discovering a problem and solving it. However, the public uproar at the idea of researchers being given funding to investigate problems that do not even exist can be imagined. It is clear that the proportion of hits achieved by such funding would be low unless ways were found of excluding the gadflies. One approach is to give funds only to people with a proven track record, but in addition to introducing a 'catch-22' situation (a track record is necessary for funding; funding is necessary for a track record), this approach would tend to set up an élite old guard and thus lock out the new and fresh (see the discussion of expertise and creativity in Chapter 2, pp 45–46). This could be dealt with by providing starter funds for beginners.

Students themselves are part of the problem. Many seem to have great difficulty in grasping that producing novelty can require a knowledge and skill base, ie in differentiating between pseudocreativity, quasicreativity and effective novelty. In the Cropley and Cropley (2000) case study, for instance, attendance at lectures was down to about one-third towards the end of the semester and many students completed their laboratory work – to their own satisfaction at least – in one or two weeks. Many of these students were then indignant when banal, trivial, ignorant and superficial work received low grades, adopting the position that since the seminar was concerned with creativity the instructors should accept the first thoughts that came into the students' heads or regard all answers as of equal value.

A great deal remains to be done if fostering creativity is to become more than a rallying cry. Above all, creativity must be taken seriously. I hope that this book will make a contribution to achieving progress in the desired direction.

References

Abra, J (1994) Collaboration in creative work: an initiative for investigation, *Creativity Research Journal*, **7**, pp 1–20

Ai, X(1999) Creativity and academic achievement: an investigation of gender differences, *Creativity Research Journal*, **12**, pp 329–38

Albert, R S (1990) Identity, experiences, and career choice among the exceptionally gifted and talented, in *Theories of Creativity*, ed M A Runco, pp 13–34, Sage, Newbury Park, CA

Albert, R S and Runco, M A (1989) Independence and the creative potential of gifted and exceptionally gifted boys, *Journal of Youth and Adolescence*, **18**, pp 221–30

Altshuller, G S (1984) *Creativity as an Exact Science*, Gordon and Breach, New York

Amabile, T M (1996) *Creativity in Context*, Westview Press, Boulder, CO

Amabile, T M, Goldfarb, P and Brackfield, S C (1990) Social influences on creativity: evaluation, coaction, surveillance, *Creativity Research Journal*, **3**, pp 6–21

Anderson, C C and Cropley, A J (1966) Some correlates of originality, *Australian Journal of Psychology*, **18**, pp 218–27

Anderson, J R (1976) *Language, Memory and Thought*, Erlbaum, Hillsdale, NJ

Anderson, J R (1993) *Rules of the Mind*, Erlbaum, Hillsdale, NJ

Anderson, R S (1998) Why talk about different ways to grade: the shift from traditional assessment to alternative assessment, in *Changing the Way We Grade Student Performance: Classroom assessment and the new learning paradigm*, ed R S Anderson and B W Speck, pp 5–16, Jossey-Bass, San Francisco

Andreasen, N C (1987) Creativity and mental illness: prevalence rates in writers and their first degree relatives, *American Journal of Psychiatry*, **144**, pp 1288–92

Andreasen, N C and Powers, P S (1974) Over-inclusive thinking in mania and schizophrenia, *British Journal of Psychiatry*, **125**, pp 452–56

Anthony, E J (1987) Risk, vulnerability and resilience: an overview, in *The Invulnerable Child*, ed E J Anthony and B J Cohen, pp 3–48, Guilford Press, New York

Arieti, S (1976) *Creativity: The magic synthesis*, Basic Books, New York

Austin, J H (1978) *Chase, Chance, and Creativity*, Columbia University Press, New York

Auzmendi, E, Villa, A and Abedi, J (1996) Reliability and validity of a newly constructed multiple-choice creativity instrument, *Creativity Research Journal*, **9**, pp 89–96

Ayman-Nolley, S (1992) Vygotsky's perspective on the development of imagination and creativity, *Creativity Research Journal*, **5**, pp 101–09

Ayman-Nolley, S (1999) A Piagetian perspective on the dialectic process of creativity, *Creativity Research Journal*, **12**, pp 267–76

Baldwin, A Y (1985) Programs for the gifted and talented: issues concerning minority populations, in *The Gifted and Talented: Developmental perspectives*, ed F D Horowitz and M O'Brien, pp 223–50, American Psychological Association, Washington, DC

Baltes, P B, Reese, H W and Lipsitt, L P (1980) Lifespan developmental psychology, *Annual Review of Psychology*, **31**, pp 65–110

Baltes, P B and Smith, J (1990) Towards a psychology of wisdom and its ontogenesis, in *Wisdom: Its nature, origins and development*, ed R J Sternberg, pp 87–120, Cambridge University Press, Cambridge, MA

Barr, R B and Tagg, J (1995) From teaching to learning: a new paradigm for undergraduate education, *Change*, **27** (6), pp 13–25

Barron, F X (1963) *Creativity and Psychological Health*, Van Nostrand, New York

Barron, F X (1969) *Creative Person and Creative Process*, Holt, Rinehart and Winston, New York

Barron, F X (1972) *Artists in the Making*, Seminar Press, New York

Barron, F X and Harrington, D M (1981) Creativity, intelligence and personality, *Annual Review of Psychology*, **32**, pp 439–76

Bartlett, F C (1932) *Remembering*, Cambridge University Press, Cambridge

Basadur, M, Graen, G B and Scandura, T (1986) Training effects of attitudes toward divergent thinking among manufacturing engineers, *Journal of Applied Psychology*, **71**, pp 612–17

Basadur, M and Hausdorf, P A (1996) Measuring divergent thinking attitudes related to creative problem solving and innovation management, *Creativity Research Journal*, **9**, pp 21–32

Berlyne, D E (1962) *Conflict, Arousal and Curiosity*, McGraw Hill, New York

Besemer, S P (1998) Creative Product Analysis Matrix: testing the model structure and a comparison among products – three novel chairs, *Creativity Research Journal*, **11**, pp 333–46

Besemer, S P and O'Quin, K (1987) Creative product analysis: testing a model by developing a judging instrument, in *Frontiers of Creativity Research: Beyond the basics*, ed S G Isaksen, pp 367–89, Bearly, Buffalo, NY

Besemer, S P and O'Quin, K (1999) Confirming the three-factor Creative Product Analysis Matrix model in an American sample, *Creativity Research Journal*, **12**, pp 287–96

Besemer, S P and Treffinger, D J (1981) Analysis of creative products: review and synthesis, *Journal of Creative Behavior*, **16**, pp 68–73

Biermann, K-R (1985) Über Stigmata der Kreativität bei Mathematikern des 17. bis 19. Jahrhunderts [On indicators of creativity in mathematicians of the 17th to 19th centuries], *Rostocker Mathematik Kolloquium* [Rostock Mathematics Colloquium], **27**, pp 5–22

Birch, H (1975) The relation of previous experience to insightful problem solving, *Journal of Comparative Psychology*, **38**, pp 367–83

Birren, J E and Fisher, L M (1990) The elements of wisdom: overview and integration, in *Wisdom: Its nature, origins and development*, ed R J Sternberg, pp 317–22, Cambridge University Press, Cambridge, MA

Bligh, D A (1998) *What's the Use of Lectures?*, 5th edn, Intellect, Exeter

Bloom, B S (1985) *Developing Talent in Young People*, Ballantine, New York

Bloomberg, M (1967) An inquiry into the relationship between field independence–dependence and creativity, *Journal of Psychology*, **67**, pp 27–140

Bosman, E A and Charness, N (1996) Age-related differences in skilled performance and skill acquisition, in *Perspectives on Cognitive Change in Adulthood and Aging*, ed F Blanchard-Fields and T M Hess, pp 428–53, McGraw-Hill, New York

Botkin, J W, Elmandjra, M and Malitza, M (1979) *No Limits to Learning*, Pergamon, Oxford

Bowlby, J (1979) *The Making and Breaking of Affectional Bonds*, Tavistock, London

Brophy, D R (1998) Understanding, measuring and enhancing individual creative problem-solving efforts, *Creativity Research Journal*, **11**, pp 123–50

Brown, R T (1989) Creativity: what are we to measure?, in *Handbook of Creativity*, ed J A Glover, R R Ronning and C R Reynolds, pp 3–32, Plenum Press, New York

Bruner, J S (1962) The conditions of creativity, in *Contemporary Approaches to Cognition*, ed H Gruber, G Terrell and M Wertheimer, pp 1–30, Atheneum, New York

Bruner, J S (1964) The course of cognitive growth, *American Psychologist*, **19**, pp 1–14

Bruner, J S (1975) Child development: play is serious business, *Psychology Today*, **8**, pp 80–83

Burkhardt, H (1985) *Gleichheitswahn Parteienwahn* [Sameness Psychosis], Hohenrain, Tübingen

Burt, C (1970) Critical note, in *Creativity*, ed P Vernon, pp 203–16, Penguin, New York

Butler, D L and Kline, M A (1998) Good versus creative solutions: a comparison of brainstorming, hierarchical, and perspective-changing heuristics, *Creativity Research Journal*, **11**, pp 325–31

Byrd, R E (1986) *Creativity and Risk-taking*, Pfeiffer International Publishers, San Diego, CA

Camp, G C (1994) A longitudinal study of correlates of creativity, *Creativity Research Journal*, **7**, pp 125–44

Candy, P C, Crebert, R G and O'Leary, J O (1994) *Developing Lifelong Learners through Undergraduate Education*, National Board of Employment, Education and Training, Canberra, Australia

Carroll, J B (1993) *Human Cognitive Abilities*, Cambridge University Press, New York

Case, R (1978) Intellectual development from birth to adulthood: a neo-Piagetian interpretation, in *Children's Thinking: What develops?*, ed R S Siegler, pp 37–71, Erlbaum, Hillsdale, NJ

Cattell, R B (1971) *Abilities: Their structure, growth, and action*, Houghton Mifflin, Boston

Cattell, R B and Butcher, H J (1968) *The Prediction of Achievement and Creativity*, Bobbs-Merrill, New York

Cattell, R B and Drevdahl, J E (1955) A comparison of the personality profile of eminent researchers with that of eminent teachers and administrators, and of the general public, *British Journal of Psychology*, **46**, pp 248–61

Chi, M T H, Glaser, R and Farr, M J (1988) (eds) *The Nature of Expertise*, Erlbaum, Hillsdale, NJ

Christensen, P R, Merrifield, P R and Guilford, J P (1953) *Consequences Form A–1*, Sheridan, Beverly Hills, CA

Clapham, M M (1997) Ideational skills training: a key element in creativity training programs, *Creativity Research Journal*, **10**, pp 33–44

Clapham, M M and Schuster, D H (1992) Can engineering students be trained to think more creatively?, *Journal of Creative Behavior*, **26**, pp 156–62

Clark, C (1996) Working with able learners in regular classrooms, *Gifted and Talented International*, **11**, pp 34–38

Colangelo, N and Dettman, D F (1983) A review of research on parents and families of gifted children, *Exceptional Children*, **50**, pp 20–27

Colangelo, N *et al* (1992) The Iowa Inventiveness Inventory: toward a measure of mechanical inventiveness, *Creativity Research Journal*, **5**, pp 157–64

Cole, S (1979) Age and scientific performance, *American Journal of Sociology*, **84**, pp 958–77

Commons, M L, Richards, F A and Kuhn, D (1982) Systematic and metasystematic reasoning: a case for levels of reasoning beyond Piaget's stage of formal operations, *Child Development*, **53**, pp 1058–69

Cornelius, S W and Crespi, A (1987) Everyday problem-solving in adulthood and old age, *Psychology and Aging*, **2**, pp 144–53

Cox, C M (1926) *Genetic Studies of Genius: The early mental traits of three hundred geniuses*, Stanford University Press, Palo Alto, CA

Cropley, A J (1966) Creativity and intelligence, *British Journal of Educational Psychology*, **36**, pp 259–66

Cropley, A J (1967) *Creativity*, Longman, London

Cropley, A J (1972a) Creativity test scores under timed and untimed conditions, *Australian Journal of Psychology*, **24**, pp 31–36

Cropley, A J (1972b) A five-year longitudinal study of the validity of creativity tests, *Developmental Psychology*, **6**, pp 119–24

Cropley, A J (1990) Creativity and mental health in everyday life, *Creativity Research Journal*, **3**, pp 167–78

Cropley, A J (1992a) Glück und Kreativität: Förderung von Aufgeschlossenheit für den zündenden Gedanken [Luck and creativity: fostering openness for the spark of inspiration], in *Begabungen entwickeln, erkennen und fördern* [Developing, Recognizing and Fostering Gifts], ed K Urban, pp 216–21, University of Hannover, Faculty of Education, Hannover

Cropley, A J (1992b) *More Ways than One: Fostering creativity in the classroom*, Ablex, Norwood, NJ

Cropley, A J (1994) Creative intelligence: a concept of 'true' giftedness, *European Journal for High Ability*, **5**, pp 6–23

Cropley, A J (1997a) Creativity: a bundle of paradoxes, *Gifted and Talented International*, **12**, pp 8–14

Cropley, A J (1997b) Fostering creativity in the classroom: general principles, in *The Creativity Research Handbook*, ed M A Runco, pp 83–114, Hampton Press, Creskill, NJ

Cropley, A J (1999) Creativity and cognition: producing effective novelty, *Roeper Review*, **21**, pp 253–60

Cropley, A J and Cropley, D H (2000) Fostering creativity in engineering undergraduates, *High Ability Studies*, **11**, pp 207–19

Cropley, A J and Kahl, T N (1983) Distance education and distance learning: some psychological considerations, *Distance Education*, **4**, pp 27–39

Cropley, A J and Kahl, T N (1986) Face-to-face vs. distance learning: psychological consequences and practical implications, *Distance Education*, **7**, pp 38–48

Cropley, A J and Sikand, J S (1973) Creativity and schizophrenia, *Journal of Consulting and Clinical Psychology*, **40**, pp 462–68

Cropley, A J and Urban, K K (2000) Programs and strategies for nurturing creativity, in *International Handbook of Giftedness and Talent*, 2nd edn, ed K A Heller *et al*, pp 481–94, Pergamon, New York

Crozier, W R (1999) Age and individual differences in artistic productivity: trends within a sample of British novelists, *Creativity Research Journal*, **12**, pp 197–204

Csikszentmihalyi, M (1988) Society, culture, and person: a system view of creativity, in *The Nature of Creativity*, ed R J Sternberg, pp 325–39, Cambridge University Press, New York

Csikszentmihalyi, M (1996) *Creativity: Flow and the psychology of discovery and invention*, Harper Collins, New York

Dacey, J S (1989) *Fundamentals of Creative Thinking*, Lexington Press, Lexington, MA

Davis, G A and Rimm, S B (1982) Group Inventory for Finding Interests (GIFFI) I and II: instruments for identifying creative potential in junior and senior high school, *Journal of Creative Behavior*, **16**, pp 50–57

Davis, G A and Rimm, S B (1998) *Education of the Gifted and Talented*, Allyn and Bacon, Needham Heights, MA

deBono, E (1970) *Lateral Thinking*, Harper and Row, New York

deBono, E (1978) *Teaching Thinking*, Pelican, London

deBono, E (1991) *Handbook for the Positive Revolution*, Viking, New York

Dellas, M and Gaier, E L (1970) Identification of creativity: the individual, *Psychological Bulletin*, **73**, pp 55–73

Dennis, W (1966) Creative productivity between the ages of 20 and 80, *Journal of Gerontology*, **21**, pp 1–8

Diaz de Chumaceiro, C L (1999) Research on career paths: serendipity and its analog, *Creativity Research Journal*, **12**, pp 227–29

Dillon, J T (1982) Problem finding and solving, *Journal of Creative Behavior*, **16**, pp 97–111

Domino, G (1994) Assessment of creativity using the ACL: a comparison of four scales, *Creativity Research Journal*, **7**, pp 21–23

Doolittle, J H (1990) *Creative Reasoning Test*, Midwest Publications/Critical Thinking Press, Pacific Grove, CA

Drevdahl, J E and Cattell, R B (1958) Personality and creativity: artists and writers, *Journal of Clinical Psychology*, **14**, pp 107–11

Dudeck, S Z and Hall, W B (1991) Personality consistency: eminent architects 25 years later, *Creativity Research Journal*, **4**, pp 213–31

Eberle, B and Standish, C W (1985) *CPS for Kids*, Good Apple, Carthage, IL

Eiduson, B T (1958) Artist and non-artist: a comparative study, *Journal of Personality*, **26**, pp 13–28

Eisenberger, R and Armeli, S (1997) Can salient reward increase creative performance without reducing intrinsic creative interest?, *Journal of Personality and Social Psychology*, **72**, pp 652–63

Ellis, H A (1926) *A Study of British Genius*, Houghton Mifflin, New York

Elshout, J (1990) Expertise and giftedness, *European Journal for High Ability*, **1**, pp 197–203

Elton, L (1983) Improving the cost-effectiveness of laboratory teaching, *Studies in Higher Education*, **8**, pp 79–85

Engle, D E, Mah, J J and Sadri, G (1997) An empirical comparison of entrepreneurs and employees: implications for innovation, *Creativity Research Journal*, **10**, pp 45–49

Ericsson, K A and Smith, J (1991) *Toward a General Theory of Expertise: Prospects and limits*, Cambridge University Press, Cambridge

European Commission (1996) European year of lifelong learning, *Magazine for Education, Training and Youth in Europe*, **5**, pp 8–10

Exley, K and Dennick, R (1996) *Innovations in Teaching Medical Science*, Staff and Educational Development Association, Birmingham

Eysenck, H J (1940) The general factor in aesthetic judgments, *British Journal of Psychology*, **31**, pp 94–102

Eysenck, H J (1997) Creativity and personality, in *The Creativity Research Handbook*, vol 1, ed M A Runco, pp 41–66, Hampton Press, Cresskill, NJ

Facaoaru, C (1985) *Kreativität in Wissenschaft und Technik* [Creativity in Science and Technology], Huber, Bern

Facaoaru, C and Bittner, R (1987) Kognitionspsychologische Ansätze der Hochbegabungsdiagnostik [Cognitive approaches to assessing giftedness], *Zeitschrift für differentielle und diagnostische Psychologie* [Journal for Personality and Assessment], **8** (3), pp 193–205

Facaoaru, C (1985) *Kreativitaet und Technik*, Huber, Bern

Farisha, B (1978) Mental imagery and creativity: review and speculation, *Journal of Mental Imagery*, **2**, pp 209–38

Feist, G J (1993) A structural model of scientific eminence, *Psychological Science*, **4**, pp 366–71

Feist, G J and Runco, M A (1993) Trends in the creativity literature: an analysis of research in the *Journal of Creative Behavior* (1967–1989), *Creativity Research Journal*, **6**, pp 271–86

Feldhusen, J F (1995) Creativity: a knowledge base, metacognitive skills, and personality factors, *Journal of Creative Behavior*, **29**, pp 255–68

Feldhusen, J F and Goh, B E (1995) Assessing and accessing creativity: an integrative review of theory, research, and development, *Creativity Research Journal*, **8**, pp 231–47

Feldhusen, J F and Treffinger, D J (1975) Teachers' attitudes and practices in teaching creativity and problem solving to economically disadvantaged and minority children, *Psychological Reports*, **37**, pp 1161–62

Ferrier, B, Marrin, M and Seidman, J (1988) Student autonomy in learning medicine: some participants' experiences, in *Developing Student Autonomy in Learning*, 2nd edn, ed D Boud, pp 156–71, Kogan Page, London

Finke, R A, Ward, T B and Smith, S M (1992) *Creative Cognition*, MIT Press, Boston, MA

Frederiksen, J R and Collins, A (1996) Designing an assessment system for the future workplace, in *Linking School and Work*, ed L B Resnick and J G Wirt, pp 51–62, Jossey-Bass, San Francisco

Freud, S (1947) *Leonardo da Vinci: A study in psychosexuality* (1910), Random House, New York

Fromm, E (1980) *Greatness and Limitations of Freud's Thought*, New American Library, New York

Fromm, E (1998) Lost and found half a century later: letters by Freud and Einstein, *American Psychologist*, **53**, pp 1195–98

Gardner, H (1982) *Art, Mind and Brain*, Basic Books, New York

Gardner, H (1983) *Frames of Mind: The theory of multiple intelligences*, Basic Books, New York

Getzels, J W and Csikszentmihalyi, M (1976) *The Creative Vision: A longitudinal study of problem finding in art*, Wiley, New York

Getzels, J W and Jackson, P W (1962) *Creativity and Intelligence*, Wiley, New York

Ghiselin, B (1955) *The Creative Process*, Mentor, New York

Gibson, J and Light, P (1967) Intelligence among university scientists, *Nature*, **213**, pp 441–43

Glover, J A, Ronning, R R and Reynolds, C R (1989) (eds) *Handbook of Creativity*, Plenum, New York

Gluskinos, U M (1971) Criteria for student engineering creativity and their relationship to college grades, *Journal of Educational Measurement*, **8**, pp 189–95

Goertzel, M C, Goertzel, V and Goertzel, T C (1978) *300 Eminent Personalities*, Jossey-Bass, San Francisco

Götz, K O (1985) *Visual Aesthetic Sensitivity Test (VAST)*, 4th edn, Concept Verlag, Düsseldorf

Götz, K O and Götz, K (1979) Personality characteristics of professional artists, *Perceptual and Motor Skills*, **49**, pp 327–34

Gough, H G and Heilbrun, A B (1983) *The Adjective Check List Manual*, 2nd edn, Consulting Psychologists Press Services, Palo Alto, CA

Government of Australia (1999) *Higher Education Funding Report, 1999*, Government Printer, Canberra

Graham, B, Sawyers, J and DeBord, K B (1989) Teachers' creativity, playfulness, and style of interaction, *Creativity Research Journal*, **2**, pp 41–50

Green, K C (1999) When wishes come true: colleges and the convergence of access, lifelong learning, and technology, *Change*, **31** (1), pp 10–15

Gruber, H E and Davis, S N (1988) Inching our way up Mount Olympus: the evolving-systems approach to creative thinking, in *The Nature of Creativity*, ed R J Sternberg, pp 243–70, Cambridge University Press, New York

Grudin, R (1990) *The Grace of Great Things: Creativity and innovation*, Ticknor and Fields, New York

Guilford, J P (1950) Creativity, *American Psychologist*, **5**, pp 444–54

Guilford, J P (1959) Traits of creativity, in *Creativity and its Cultivation*, ed H H Anderson, pp 142–61, Harper, New York

Guilford, J P (1967) *The Nature of Human Intelligence*, McGraw Hill, New York

Guilford, J P (1976) *Creativity Tests for Children*, Sheridan Psychological Services, Orange, CA

Guilford, J P and Christensen, P R (1973) The one-way relation between creative potential and IQ, *Journal of Creative Behavior*, **7**, pp 247–52

Hassenstein, M (1988) *Bausteine zu einer Naturgeschichte der Intelligenz* [Building Blocks for a Natural History of Creativity], Deutsche Verlags-Anstalt, Stuttgart

Hazel, E and Baillie, C (1998) *Improving Teaching and Learning in Laboratories*, Higher Education Research and Development Society of Australasia, Jamison Centre, Australia

Heath, D H (1977) Academic predictors of adult maturity and competence, *Journal of Higher Education*, **48**, pp 613–52

Heinelt, G (1974) *Kreative Lehrer/kreative Schüler* [Creative Teachers/Creative Students], Herder, Freiburg

Heller, K A (1994) Können wir zur Erklärung außergewöhnlicher Schul-, Studien- und Berufsleistungen auf das hypothetische Konstrukt 'Kreativität' verzichten? [Can we do without the hypothetical construct 'creativity' in explaining exceptional school, university and vocational achievements?], *Empirische Pädagogik* [Experimental Instruction], **8**, pp 361–98

Helson, R (1983) Creative mathematicians, in *Genius and Eminence: The social psychology of creativity and exceptional achievement*, ed R S Albert, pp 311–30, Pergamon, Elmsford, NY

Helson, R (1996) In search of the creative personality, *Creativity Research Journal*, **9**, pp 295–306

Helson, R (1999) A longitudinal study of creative personality in women, *Creativity Research Journal*, **12**, pp 89–102

Henle, M (1974) The cognitive approach: the snail beneath the shell, in *Essays in Creativity*, ed S Rosner and L E Aber, pp 23–44, North River Press, Croton on Hudson, NY

Hennessey, B A (1994) The consensual assessment technique: an examination of the relationships between ratings of product and process creativity, *Creativity Research Journal*, **7**, pp 193–208

Hequet, M (1995) Doing more with less, *Training*, October, pp 76–82

Heron, W (1957) The pathology of boredom, *Scientific American*, January, pp 52–56

Herrmann, W (1987) Auswirkungen verschiedener Fussballtrainingsstile auf Leistungsmotivation [Effects of different styles for coaching football on motivation], University of Hamburg, Unpublished Master's thesis

Heston, L L (1966) Psychiatric disorders in foster-home reared children of schizophrenic mothers, *British Journal of Psychiatry*, **112**, pp 819–25

Hocevar, D (1981) Measurement of creativity: review and critique, *Journal of Personality Assessment*, **45**, pp 450–64

Hocevar, D and Bachelor, P (1989) A taxonomy and critique of measurements used in the study of creativity, in *Handbook of Creativity*, ed J A Glover, R R Ronning and C R Reynolds, pp 53–76, Plenum, New York

Horn, J L (1982) The aging of human abilities, in *Handbook of Developmental Psychology*, ed B J Wolman, pp 287–308, Prentice Hall, Englewood Cliffs, NJ

Horn, J L (1988) Major issues before us now and for the next decade, Paper presented at International Seminar on Intelligence, August, Melbourne

Horner, K L, Rushton, J P and Vernon, PA (1986) Relation between aging and research productivity of academic psychologists, *Psychology and Aging*, **1**, pp 319–24

Howe, M J A and Sloboda, J A (1991) Early signs of talents and special interests in the lives of young musicians, *European Journal for High Ability*, **2**, pp 102–11

Howieson, N (1984) Is Western Australia neglecting the creative potential of its youth?, Paper presented at the 1984 Annual Conference of the Australian Psychological Society, August 12–17, Perth

Hruby, G G (1999) Review of Jensen, E (1998): teaching with the brain in mind, *Roeper Review*, **21**, pp 326–27

Huczynski, W (1983) *Encyclopedia of Management Development Methods*, Gower, Aldershot

Hudson, L (1963) Personality and scientific aptitude, *Nature*, **199**, pp 913–14

Hudson, L (1968) *Contrary Imaginations*, Methuen, London

Isen, A M, Daubman, K A and Nowicki, G P (1987) Positive affect facilitates creative problem solving, *Journal of Personality and Social Psychology*, **52**, pp 1122–31

Jackson, P W and Messick, S (1965) The person, the product, and the response: conceptual problems in the assessment of creativity, *Journal of Personality*, **33**, pp 309–29

Jamison, K R (1993) *Touched with Fire: Depressive illness and the artistic temperament*, Free Press, New York

Jay, E S and Perkins, D N (1997) Problem finding: the search for mechanisms, in *The Creativity Research Handbook*, vol 1, ed M A Runco, pp 257–94, Hampton Press, Cresskill, NJ

Johnson, D L (1979) *The Creativity Checklist*, Stoelting, Wood Dale, IL

Joussemet, M and Koestner, R (1999) Effect of expected rewards on children's creativity, *Creativity Research Journal*, **12**, pp 231–40

Juda, A (1949) The relationship between highest mental capacity and psychic abnormalities, *American Journal of Psychiatry*, **106**, pp 296–307

Karlsson, J L (1970) Genetic associations of giftedness and creativity in schizophrenia, *Hereditas*, **66**, pp 177–82

Kasof, J (1997) Creativity and breadth of attention, *Creativity Research Journal*, **10**, pp 303–15

Kirschenbaum, R J (1989) *Understanding the Creative Activity of Students*, Creative Learning Press, Mansfield, CT

Kirton, M J (1989) (ed) *Adaptors and Innovators: Styles of creativity and problem-solving*, Routledge, London

Kitto, J, Lok, D and Rudowicz, E (1994) Measuring creative thinking: an activity-based approach, *Creativity Research Journal*, **7**, pp 59–69

Knapper, C K and Cropley, A J (2000) *Lifelong Learning and Higher Education*, Kogan Page, London

Knowles, M S (1975) Non-traditional study: issues and relations, *Adult Leadership*, **23**, pp 232–35

Koestler, A (1964) *The Act of Creation*, Macmillan, New York

Kogan, N (1983) Stylistic variation in childhood and adolescence: creativity, metaphor, and cognitive styles, in *Handbook of Child Psychology*, vol 3, ed P Mussen, pp 631–706, Wiley, New York

Kramer, J J and Conoley, J C (1989) (eds) *The 11th Mental Measurements Yearbook*, University of Nebraska Press, Lincoln

Krampen, G, Freilinger, J and Wilmes, L (1988) Kreativitätstest für Vorschul- und Schulkinder (KVS): Testentwicklung, Handanweisung, Testheft [Creativity test for preschool and schoolchildren (KVS): test development, administration instructions, test booklet], *Trierer Psychologische Berichte* [Trier Psychological Reports], **15** (Whole No 7)

Kris, E (1950) On preconscious mental processes, *Psychoanalytic Quarterly*, **19**, pp 542–51

Krystal, H (1988) On some roots of creativity, *Psychiatric Clinics of North America*, **11**, pp 475–91

Kubie, L (1958) *Neurotic Distortion of the Creative Process*, University of Kansas Press, Lawrence, KS

Kumar, V K, Kemmler, D and Holman, E R (1997) The Creativity Styles Questionnaire revised, *Creativity Research Journal*, **10**, pp 51–58

Langer, G *et al* (1989) Conditional teaching and mindful learning, *Creativity Research Journal*, **2**, pp 139–50

Langley, P W et al (1987) *Scientific Discovery: Computational explorations of the creative process*, MIT Press, Cambridge MA

Lehman, H C (1953) *Age and Achievement*, Princeton University Press, Princeton, NJ

Lehwald, G (1985) *Zur Diagnostik des Erkenntnisstrebens bei Schülern* [Identifying Thirst for Knowledge in Schoolchildren], Volk und Wissen, Berlin

Lindauer, M S (1993) The span of creativity among long-lived historical artists, *Creativity Research Journal*, **6**, pp 221–40

Lindenberger, U (2000) Intellektuelle Entwicklung über die Lebensspanne [Intellectual development over the lifespan], *Psychologische Rundschau* [Psychological Review], **51**, pp 135–45

Lombroso, C (1891) *The Man of Genius*, Scott, London

Ludwig, A M (1998) Method and madness in the arts and sciences, *Creativity Research Journal*, **11**, pp 93–102

MacKinnon, D W (1983) Creative architects, in *Genius and Eminence: The social psychology of creativity and exceptional achievement*, ed R S Albert, pp 291–301, Pergamon, Elmsford, NY

Mansfield, R S, Busse, T V and Krepelka, E J (1978) The effectiveness of creativity training, *Review of Educational Research*, **48**, pp 517–36

Martinson, O (1995) Cognitive styles and experience in solving insight problems: replication and extension, *Creativity Research Journal*, **8**, pp 291–98

Masi, J V (1989) Teaching the process of creativity in the engineering classroom, in *Proceedings of the 1989 International Association for Engineering Education Frontiers in Education Conference*, ed L P Grayson and J M Biedenbach, pp 288–92, IEEE, Springfield, MA

Maslow, A H (1973) Creativity in self-actualizing people, in *The Creative Question*, ed A Rothenberg and C R Hausman, pp 86–92, Duke University Press, Durham, NC

May, R (1976) *The Courage to Create*, Bantam, New York

McCrae, R R (1987) Creativity, divergent thinking and openness to experience, *Journal of Personality and Social Psychology*, **52**, pp 1258–65

McLaren, R B (1993) The dark side of creativity, *Creativity Research Journal*, **6**, pp 137–44

McMullan, W E (1978) Creative individuals: paradoxical personages, *Journal of Creative Behavior*, **10**, pp 265–75

McNeill, T F (1971) Prebirth and postbirth influence on the relationship between creative ability and recorded mental illness, *Journal of Personality*, **39**, pp 391–406

Mednick, S A (1962) The associative basis of creativity, *Psychological Review*, **69**, pp 220–32

Meeker, M (1985) *Structure of Intellect Learning Abilities Test*, Western Psychological Services, Los Angeles

Mehlhorn, G and Mehlhorn, H-G (1985) *Begabung, Schöpfertum, Persönlichkeit* [Giftedness, Creativity, Personality], Volk und Wissen, Berlin

Mehlhorn, H-G *et al* (1988) *Persönlichkeitsentwicklung Hochbegabter* [Personality Development of Gifted Individuals], Volk und Wissen, Berlin

Meisgaier, C and Meisgaier, C (1997) Personality factors associated with giftedness and creativity, Paper presented at the 12th World Conference on Gifted and Talented Children, July 29–August 2, Seattle, Washington

Messick, S (1994) The matter of style: manifestations of personality in cognition, learning, and teaching, *Educational Psychologist*, **29**, pp 121–36

Mezirow, J *et al* (1990) *Fostering Critical Reflection in Adulthood*, Jossey Bass, San Francisco

Michael, W B and Colson, K R (1979) The development and validation of a life experience inventory for the identification of creative electrical engineers, *Educational and Psychological Measurement*, **39**, pp 463–70

Michalko, M (1996) *Thinkertoys*, Ten Speed Press, Berkeley, CA

Michalko, M (1998) *Cracking Creativity*, Ten Speed Press, Berkeley, CA

Milgram, R M (1990) Creativity: an idea whose time has come and gone?, in *Theories of Creativity*, ed M A Runco and R S Albert, pp 215–33, Sage, Newbury Park, CA

Milgram, R M and Hong, E (1999) Creative out-of-school activities in intellectually gifted adolescents as predictors of their life accomplishments in young adults: a longitudinal study, *Creativity Research Journal*, **12**, pp 77–88

Miller, G A (1956) The magical number seven, plus or minus two: some limits on our capacity for processing information, *Psychological Review*, **63**, pp 81–97

Miller, A I (1992) Scientific creativity: a comparative study of Henri Poincaré and Albert Einstein, *Creativity Research Journal*, **5**, pp 385–418
Morgan, A (1983) Theoretical aspects of project-based learning in higher education, *British Journal of Educational Technology*, **1**, pp 68–78
Morgan, D N (1953) Creativity today, *Journal of Aesthetics*, **12**, pp 1–24
Motamedi, K (1982) Extending the concept of creativity, *Journal of Creative Behavior*, **16**, pp 75–88
Moustakis, C E (1977) *Creative Life*, Van Nostrand, New York
Mumford, M D and Gustafson, S B (1988) Creativity syndrome: integration, application, and innovation, *Psychological Bulletin*, **103**, pp 27–43
Mumford, M D *et al* (1997) Process-based measures of creative problem-solving skills: IV Category Combination, *Creativity Research Journal*, **10**, pp 59–71
Mumford, M D *et al* (1998) Domain-based scoring of divergent-thinking tests: validation evidence in an occupational sample, *Creativity Research Journal*, **11**, pp 151–63
Munroe, A S (1995) Is your design a life sentence?, *Machine Design*, 26 January, p 156
Myers, I B and McCaulley, M H (1985) *Manual: A guide to the development and use of the Myers–Briggs Type Indicator*, Consulting Psychologists Press, Palo Alto, CA
Nardi, K and Martindale, C (1981) Creativity and preference for tones varying in dissonance and intensity, Paper presented at Eastern Psychological Association convention, New York
Necka, E (1986) On the nature of creative talent, in *Giftedness: A continuing worldwide challenge*, ed A J Cropley *et al*, pp 131–40, Trillium, New York
Neff, G (1975) Kreativität und Gruppe [Creativity and the group], in *Kreativität in Schule and Gesellschaft* [Creativity in School and Society], ed G Neff, pp 17–29, Otto Maier, Ravensburg
Neice, D C and Murray, T S (1997) Literary proficiency and adults' readiness to learn, in *New Patterns of Adult Learning: A six-country comparative study*, ed P Belanger and A C Tuijnman, pp 129–61, Pergamon, Oxford
Newell, A, Shaw, J C and Simon, H A (1962) The processes of creative thinking, in *Contemporary Approaches to Creative Thinking*, ed H E Gruber, G Terrell and M Wertheimer, pp 63–119, Atherton, New York
Nichols, J G (1972) Creativity in the person who will never produce anything original and useful: the concept of creativity as a normally distributed trait, *American Psychologist*, **27**, pp 717–27
Obuche, N M (1986) The ideal pupil as perceived by Nigerian (Igbo) teachers and Torrance's creative personality, *International Review of Education*, **32**, pp 191–96
O'Neil, H F, Abedi, J and Spielberger, C D (1994) The measurement and teaching of creativity, in *Motivation: Theory and research*, ed H F O'Neil and M Drillings, pp 245–63, Erlbaum, Hillsdale, NJ
Oral, G and Guncer, B (1993) Relationship between creativity and nonconformity to school discipline as perceived by teachers of Turkish elementary school children, by controlling for their grade and sex, *Journal of Instructional Psychology*, **20**, pp 208–14
Osborn, A F (1953) *Applied Imagination*, Scribner's, New York
Parloff, M B *et al* (1968) Personality characteristics which differentiate creative male adolescents and adults, *Journal of Personality*, **36**, pp 530–52

Parnes, S J (1981) *Magic of your Mind*, Creative Education Foundation, Buffalo, NY
Perkins, D N (1981) *The Mind's Best Work*, Harvard University Press, Cambridge, MA
Perlmutter, M (1988) Cognitive potential throughout life, in *Emergent Theories of Aging*, ed J Birren and V Bengston, pp 230–41, Erlbaum, Hillsdale, NJ
Petersen, S (1989) Motivation von Laienautoren [Motivation of hobby authors], Unpublished Master's thesis, University of Hamburg
Plucker, J A (1999) Is the proof in the pudding? Reanalysis of Torrance's (1958 to present) longitudinal data, *Creativity Research Journal*, **12**, pp 103–14
Policastro, E (1995) Creative intuition: an integrative review, *Creativity Research Journal*, **8**, pp 99–114
Puccio, G J, Treffinger, D J and Talbot, R J (1995) Exploratory examination of the relationship between creativity styles and creative products, *Creativity Research Journal*, **8**, pp 152–57
Renzulli, J S (1986) The three-ring conception of giftedness: a developmental model for creative productivity, in *Conceptions of Giftedness*, ed R J Sternberg and J E Davidson, pp 53–92, Cambridge University Press, Cambridge
Resnick, L B (1987) *Education and Learning to Think*, National Academy Press, Washington, DC
Richards, R *et al* (1988) Assessing everyday creativity: characteristics of the Lifetime Creativity Scales and validation with three large samples, *Journal of Personality and Social Psychology*, **54**, pp 476–85
Rickards, T J (1994) Creativity from a business school perspective: past, present and future, in *Nurturing and Developing Creativity: The emergence of a discipline*, ed S G Isaksen *et al*, pp 155–76, Ablex, Norwood, NJ
Rimm, S and Davis, G A (1980) Five years of international research with GIFT: an instrument for the identification of creativity, *Journal of Creative Behavior*, **14**, pp 35–46
Roe, A (1952) *The Making of a Scientist*, Dodd Mead, New York
Roe, A (1953) A psychological study of eminent psychologists and anthropologists, and a comparison with biological and physical scientists, *Psychological Monographs: General and applied*, **67** (Whole No 352)
Rogers, C R (1961) *On Becoming a Person*, Houghton Mifflin, Boston
Root-Bernstein, R S (1989) *Discovery*, Cambridge University Press, Cambridge, MA
Root-Bernstein, R S, Bernstein, M and Garnier, H (1993) Identification of scientists making long-term high-impact contributions, with notes on their methods of working, *Creativity Research Journal*, **6**, pp 329–43
Rosenblatt, E and Winner, E (1988) The art of children's drawing, *Journal of Aesthetic Education*, **22**, pp 3–15
Rosenblatt, L M (1986) Writing and reading: the transactional theory, Paper at the Reading/Writing Conference, October, Urbana, Illinois
Rosenman, M F (1988) Serendipity and scientific discovery, *Journal of Creative Behavior*, **22**, pp 132–38
Rostan, S M (1994) Problem finding, problem solving and cognitive controls: an empirical investigation of critically acclaimed productivity, *Creativity Research Journal*, **7**, pp 97–110

Rothenberg, A (1983) Psychopathology and creative cognition: a comparison of hospitalised patients, Nobel laureates and controls, *Archives of General Psychiatry*, **40**, pp 937–42

Rothenberg, A (1988) Creativity and the homospatial process: experimental studies, *Psychiatric Clinics of North America*, **11**, pp 443–60

Rubinstein, M F (1980) A decade of experience in teaching an interdisciplinary problem solving course, in *Problem Solving and Education*, ed D T Turna and F Reif, pp 35–48, Erlbaum, Hillsdale, NJ

Runco, M A (1987) Interrater agreement on a socially valid measure of students' creativity, *Psychological Reports*, **61**, pp 1009–10

Runco, M A (1995) Creativity need not be social, in *Social Creativity*, ed A Montuori and R Purser, pp 184–98, Hampton Press, Creskill, NJ

Runco, M A and Albert, R S (1986) The threshold hypothesis regarding creativity and intelligence: an empirical test with gifted and nongifted children, *Creative Child and Adult Quarterly*, **11**, pp 212–18

Runco, M A and Charles, R E (1997) Developmental trends in creative potential and creative performance, in *The Creativity Research Handbook*, vol 1, ed M A Runco, pp 115–52, Hampton Press, Creskill, NJ

Runco, M A, Okuda, S M and Thurston, B J (1991) Environmental cues and divergent thinking, in *Divergent Thinking*, ed M A Runco, pp 79–85, Ablex, Norwood, NJ

Russ, S W, Robins, A L and Christiano, B A (1999) Pretend play: longitudinal prediction of creativity and affect in fantasy in children, *Creativity Research Journal*, **12**, pp 129–39

Ryhammer, L and Smith, G J W (1999) Creativity and other personality functions as defined by percept-genetic techniques and their relation to organizational conditions, *Creativity Research Journal*, **12**, pp 277–86

Sattler, J M (1992) *Assessment of Children*, Author, San Diego, CA

Schaefer, C E and Anastasi, A (1968) A biographical inventory for identifying creativity in adolescent boys, *Journal of Applied Psychology*, **52**, pp 42–48

Schaefer, C I (1971) *The Creative Attitude Survey*, Psychologists and Educators Inc, Jacksonville, IL

Scheliga, J (1988) Musikmachen und die Förderung von Kreativität [Making music and fostering creativity], Unpublished Master's thesis, University of Hamburg

Schubert, D S, Wagner, H E and Schubert, H J (1988) Family constellation and creativity: increased quantity of creativity among lastborns, *Creative Child and Adult Quarterly*, **13**, pp 97–103

Schwarzkopf, D (1981) Selbstentfaltung durch kreatives Gestalten [Self-development through creative handwork], Unpublished Master's thesis, University of Hamburg

Scott, C L (1999) Teachers' biases toward creative children, *Creativity Research Journal*, **12**, pp 321–28

Seitz, J A (1997) The development of metaphoric understanding: implications for a theory of creativity, *Creativity Research Journal*, **10**, pp 347–53

Shaughnessy, M F (1988) Intra and interpersonal intelligences and creativity, *Creative Child and Adult Quarterly*, **13**, pp 104–15

Shaughnessy, M F and Manz, A F (1991) Personological research on creativity in the performing and fine arts, *European Journal for High Ability*, **2**, pp 91–101

Shaw, M P (1989) The Eureka process: a structure for the creative experience in science and engineering, *Creativity Research Journal*, **2**, pp 286–98

Shoumakova, N and Stetsenko, A (1993) Exceptional children: promoting creativity in a school training context, in *Symposium Abstracts of the Twelfth Biennial Meeting of ISSBD*, ed International Society for the Study of Behavioural Development (ISSBD), p 23, ISSBD, Recife, Brazil

Sierwald, W (1989) Kreative Hochbegabung: Identifikation, Entwicklung und Förderung kreativ Hochbegabter [Creative giftedness: identifying, developing and fostering the creatively gifted], Paper presented at the second annual meeting of the working group Educational Psychology of the German Psychological Society, September, Munich

Simon, H A (1989) The scientist as a problem solver, in *Complex Information Processing*, ed D Klahr and K Kotovsky, pp 375–98, Erlbaum, Hillsdale, NJ

Simonton, D K (1988a) Age and outstanding achievement: what do we know after a century of research?, *Psychological Bulletin*, **104**, pp 251–67

Simonton, D K (1988b) *Scientific Genius: A psychology of science*, Cambridge University Press, New York

Simonton, D K (1994) *Greatness: Who makes history and why*?, Guilford, New York

Simonton, D K (1997) Historiometric studies of creative genius, in *The Creativity Research Handbook*, vol 1, ed M A Runco, pp 3–28, Hampton Press, Creskill, NJ

Simonton, D K (1998) Masterpieces in music and literature: historiometric inquiries, *Creativity Research Journal*, **11**, pp 103–10

Smith, G J W and Carlsson, I (1983) Creativity and anxiety: an experimental study, *Scandinavian Journal of Psychology*, **24**, pp 107–15

Smith, G J W and Carlsson, I (1990) The creative process, *Psychological Issues* (Monograph 57), International Universities Press, New York

Smith, G J W and Fäldt, E (1999) Self-description or projection: comparison of two methods to estimate creativity, *Creativity Research Journal*, **12**, pp 297–302

Smith, J M and Schaefer, C E (1969) Development of a creativity scale for the Adjective Check List, *Psychological Reports*, **25**, pp 87–92

Snyder, B (1967) Creative students in science and engineering, *Universities Quarterly*, **21**, pp 205–18

Steiner, C J (1998) Educating for innovation and management: the engineering educators' dilemma, *International Association for Engineering Education Transactions in Education*, **41**, pp 1–7

Sternberg, R J (1988) *The Nature of Creativity*, Cambridge University Press, New York

Sternberg, R J (1997) Intelligence and lifelong learning: what's new and how can we use it?, *American Psychologist*, **52**, pp 1134–39

Sternberg, R J (1999) A propulsion model of types of creative contributions, *Review of General Psychology*, **3** (2), pp 83–100

Sternberg, R J and Dowing, D C (1982) The development of higher order reasoning in adolescence, *Child Development*, **53**, pp 209–21

Sternberg, R J and Lubart, T I (1995) *Defying the Crowd: Cultivating creativity in a culture of conformity*, Free Press, New York

Stone, B G (1980) Relationship between creativity and classroom behavior, *Psychology in the Schools*, **17**, pp 106–08

Suchman, R J (1961) Inquiry training: building skills for autonomous discovery, *Merrill-Palmer Quarterly*, **7**, pp 147–69

Sweetland, R C and Keyser, D J (1991) *A Comprehensive Reference for Assessment in Psychology*, Education and Business, Pro-Ed, Austin, TX

Tannenbaum, R S (1999) Education or training: reflections on a life in computing, *Educom Review*, **34** (1), pp 10–14

Tardif, T Z and Sternberg, R J (1988) What do we know about creativity?, in *The Nature of Creativity*, ed R J Sternberg, pp 429–40, Cambridge University Press, New York

Taylor, I A (1975) An emerging view of creative actions, in *Perspectives in Creativity*, ed I A Taylor and J W Getzels, pp 297–325, Aldine, Chicago

Thakray, J (1995) That vital spark (creativity enhancement in business), *Management Today*, July, pp 56–58

Thorndike, R L (1963) The measurement of creativity, *Teachers College Record*, **64**, pp 422–24

Torrance, E P (1965) *The Minnesota Studies of Creative Thinking: Widening horizons in creativity*, Wiley, New York

Torrance, E P (1968) A longitudinal examination of the fourth-grade slump in creativity, *Gifted Child Quarterly*, **12**, pp 195–99

Torrance, E P (1979) *The Search for Satori and Creativity*, Creative Education Foundation, Buffalo, NY

Torrance, E P (1992) A national climate for creativity and invention, *Gifted Child Today*, January–February, pp 10–14

Torrance, E P (1999) *Torrance Test of Creative Thinking: Norms and technical manual*, Scholastic Testing Services, Bensenville, IL

Torrance, E P and Goff, K (1989) A quiet revolution, *Journal of Creative Behavior*, **23**, pp 136–45

Torrance, E P and Hall, L K (1980) Assessing the further reaches of creative potential, *Journal of Creative Behavior*, **14**, pp 1–19

Torrance, E P and Safter, H T (1999) *Making the Creative Leap Beyond*, Creative Education Foundation Press, Buffalo, NY

Treffinger, D J (1985) Review of Torrance Tests of Creative Thinking, in *Ninth Mental Measurements Yearbook*, ed J V Mitchell, pp 1632–34, Buros Institute of Mental Measurement, University of Nebraska, Lincoln, NB

Treffinger, D J (1995) Creative problem solving: overview and educational implications, *Educational Psychology Review*, **7**, pp 301–12

Treffinger, D J, Feldhusen, J F and Isaksen, S G (1990) Organisation and structure of productive thinking, *Creative Learning Today*, **4** (2), pp 6–8

Treffinger, D J, Isaksen, S G and Dorval, K B (1995) *Creative Problem Solving: An introduction*, Center for Creative Learning, Sarasota, FL

Treffinger, D J, Isaksen, S G and Firestien, R L (1983) Theoretical perspectives on creative learning and its facilitation, *Journal of Creative Behavior*, **17**, pp 9–17

Treffinger, D J, Sortore, M R and Cross, J A (1993) Programs and strategies for nurturing creativity, in *International Handbook for Research on Giftedness and Talent*, ed K Heller, F J Mönks and A H Passow, pp 555–67, Pergamon, Oxford

Tweney, R D (1996) Presymbolic process in scientific creativity, *Creativity Research Journal*, **9**, pp 163–72

United States Patent and Trademark Office (1990) *The Inventive Thinking Curriculum Project*, US Patent and Trademark Office, Washington, DC

Urban, K K (1990) Recent trends in creativity research and theory in Western Europe, *European Journal for High Ability*, **1**, pp 99–113

Urban, K K (1991) On the development of creativity in children, *Creativity Research Journal*, **4**, pp 177–91

Urban, K K (1994) Recent trends in creativity research and theory, in *Competence and Responsibility*, 2nd edn, ed K A Heller and E A Hany, pp 55–67, Hogrefe and Huber, Seattle

Urban, K K (1995a) Different models in describing, exploring, explaining and nurturing creativity in society, *European Journal for High Ability*, **6**, pp 143–59

Urban, K K (1995b) Openness: a 'magic formula' for an adequate development and promotion of giftedness and talents?!, *Gifted and Talented International*, **10**, pp 15–19

Urban, K K (1996) Encouraging and nurturing creativity in school and workplace, in *Optimizing Excellence in Human Resource Development*, ed U Munander and C Semiawan, pp 78–97, University of Indonesia Press, Jakarta

Urban, K K (1997) Modelling creativity: the convergence of divergence or the art of balancing, in *Maximizing Potential: Lengthening and strengthening our stride*, ed J Chan, R Li and J Spinks, pp 39–50, University of Hong Kong Social Sciences Research Centre, Hong Kong

Urban, K K (in press) Towards a componential model of creativity, in *Creative Intelligence: Toward a theoretical integration*, ed D Ambrose, L M Cohen and A J Tannenbaum, Hampton Press, Creskill, NJ

Urban, K K and Jellen, H G (1996) *Test for Creative Thinking – Drawing Production (TCT–DP)*, Swets and Zeitlinger, Lisse, Netherlands

van der Heijden, B I J M (2000) The development and psychometric evaluation of a multi-dimensional measurement instrument of professional expertise, *High Ability Studies*, **11**, pp 9–39

Vosburg, S K (1998) Mood and quantity and quality of ideas, *Creativity Research Journal*, **11**, pp 315–24

Walberg, H J and Stariha, W E (1992) Productive human capital: learning, creativity and eminence, *Creativity Research Journal*, **5**, pp 323–40

Walder, R (1965) Schizophrenic and creative thinking, in *The Creative Imagination*, ed H M Ruitenbeck, pp 123–36, Quadrangle, Chicago, IL

Wales, C E, Nardi, A H and Stager, R A (1993) Emphasizing critical thinking and problem solving, in *Educating Professionals: Responding to new expectations for competence and accountability*, ed L Curry and J Wergin, pp 178–211, Jossey-Bass, San Francisco

Wallace, D B and Gruber, H E (1989) (eds) *Creative People at Work: Twelve cognitive case studies*, Oxford University Press, New York

Wallach, M A (1976) Tests tell us little about talent, *American Scientist*, January–February, pp 57–63

Wallach, M A and Wing, C W (1969) *The Talented Student*, Holt, Rinehart and Winston, New York

Wallach, M M and Kogan, N (1965) *Modes of Thinking in Young Children*, Holt, Rinehart and Winston, New York

Wallas, G (1926) *The Art of Thought*, Harcourt Brace, New York

Ward, T B, Saunders, K N and Dodds, R A (1999) Creative cognition in gifted adolescents, *Roeper Review*, **21**, pp 260–66

Weeks, D J and Ward, K (1988) *Eccentrics: The scientific investigation*, Stirling University Press, Stirling, UK

Weisberg, R W (1986) *Creativity*, Freeman, New York

Welsh, G S (1975) *Creativity and Intelligence: A personality approach*, Institute for Research in Social Science, Chapel Hill, NC

Westby, E L and Dawson, V L (1995) Creativity: asset or burden in the classroom?, *Creativity Research Journal*, **8**, pp 1–10

Williams, F E (1972) *A Total Creativity Program for Individualizing and Humanizing the Learning Process*, Educational Technology Publications, Englewood Cliffs, NJ

Williams, F E (1980) *The Creativity Assessment Packet*, Psychologists and Educators Inc, Chesterfield, MO

Williams, G (1977) *Towards Lifelong Education: A new role for higher education institutions*, Unesco, Paris

Woods, D R (1983) Introducing explicit training in problem solving into our courses, *Higher Education Research and Development*, **2**, pp 79–102

Woody, R H (1999) The musician's personality, *Creativity Research Journal*, **12**, pp 241–50

Yager, R E (1989) Development of student creative skills, *Creativity Research Journal*, **2**, pp 196–203

INDEX